Asa Hull

Devotional Chimes

a choice collection of new and standard hymns and tunes, adapted to all occasions

of social worship, family devotions and congregations

Asa Hull

Devotional Chimes
a choice collection of new and standard hymns and tunes, adapted to all occasions of social worship, family devotions and congregations

ISBN/EAN: 9783337286316

Printed in Europe, USA, Canada, Australia, Japan

Cover: Foto ©Lupo / pixelio.de

More available books at **www.hansebooks.com**

THE DEVOTIONAL CHIMES.

A CHOICE COLLECTION OF

New and Standard Hymns and Tunes,

ADAPTED TO ALL OCCASIONS OF

SOCIAL WORSHIP, FAMILY DEVOTIONS,

AND

CONGREGATIONAL SINGING,

BY

ASA HULL,

Author of "*Pilgrim's Harp*," "*Sparkling Rubies*," "*Casket of Sunday-School Melodies*," etc.

PHILADELPHIA:

PUBLISHED BY ASA HULL, 909 RACE STREET.
FOR SALE AT THE PHILA. M. E. BOOK-ROOM,
J. B. McCULLOUGH, Agent, 1018 Arch Street.

| BOSTON: | NEW YORK: | CHICAGO: |
| O. DITSON & CO. | C. H. DITSON & CO. | LYON & HEALY. |

Entered, according to Act of Congress, in the year 1873, by OLIVER DITSON & CO., in the Office of the Librarian of Congress, at Washington.

PREFACE.

The very general demand for an improved edition of the PILGRIM'S HARP, in which the new and popular music issued since the "HARP" was published, four years ago, should be introduced, has induced us to prepare this volume.

In this way, alone, could we remedy the small type of the "HARP," and supply the lack of hymns, which are the only defects brought to our notice in connection with that work.

In DEVOTIONAL CHIMES we have overcome these difficulties without materially enlarging or overcrowding its pages, but have been compelled to increase the number of pages to make room for the large number of hymns added, mainly to the second part. It is believed that the "CHIMES" will be found one of the best Hymn and Tune Books extant for Congregational singing, and without a rival for Social Worship and Family devotions. The hymns have been selected with reference to their intrinsic worth, without regard to their denominational associations, and we trust they will be found alike acceptable to all. The selection of the old standard tunes has been made with great care, and are such as our experience and observation indicated as the essence of the great mass at our command to select from; yet in our limited space we could hardly expect to find room for a class of tunes that have only a local popularity.

In the department of new and popular Music, we have given the useful preference over the merely sensational, yet we think it will be found both spirited and spiritual in its tendencies. We acknowledge our obligations to Messrs. O. Ditson & Co., for permission to use the music by Dr. L. Mason, and other authors represented by them; Messrs. Bigelow & Main, for permission to use Music by Rev. R. Lowry, and W. B. Bradbury, and others, whose names appear over their respective compositions.

THE AUTHOR.

Entered, according to Act of Congress, in the year, 1873, by O. DITSON & CO., in the office of the Librarian of Congress, at Washington.

J. M. ARMSTRONG, Music Typographer, 129 So. Eighth St., Philadelphia.

DEVOTIONAL CHIMES.

WHAT HAST THOU DONE?
Music by Asa Hull.

1. I gave my life for thee— My precious blood I shed,
That thou might'st ransomed be, And quickened from the dead;
I gave my life for thee; What hast thou done for me?

2. I spent long years for thee, In wea-ri-ness and woe;
That one e-ter-ni-ty Of joy thou mightest know;
I spent long years for thee; Hast thou spent one for me?

3.
I suffered much for thee,
  Yes, more than tongue can tell,
Of bitterest agony,
  To rescue thee from hell;
I suffered much for thee;
What dost thou bear for me?

4.
O, let thy life be given,
  Thy years for me be spent,
World-fetters all be riven,
  And joy with suffering blent;
Give thou thyself to me,
And I will welcome thee!

LEAD ME TO THE ROCK.

Words by R. A. SEARLES.
Music by ASA HULL.

1. When mountains of doubt hem me in on each side, And waves of affliction roll in like a tide; When vainly I seek some new pathway to try,
2. When storms of deep trouble rage fiercely around, When forebodings of ill in my spirit abound; When the hopes of a lifetime are blighted and die,

Rall. *a tempo.*

Chorus.

Oh, lead me to the Rock that is higher than I. Oh, lead me to the Rock, Oh, lead me to the Rock, Oh, lead me to the Rock that is higher than I.
Oh, lead me to the Rock that is higher than I. Oh, lead me, etc.

Rit.

Oh, lead me to the Rock, Oh, lead me to the Rock that is higher than I.

ALL FOR JESUS!

Words by MARY D. JAMES.   For Male Voices.   Music by ASA HULL.

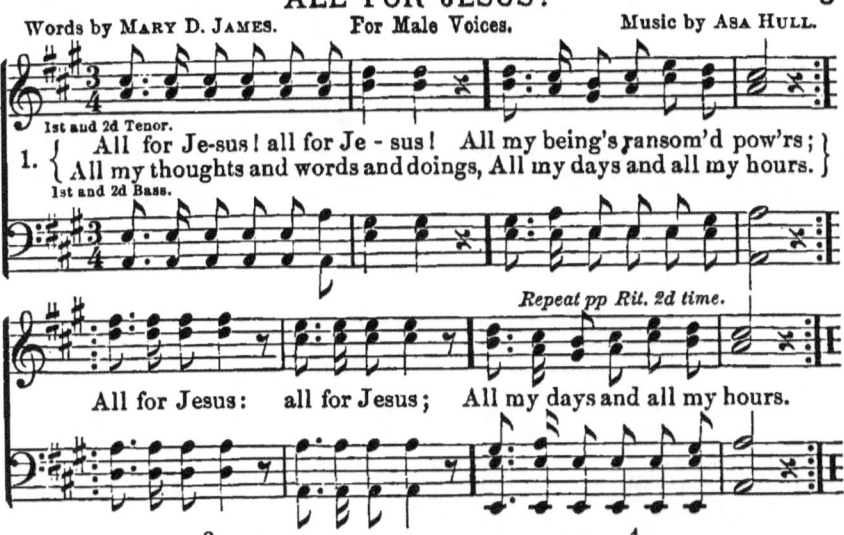

2.
Let my hands perform his bidding;
Let my feet run in his ways;
Let my eyes see Jesus only;
Let my lips speak forth his praise.
All for Jesus! all for Jesus!
Let my lips speak forth his praise.

3.
Worldlings prize their gems of beauty,
Cling to gilded toys of dust, [sure;
Boast of wealth, and fame, and plea-
Only Jesus will I trust.
Only Jesus! only Jesus!
Only Jesus will I trust.

4.
Since my eyes were fixed on Jesus,
I've lost sight of all beside,—
So enchained my spirit's vision,
Looking at the crucified.
All for Jesus! all for Jesus!
All for Jesus, crucified!

5.
Oh, what wonder! how amazing!
Jesus, glorious King of kings,
Deigns to call me his beloved,
Lets me rest beneath his wings.
All for Jesus! all for Jesus!
Resting now beneath his wings.

LEAD ME TO THE ROCK.—Concluded.

3. The sun of prosperity brightly may shine,
   And my heart round its treasures too closely may twine,—
   When my hopes are in danger of rising too high,
   Oh, lead me to the Rock that is higher than I.
      Oh, lead me to the Rock, etc.

4. When nearing the shore of the river of death,
   And the moments fly swiftly with each labored breath,
   When losing my hold of each dear earthly tie,
   Oh, lead me to the Rock that is higher than I.
      Oh, lead me to the Rock, etc.

5. Whatever my lot, be it wearily sad,
   Or actively busy or joyously glad;
   In each joy and sorrow, my God, be thou nigh,
   And lead me to the Rock that is higher than I.
      Oh, lead me to the Rock, etc.

6. RESTING AT THE CROSS.

WM. J. KIRKPATRICK.

1. To the cross of Christ, my Sa-viour, I had bro't my wea-ry soul,
2. At the cross, while meekly bow-ing, Je-sus, smiling, bade me live;

Burden'd, faint, and broken-hearted, Praying, "Je-sus make me whole."
I have died for your transgressions, And I free-ly all for-give.

Chorus.

Glo-ry, glo-ry be to Je-sus, I am counting all but dross,

I have found a full sal-va-tion, I am rest-ing at the cross;

I'm resting, ---- I'm resting, ---- I'm resting at the cross.
　　　　at the cross,　　　　at the cross,

WITHERED LEAVES.

Music by Asa Hull.

1. Nothing but leaves! the spir-it grieves Over a wast-ed life;
2. Nothing but leaves! no gather'd sheaves Of life's fair rip'ning grain;

O'er sins indulged while conscience slept, O'er vows and promises unkept,
We sow our seeds, lo! tares and weeds; Words, idle words, for honest deeds;

And reaps from years of strife Nothing but leaves! nothing but leaves!
We reap with toil and pain Nothing but leaves! nothing but leaves!

3.
Nothing but leaves! sad memory weaves
No vail to hide the past;
And as we trace our weary way,
Counting each lost and misspent day,
Sadly we find at last,
    Nothing but leaves!

4.
Ah! who shall thus the Master meet,
Bearing but withered leaves?
Ah! who shall at the Saviour's feet,
Before the awful judgment seat,
Lay down, for golden sheaves,
    Nothing but leaves?

RESTING AT THE CROSS.—Concluded.

3.
At the cross, while prostrate lying,
Jesus' blood flowed o'er my soul;
All my guilt and sin were covered,
And he whispered, "Child, be whole."
Glory, glory be to Jesus, etc.

4.
At the cross I'm calmly trusting;
Every moment now is sweet;
I am tasting of his glory:
I am resting at his feet.
Glory, glory be to Jesus, etc.

WORK WHILE THE DAY LASTS.

Music by Asa Hull.

There are lonely hearts to cher-ish While the days are going by;
There are weary souls who per-ish While the days are going by;
If a smile we can re-new As our journey we pur-sue,
Oh, the good we all may do, While the days are go-ing by.
While the days are go-ing by, While the days are go-ing by;

2.
There's no time for idle scorning,
  While the days are going by;
Let your face be like the morning,
  While the days are going by;
Oh, the world is full of sighs,
Full of sad and weeping eyes,—
Help your fallen brothers rise,
  While the days are going by.
:||:While the days are going by,:||:
  Help your fallen brothers rise, etc.

3.
All the loving links that bind us,
  While the days are going by;
One by one we leave behind us
  While the days are going by;
But the seed of good we sow,
Both in shade and shine will grow,
And will keep our hearts aglow,
  While the days are going by.
:||:While the days are going by,:||:
  It will keep our hearts aglow, etc.

CLINGING TO JESUS.

Words by Rev. W. H. BURRELL.
Music by ASA HULL.

1. While clinging to Jesus with un-yield-ing hold, How sweetly I dwell in his heavenly fold; Our union is perfect all foes we de-fy,
2. The storms may be fearful and my trials se-vere, No bow in the heavens to comfort or cheer; Tho' clouds of temptation spread over the sky,

Chorus.

We cling to each other, my Jesus and I.
We cling to each other, my Jesus and I. My Jesus and I, my Jesus and I; We cling to each oth-er, my Jesus and I.

3. Dear friends and companions, though most closely allied,
May sever their friendship, each other deride;
Their long cherished union may suddenly die,—
We cling to each other, my Jesus and I.—My Jesus and I, etc.

4. Contentions and strivings in the world may prevail;
True kindness and love everywhere sadly fail;
In union immortal, continued on high,
We cling to each other, my Jesus and I.—My Jesus and I, etc.

THE CLEANSING WAVE.

Words by Mrs. Phœbe Palmer. Music by Mrs. J. F. Knapp.

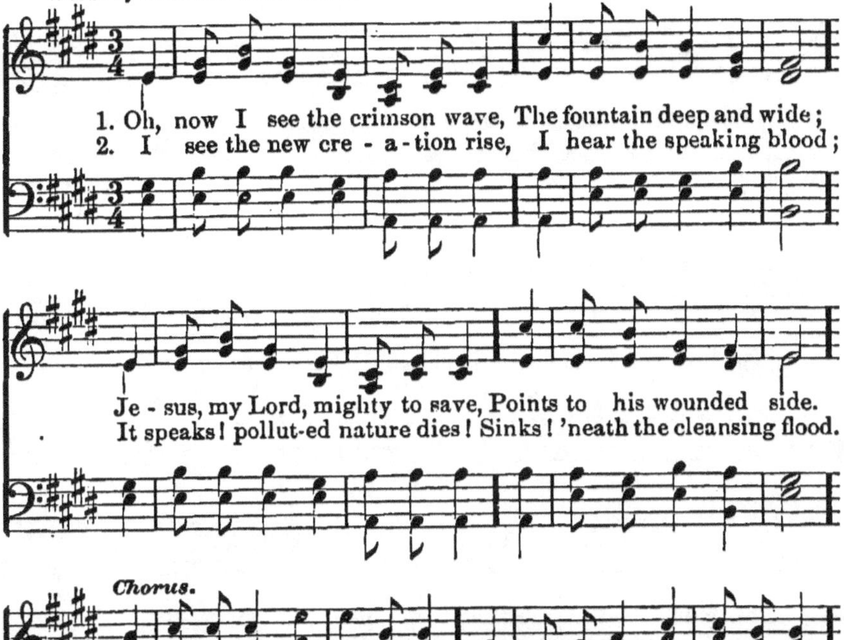

1. Oh, now I see the crimson wave, The fountain deep and wide;
Je - sus, my Lord, mighty to save, Points to his wounded side.

2. I see the new cre - a - tion rise, I hear the speaking blood;
It speaks! pollut-ed nature dies! Sinks! 'neath the cleansing flood.

Chorus.

The cleansing stream, I see, I see! I plunge, and oh, it cleanseth me!
Oh, praise the Lord, it cleanseth me! It cleanseth me, yes, cleanseth me!

3.
I rise to walk in heaven's own light,
  Above the world and sin, [white,
With heart made pure, and garments
  And Christ enthroned within.
    The cleansing stream, etc.

4.
Amazing grace! 'tis heaven below
  To feel the blood applied;
And Jesus, only Jesus know,
  My Jesus crucified.
    The cleansing stream, etc.

From "Guide to Holiness," by permission,

2.
Behold, how many seek its brink,
  To find a cure for sin;
And all the world may come and drink,
  And be renewed within.
    The fountain, etc.

3.
Come, trembling soul, and find a cure
  For all your ills and woes;
The promises of God are sure;
  For you the fountain flows.
    The fountain, etc.

4.
Poor, sinful, thirsty, fainting souls,
  Are freely welcomed here;
Salvation like a river rolls,
  Abundant, free, and clear.
    The fountain, etc.

5.
Come, then, with all your wants and wounds;
  Your every burden bring;
Here love, unchanging love, abounds,
  A deep celestial spring.
    The fountain, etc.

"HOW CAN I KEEP FROM SINGING." 13

Rev. R. Lowry.

1. My life flows on in endless song; Above Earth's lamentation,
I catch the sweet, tho' far-off, hymn That hails a new creation;
Thro' all the tumult and the strife I hear the music ringing;
It finds an echo in my soul—How can I keep from singing?

2.
What tho' my joys and comforts die?
  The Lord my Saviour liveth;
What tho' the darkness gather round?
  Songs in the night he giveth;
No storm can shake my inmost calm,
  While to that refuge clinging;
Since Christ is Lord of heaven and earth,
  How can I keep from singing?

3.
I lift my eyes; the cloud grows thin;
  I see the blue above it;
And day by day this pathway smooths,
  Since first I learned to love it;
The peace of Christ makes fresh my heart,
  A fountain ever springing;
All things are mine since I am his—
  How can I keep from singing?

WHITER THAN SNOW.

Words by JAMES NICHOLSON. Music by JNO. R. SWENEY.

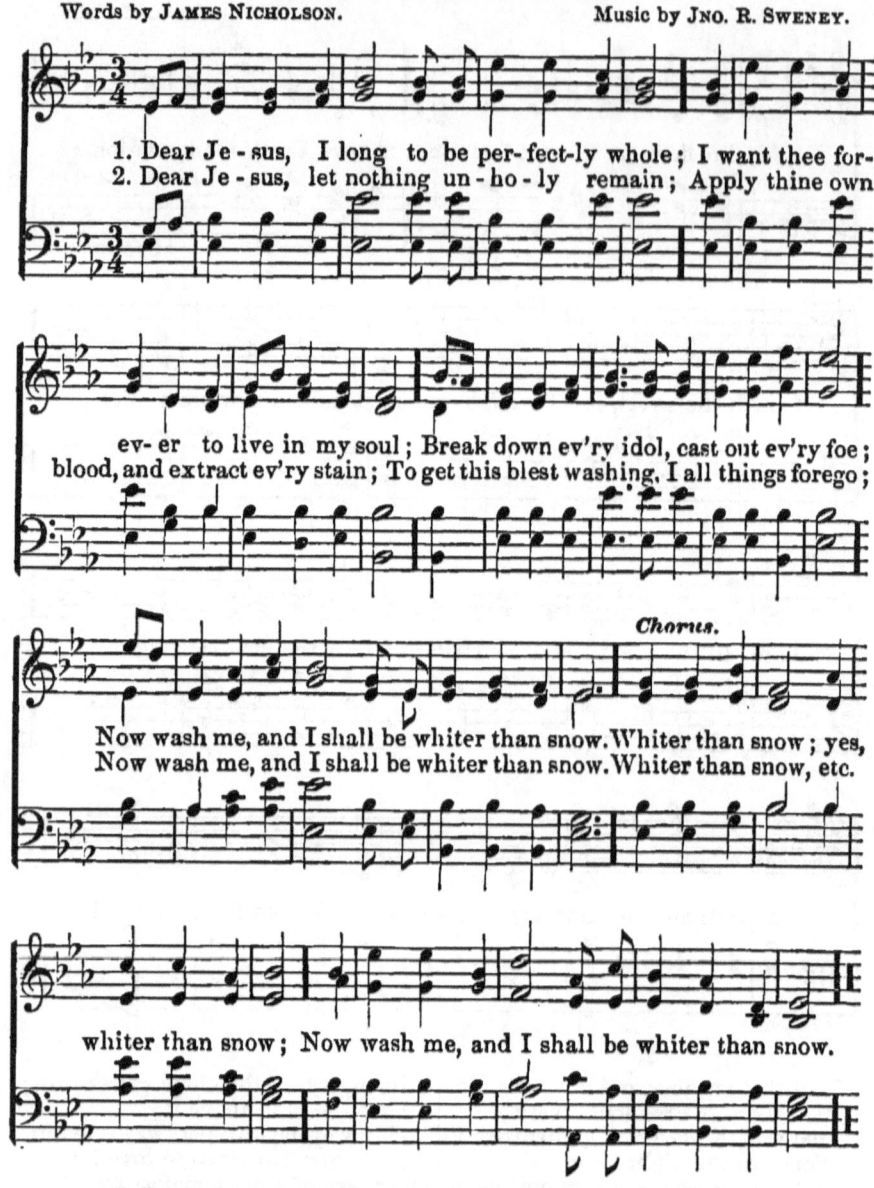

1. Dear Je-sus, I long to be per-fect-ly whole; I want thee for-ev-er to live in my soul; Break down ev'ry idol, cast out ev'ry foe;
2. Dear Je-sus, let nothing un-ho-ly remain; Apply thine own blood, and extract ev'ry stain; To get this blest washing, I all things forego;

Chorus.

Now wash me, and I shall be whiter than snow. Whiter than snow; yes, whiter than snow; Now wash me, and I shall be whiter than snow.
Now wash me, and I shall be whiter than snow. Whiter than snow, etc.

3. Dear Jesus, come down from thy throne in the skies,
And help me to make a complete sacrifice;
I give up myself, and whatever I know,—
Now wash me, and I shall be whiter than snow.
Whiter than snow; yes, whiter, etc.

THE LORD WILL PROVIDE.   15
Prof. C. S. Harrington.

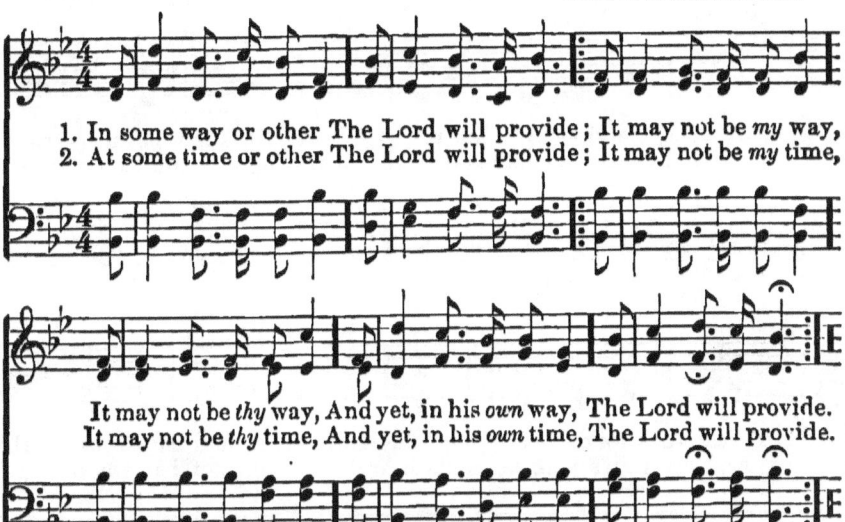

1. In some way or other The Lord will provide; It may not be *my* way,
2. At some time or other The Lord will provide; It may not be *my* time,

It may not be *thy* way, And yet, in his *own* way, The Lord will provide.
It may not be *thy* time, And yet, in his *own* time, The Lord will provide.

3. Despond, then, no longer;
    The Lord will provide;
  And this be the token—
  No word he hath spoken
  Was ever yet broken,—
    The Lord will provide.
  It may not be *my* way,
  It may not be *thy* way,
  And yet, in his *own* way,
    The Lord will provide.

4. March on, then, right boldly;
    The sea shall divide;
  The pathway made glorious
  With shoutings victorious,
  We'll join in the chorus,
    The Lord will provide.
  It may not be *my* way,
  It may not be *thy* way,
  And yet, in his *own* way,
    The Lord will provide.

WHITER THAN SNOW.—Concluded.

4. Dear Jesus, thou see'st I patiently wait;
  Come now, and within me a new heart create;
  To those who have sought thee, thou never saidst no,—
  Now wash me, and I shall be whiter than snow.—*Chorus.*

5. Dear Jesus, for this I most humbly entreat;
  I wait, blessed Lord, at thy crucified feet;
  By faith, for my cleansing, I see thy blood flow,—
  Now wash me, and I shall be whiter than snow.—*Chorus.*

6. The blessing, by faith, I receive from above;
  Oh, glory! my soul is made perfect in love;
  My prayer has prevailed, and this moment I know
  The blood is applied, I am whiter than snow.
    Whiter than snow; yes, whiter than snow,
    Dear Jesus, thy blood makes me whiter than snow.

3.

When the darkling heavens frown,
And the wrathful winds come down,
And the fierce waves toss'd on high,
Lash themselves against the sky;
Jesus, Saviour, pilot me
Over life's tempestuous sea.

4.

When th' Apostles' fragile bark
Struggled with the billows dark;
On the stormy Galilee.
Thou didst walk upon the sea;
And when they beheld thy form,
Safe they glided through the storm.

5.

As a mother stills her child,
Thou canst hush the ocean wild;
Boist'rous waves obey thy will
When thou say'st to them, "Be still,"
Wond'rous Sovereign of the sea,
Jesus, Saviour, pilot me.

6.

When at last I near the shore,
And the fearful breakers roar,—
Thou canst calm my anxious breast,
And conduct me to my rest.
Then, dear Saviour, pilot me
Over Death's tempestuous sea.

JESUS LOVES EVEN ME.   17

From "THE CHARM," by permission.   Words and Music by P. P. BLISS.

1. { I am so glad that our Father in Heav'n, Tells of his love in the Book he has giv'n;
   { Wonderful things in the Bible I see; This is the dearest, that Jesus loves me. }
   I am so glad that Jesus loves me, Jesus loves me, Jesus loves me;
   I am so glad that Jesus loves me, Jesus loves even me.

2. Though I forget him and wander away,
   Kindly he follows wherever I stray;
   Back to his dear loving arms would I flee;
   When I remember that Jesus loves me.—*Chorus.*

3. Oh, if there's only one song I can sing,
   When in his beauty I see the great King;
   This shall my song in eternity be,
   Oh, what a wonder that Jesus loves me.—*Chorus.*

THE GATE THAT STANDS AJAR.

Music by Asa Hull.

3.
Press onward, then, tho' foes may frown,
　While mercy's gate is open:
Accept the cross, and win the crown,
　Love's everlasting token.
　　Amazing love! etc.

4.
Beyond the river's brink we'll lay
　The cross that here is given;
And bear the crown of life away,
　And love him more in heaven.
　　Amazing love! etc.

2.
Life may have its many pleasures,
  They are fleeting as the day;
There above are dearer treasures,
  That will never fade away.
In the path of right and duty,
  Many ills will be our fate,
But religion has a beauty,
  That will lead to mercy's gate.

3.
Up the hill ascending ever,
  With our eyes upon the goal;
Let the world's allurements never,
  Teach us to forget the soul.
Soon our toil will here be ended,
  Bright awards for us await;
When to Him we are ascended,
  Who has opened mercy's gate.

THE INVITATION.

Words by JAMES B. ROGERS. Music by ASA HULL.

1. Come to the fountain of mer-cy, Come to the ha-ven so blest;
   Ye who are burden'd and weary, Come, and in Je-sus find rest.
   Come, come, come, come, Come, and in Je-sus find rest.

2. Come, while the Spirit invites you, Yield to its plead-ing to-day;
   Turn not aside from its warn-ing, Grieve not the Spir-it a-way.
   Come, come, come, come, Grieve not the Spir-it a-way.

3. Gently the Saviour is calling,
   Weary one! "Come unto me,"
   "Cast upon me all thy burden;
   Rest I will give unto thee."
   Come, come, come, come,
   Rest he will give unto thee.

4. Bring, then, thy burden to Jesus,
   To him thy sorrow confide;
   Trusting alone in his merit,
   Come, and in Jesus abide.
   Come, come, come, come,
   Come, and in Jesus abide.

5. Safely in Jesus abiding,
   Trusting in him all thy days;
   Ever his promise will cheer thee,
   "Lo! I am with you always."
   Come, come, come, come;
   He will be with you always.

THE SAVIOUR IS PRAYING FOR THEE.—Concluded.

3.
In pain and in sickness he stands by thy bed,
And speaks of the suff'rings he bore in thy stead;
That night in the garden, that day on [the tree,
Remember, thy Saviour is praying for thee.—*Chorus.*

4.
When suns shall have vanished, no longer to shine,
Assurance of glory, believer, is thine;
When earth has departed, how blissful to see
The face of thy Saviour, who prayeth for thee.—*Chorus.*

THE HEAVENLY VISITOR.

Music by Asa Hull.

Con espressione.

1. { In the si-lent midnight watches, List! thy bo-som door!
    How it knocketh, knocketh, knocketh, (Omit.)

Knock-eth ev-er-more. Say not, 'tis thy puls-es beat-ing,

'Tis thy heart of sin; 'Tis the Spir-it's voice en-treat-ing

Thee to let the Saviour in. *Chorus.* Let Him in, - - Let Him in, - -
Let Him in,   Let Him in,

'Tis the Ho-ly Spir-it knocketh,—Rise, and let the Saviour in.

INFINITE GRACE.

Music by Asa Hull.

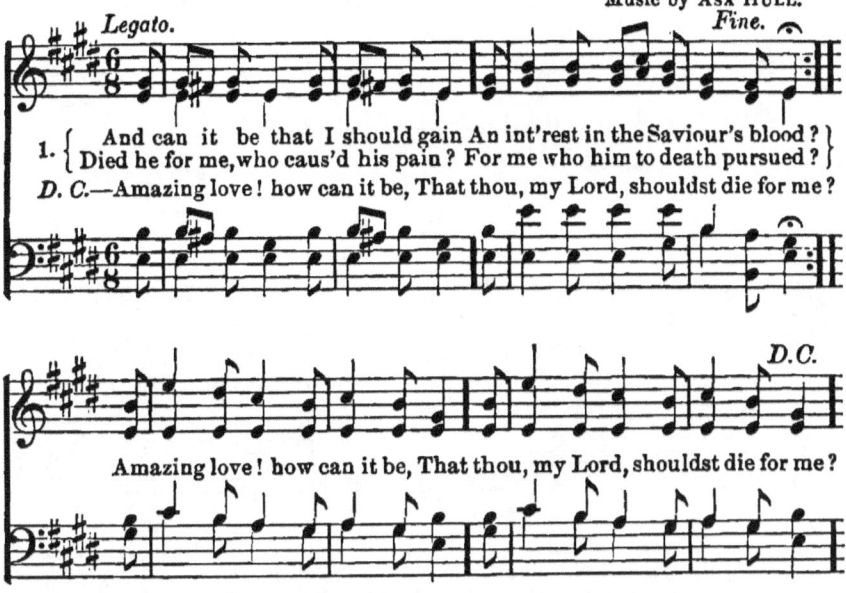

1. And can it be that I should gain An int'rest in the Saviour's blood?
Died he for me, who caus'd his pain? For me who him to death pursued?
D. C.—Amazing love! how can it be, That thou, my Lord, shouldst die for me?

Amazing love! how can it be, That thou, my Lord, shouldst die for me?

2.
'Tis myst'ry all, th' Immortal dies!
　Who can explore his strange design?
In vain the first-born seraph tries
　To sound the depths of love divine;
'Tis mercy all! let earth adore:
　Let angel minds inquire no more.

3.
He left his Father's throne above;
　(So free, so infinite his grace!)
Emptied himself of all but love,
　And bled for Adam's helpless race;
'Tis mercy all, immense and free,
　For, O my God, it found out me!

4.
Long my imprisoned spirit lay
　Fast bound in sin and nature's night:
Thine eye diffused a quick'ning ray;
　I woke: the dungeon flam'd with light;
My chains fell off, my heart was free—
　I rose, went forth, and followed thee.

5.
No condemnation now I dread;
　Jesus, with all in him, is mine;
Alive in Him my living Head,
　And clothed in righteousness divine,
Bold I approach th' eternal throne
　And claim the crown, thro' Christ my own.

THE HEAVENLY VISITOR.—Concluded.

2.
Death comes down with ruthless footstep
　To the hall and hut—
Think you death will stand there knock-
　When thy door is shut?　　　[ing
Jesus waiteth, waiteth, waiteth,
　But thy door is fast;
Grieved, away the Saviour turneth,
　Death breaks in the door at last.
　　Let him in, etc.

3.
Then 'tis time to stand entreating
　Christ to let *thee* in;
At the gate of heaven beating,
　Wailing for thy sin.
Nay, alas! thou foolish creature,
　Can it be forgot?
Jesus waited long to know thee,
　But he then will know thee not.
　　Let him in, etc.

THE ROYAL WAY.

Music by ASA HULL.

1. We may spread our couch with roses, And sleep thro' the summer day;
D.C.—For the on-ly way to heaven, Is the roy-al way of the cross.
But the soul that in sloth re-pos-es Is not in the narrow way.
If we follow the chart that is giv-en, We need not be at loss,

2.
Unto those who live in splendor,
 The cross is a heavy load;
And the feet that are soft and tender,
 Will shrink from the thorny road;
But the chains of the soul must be riven,
 And wealth must be as dross;
For the only way to heaven,
 Is the royal way of the cross.

3.
We may say we'll walk to-morrow,
 The path we refuse to-day;
And still, with our lukewarm sorrow,
 We shrink from the narrow way.
What heeded the chosen eleven,
 How fortune life might toss,
As they followed their Lord to heaven,
 By the way of the royal cross.

THE PENITENT.—Concluded.

2.
My hands hang limp and nerveless,
 My burden to remove;
My feeble knees are shaking,
 Open, and show thy love.
My eyes are dim with watching
 To catch a glimpse within;
My heavy ear is aching
 To hear thee say, "Come in."

3.
Oh! haste! unlatch, I pray thee!
 I trust thy gracious word,
"To him that knocks I'll open!"
 Thou true and faithful Lord.
The latch turns on the promise,
 The door on hinge of gold;
Oh! wondrous grace and glory!
 The half had not been told.

3.
Like the sea of Galilee,
Quickly would I yield to thee;
At thy thy feet, dear Jesus, lie
Calm and peaceful, with thee so nigh.
  To wind and wave, etc.

4.
Like the sea, the Jasper sea,
Clear as crystal I would be;
Robed in white in heav'n I'd shine,
Pure, and spotless, forever thine.
  To wind and wave, etc.

RESTING ON THE PROMISES.

Music by ASA HULL.

2
Deep beneath the running ocean,
  Deep beneath the swelling flood,
All unmoved by the commotion,
  Sit the promises of God.
We are anchored firmly to them,
  Though in tatters hang our shrouds;
Calmly we look up, and through them
  View the thunder-riven clouds.—*Cho.*

3.
This our constant heart consoleth,
  And we will not be afraid;
'Tis our Heavenly Father ruleth
  And on Him our trust is stayed.
Quiet as a peaceful river,
  Quiet as the wind-hushed seas,
In Jehovah trusting ever,
  We are kept in perfect peace.—*Cho.*

28. TAKE IT ALL TO THE LORD.

Music by Karl Reden.

2.
Have we trials and temptations?
   Is there trouble anywhere?
We should never be discouraged,
   Take it to the Lord in prayer.
Can we find a friend so faithful,
   Who will all our sorrows share?
Jesus knows our ev'ry weakness,
   Take it to the Lord in prayer.

3.
Are we weak and heavy laden,
   Cumbered with a load of care,
Precious Saviour, still our refuge,
   Take it to the Lord in prayer.
Do thy friends despise, forsake thee,
   Take it to the Lord in prayer;
In his arms he'll take and shield thee,
   Thou wilt find a solace there.

ABIDE WITH ME.

Music by ASA HULL.

1. A-bide with me; fast falls the e-ven-tide; The darkness deepens; Lord, with me a-bide; When oth-er help-ers fail, and comforts flee, Help of the helpless, O a-bide with me.
2. Swift to its close ebbs out life's lit-tle day; Earth's joys grow dim; its glo-ries pass a-way; Change and de-cay in all around I see; O thou who changest not, a-bide with me.

3. I need thy presence every passing hour;
   What but thy grace can foil the tempter's power?
   Who like thyself my guide and stay can be?
   Through cloud and sunshine, Lord, abide with me.

4. I fear no foe with thee at hand to bless;
   Ills have no weight, and tears no bitterness;
   Where is death's sting, where, grave, thy victory?
   I triumph still, if thou abide with me.

5. Hold thou thy Cross before my closing eyes:
   Shine through the gloom, and point me to the skies;
   Heaven's morning breaks, and earth's vain shadows flee;
   In life, in death, O Lord, abide with me.

ANYWHERE WITH JESUS. 31

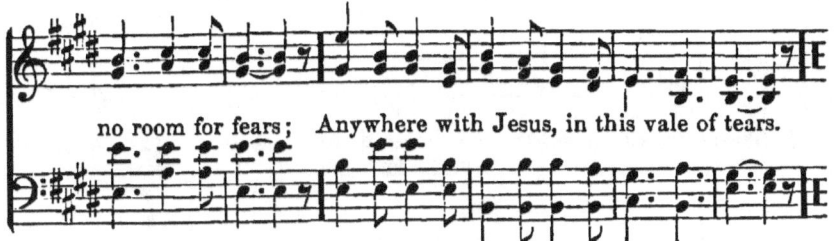

no room for fears; Anywhere with Jesus, in this vale of tears.

3. Anywhere with Jesus, though it be the tomb
With its fearful terror, with its dreaded gloom;
Though it be the weariness of a long-drawn life,
Fainting in the constant toil, drooping in the strife.—*Cho.*

4. Anywhere with Jesus, for it cannot be
Dreary, dark, or desolate, where he is with me;
He will love me alway, every need he'll supply,
Anywhere with Jesus, should I live or die.—*Cho.*

BE IN EARNEST.

Music by ASA HULL.

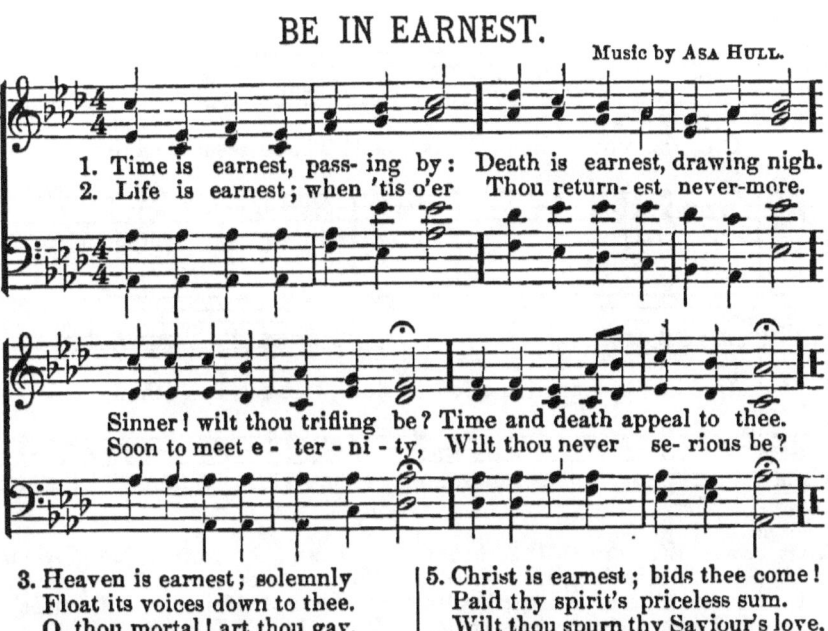

1. Time is earnest, pass-ing by: Death is earnest, drawing nigh.
2. Life is earnest; when 'tis o'er Thou return-est never-more.

Sinner! wilt thou trifling be? Time and death appeal to thee.
Soon to meet e-ter-ni-ty, Wilt thou never se-rious be?

3. Heaven is earnest; solemnly
Float its voices down to thee.
O, thou mortal! art thou gay,
Sporting thro' thine earthly day!

4. God is earnest; kneel and pray,
Ere thy season pass away;
Ere be set his judgment throne—
Vengeance ready, mercy gone!

5. Christ is earnest; bids thee come!
Paid thy spirit's priceless sum.
Wilt thou spurn thy Saviour's love,
Pleading with thee from above?

6. Thou refusest, wretched one!
Thou despisest God's dear Son!
Madness! dying sinner, turn,
Lest his wrath within thee burn.

THE HALLOWED CROSS.

Arranged from Rev. J. H. STOCKTON.

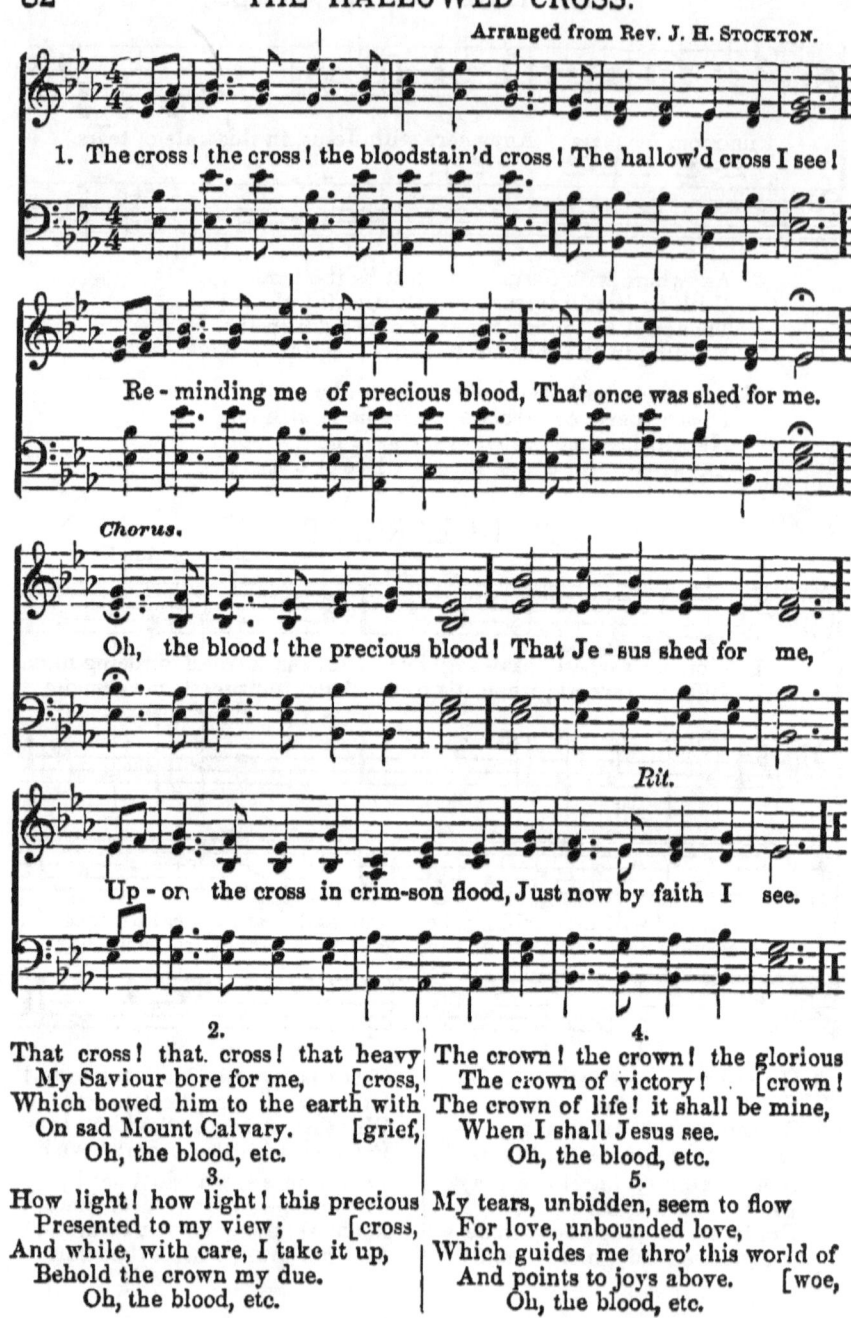

1. The cross! the cross! the bloodstain'd cross! The hallow'd cross I see!
Re-minding me of precious blood, That once was shed for me.

Chorus.
Oh, the blood! the precious blood! That Jesus shed for me,
Upon the cross in crim-son flood, Just now by faith I see.

2.
That cross! that cross! that heavy cross,
My Saviour bore for me, [cross,
Which bowed him to the earth with grief,
On sad Mount Calvary. [grief,
Oh, the blood, etc.

3.
How light! how light! this precious cross,
Presented to my view; [cross,
And while, with care, I take it up,
Behold the crown my due.
Oh, the blood, etc.

4.
The crown! the crown! the glorious crown,
The crown of victory! [crown!
The crown of life! it shall be mine,
When I shall Jesus see.
Oh, the blood, etc.

5.
My tears, unbidden, seem to flow
For love, unbounded love,
Which guides me thro' this world of woe,
And points to joys above. [woe,
Oh, the blood, etc.

"WHO'LL STAND UP FOR JESUS?"

Rev. L. Hartsough.

1. O, who'll stand up for Jesus, The lowly Nazarene?
2. O, who will follow Jesus, Amid reproach and shame,

And raise the blood-stain'd banner Amid the hosts of sin?
Where others shrink or falter, Who'll glory in his name?
D.S. All hail reproach or sorrow, If Jesus leads me there.

Chorus.

The cross for Christ I'll cherish, Its crucifixion bear;

3.
Though fierce may rage the battle,
 And wild the storm may blow,
Though friends may go forever,
 Who will with Jesus go?—*Cho.*

4.
Though foes shall madly gather,
 And devils rage and roar,
Who'll choose the fiery furnace,
 With Jesus evermore?—*Cho.*

5.
My all to Christ I've given,
 My talents, time, and voice,
Myself, my reputation,
 The lone way is my choice.—*Cho.*

6.
O Jesus, Jesus, Jesus,
 My all-sufficient Friend!
Come, fold me to thy bosom,
 Ev'n to the journey's end.—*Cho.*

1. SECOND HYMN, for "Hallowed Cross." 3.

There is a fountain fill'd with blood,
 Drawn from Immanuel's veins,
And sinners plung'd beneath that flood,
 Lose all their guilty stains.—*Cho.*

2.
The dying thief rejoiced to see
 That fountain in his day;
And there may I, though vile as he,
 Wash all my sins away.—*Cho.*

Thou dying Lamb, thy precious blood
 Shall never lose its power
Till all the ransom'd Church of God
 Are saved, to sin no more.—*Cho.*

4.
E'er since by faith I saw the stream
 Thy flowing wounds supply,
Redeeming love has been my theme;
 And shall be till I die.—*Cho.*

NO NIGHT IN HEAVEN.

Music by Asa Hull.

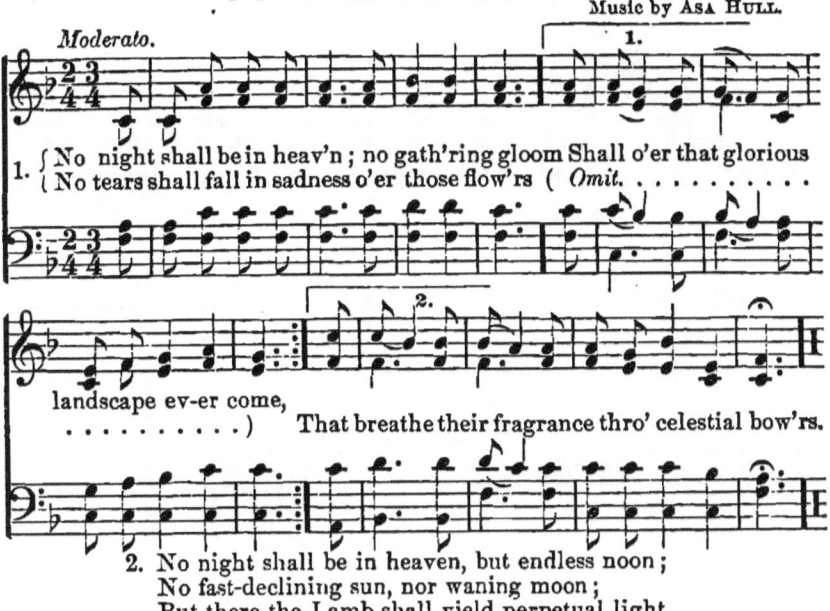

1. No night shall be in heav'n; no gath'ring gloom Shall o'er that glorious
   No tears shall fall in sadness o'er those flow'rs (*Omit*............
   landscape ev-er come,
   ....) That breathe their fragrance thro' celestial bow'rs.

2. No night shall be in heaven, but endless noon;
   No fast-declining sun, nor waning moon;
   But there the Lamb shall yield perpetual light,
   'Mid pastures green, and waters ever bright.

3. No night shall be in heaven,—no darkened room,
   No bed of death, nor silence of the tomb;
   But breezes, ever fresh with love and truth,
   Shall brace the frame with an immortal youth.

4. No night shall be in heaven; oh, had I faith
   To rest in what the faithful witness saith,
   That faith should make these hideous phantoms flee,
   And leave no night henceforth on earth to me.

PRESSING TOWARD THE PRIZE.—Concluded.

2.
Upward, upward, upward in your praises?
Looking up, looking up, looking up to Jesus;
Look up to him who hath ascended on high.
Looking up toward the prize, etc.
:||: Upward, upward still :||:
Upward, upward, upward still,
Doing God's will.

3.
Higher, higher, higher yet to things above;
Mounting up, mounting up, mounting up on wings of love;
Mount far above the clouds and storms of the earth.
Pressing on toward the prize, etc.
:||: Higher, higher still, :||:
Higher, higher, higher still,
Doing God's will.

4.
Nearer, nearer, nearer to the Saviour;
Trusting him, trusting him, trusting him forever:
And while you live keep pressing on to the prize.
Pressing on toward the prize, etc.
:||: Nearer, nearer still :||:
Nearer, nearer, nearer still,
Doing God's will.

36. I LOVE TO TELL THE STORY.

By Permission. Music by WM. G. FISCHER.

1. I love to tell the story: Of un-seen things a-bove,
Of Je-sus and his glo-ry, Of Je-sus and his love.
I love to tell the story, Be-cause I know it's true;
It sat-is-fies my long-ings, As noth-ing else would do.

2. I love to tell the story: More won-der-ful it seems,
Than all the gold-en fan-cies, Of all our gold-en dreams.
I love to tell the sto-ry: It did so much for me!
And that is just the rea-son I tell it now to thee

Chorus.

I love to tell the sto-ry 'Twill be my theme in glo-ry,

I LOVE TO TELL THE STORY.

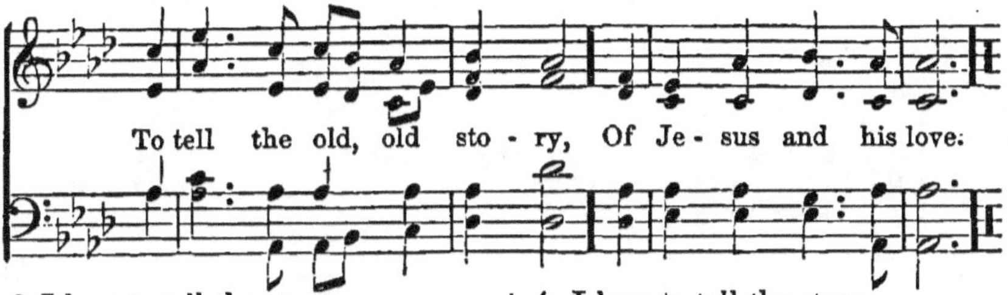

To tell the old, old sto-ry, Of Je-sus and his love.

3. I love to tell the story:
   'Tis pleasant to repeat
   What seems, each time I tell it,
   More wonderfully sweet.
   I love to tell the story:
   For some have never heard
   The Message of salvation
   From God's own holy word.—*Cho.*

4. I love to tell the story:
   For those who know it best,
   Seem hungering and thirsting
   To hear it like the rest.
   And when, in scenes of glory,
   I sing the NEW, NEW SONG.
   'Twill be—the OLD, OLD STORY
   That I have loved so long.—*Cho.*

"WE'LL DIE ON THE FIELD." Freedmen's Melody, Arr. for this work.

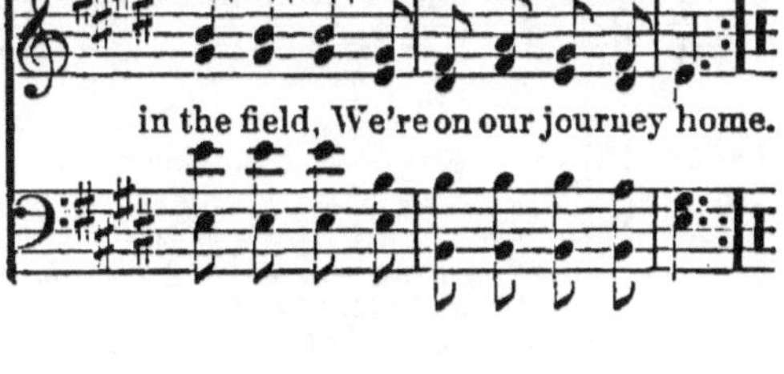

1. Oh, now I am a sol-dier, My Captain's gone be-fore,
   He's giv-en me my or-ders, And bid me not give o'er:
2. If I con-tin-ue faith-ful, A righteous crown he'll give,
   And all his va-liant soldiers E-ter-nal life shall have.

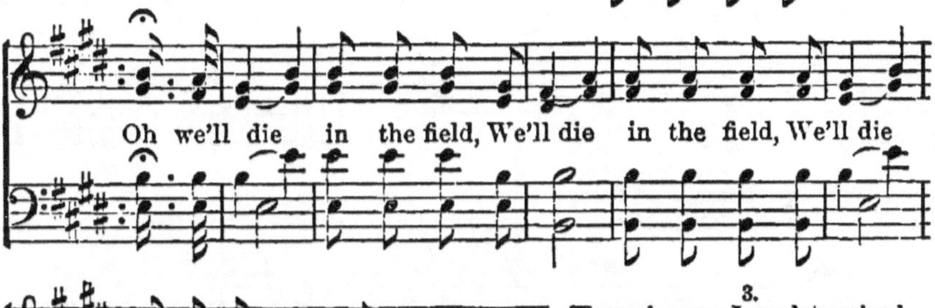

Oh we'll die in the field, We'll die in the field, We'll die in the field, We're on our journey home.

3.
Through grace I am determined
To conquer though I die!
And then away to Jesus
On wings of love I'll fly.—*Cho*

4.
Farewell to sin and sorrow,
I bid you all adieu;
And O, my friends, prove faithful,
And on your way pursue.—*Cho.*

OVER THERE.

T. C. O'Kane.

1. O, think of a home over there, By the side of the river of light,
Where the saints, all immortal and fair, Are robed in their garments of white.
O-ver there, O-ver there, O, think of a home over there,
O-ver there, Over there, over there, O, think of a home over there.

2. O, think of the friends over there, Who before us the journey have trod,
Of the songs that they breathe on the air, In their home in the palace of God.
Over there, Over there, O, think of the friends over there,
Over there, over there, O, think of the friends over there.

3.
My Saviour is now over there; [rest:
There my kindred and friends are at
Then away from my sorrow and care,
Let me fly to the land of the blest.
Over there, over there,
My Saviour is now over there.

4.
I'll soon be at home over there,
For the end of my journey I see;
Many dear to my heart, over there,
Are watching and waiting for me.
Over there, over there,
I'll soon be at home over there.

2.
I dread not the terror by night,
  No arrow can harm me by day;
His shadows has covered me quite,
  My fears he has driven away.—*Cho.*

3.
The pestilence walking about,
  When darkness has settled abroad,
Can never compel me to doubt
  The presence, and power of God. *Cho.*

4.
The wasting destruction at noon,
  No fearful foreboding can bring;
With Jesus, my soul doth commune,
  His perfect salvation I sing.—*Cho.*

5.
A thousand may fall at my side,
  And ten thousand at my right hand;
Above me his wings are spread wide,
  Beneath them in safety I stand. *Cho.*

3.
See the glory, friends of Jesus,
  On this ocean deep and wide;
But a glory, clearer, brighter,
  Lies beyond this swelling tide.
    Chorus.—Far beyond, etc.

4.
Tempests sweep across the ocean,
  Ruin is the stern decree,
But "be still" in tones of sweetness,
  Sounds across the jasper sea.
    Chorus.—Far beyond, etc.

5.
Gaze not simply on this ocean,
  Walk not only on the shore,
Launch ye boldly on its bosom,
  Trust your Pilot evermore.
    Chorus.—Far beyond, etc.

6.
Yes, launch out, ye friends of Jesus,
  Spread your sails for that blest shore;
Praise the Lord, the Pilot's with us,
  We are safe for evermore.
    Chorus.—Far beyond, etc.

42 "COME UP HITHER."

Words by E. H. NEVIN, D. D.
Music by ASA HULL.

1. "Come up hith-er!" come a-way! Thus the ransom'd spir-its sing;
2. "Come up hith-er!" come and see Heaven's glo-ries yet un-told;

Here is cloud-less, end-less day, Here is ev-er-last-ing spring.
Bright-er than the sun they be, Rich-er than the pur-est gold.

Chorus.

*"Come up hith-er," O, come a-way, "Come up hither," the angels say;

"Come up hither," O, come and see Heav'nly glories, how bright they be.

3. "Come up hither!" come and dwell
   With the living hosts above;
   Come, and let your bosoms swell
   With the burning songs of love.—*Cho.*
4. "Come up hither!" come and share
   In the sacred joys that rise
   Like an ocean everywhere,
   Through the myriads of the skies.

5. "Come up hither!" come and shine
   In the robes of spotless white;
   Palms, and harps, and crowns are thine,
   Hither! hither wing your flight.
6. "Come up hither!" hither speed!
   Rest is found in heav'n alone;
   Here is all the wealth you need, [own.
   Come, and make that wealth your

* If the Tenor is weak, about half of the Altos should sing the small notes.

THE VOICE WITHIN. 43

Words by GEO. H. SPRING. Music by J. H. ROSECRANS.

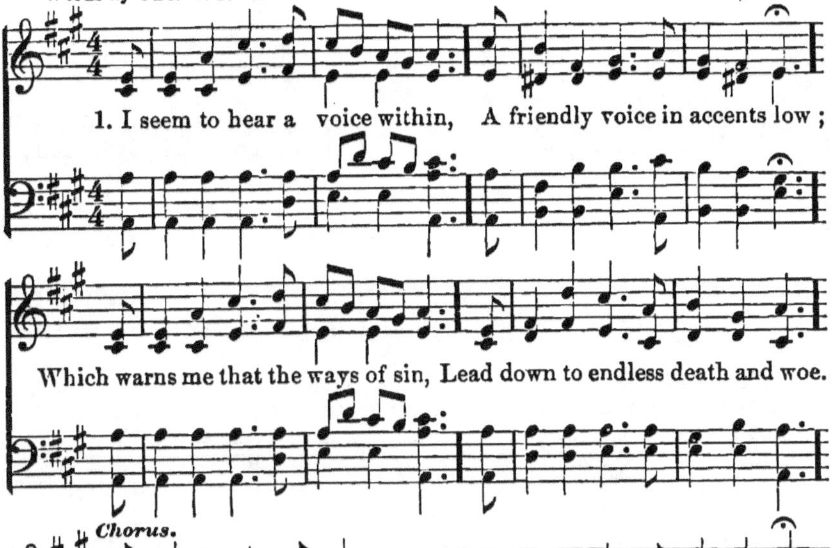

1. I seem to hear a voice within, A friendly voice in accents low;
Which warns me that the ways of sin, Lead down to endless death and woe.

Chorus.
It is the voice of love divine, That utters thus a warning kind,
That whispers to this heart of mine, Seek now, if mercy you would find.

2.
Though all around seems bright and fair,
Yet deadly evil lurks within,
And if you still retain it there,
You'll surely perish in your sin.

3.
Life's op'ning morn may smile to-day,
To-morrow gloomy death may call;
Yet now thy Maker's voice obey, [pal.
Then shall death's summons ne'er ap-

4.
Yes, go to Jesus, who was slain,
To ransom guilty ones from woe,
His blood can cleanse sin's every stain,
His friendship endless bliss bestow.

5.
Seek while thy Father waits to bless,
Seek while the Saviour will forgive,
Seek while the Spirit, rich in grace,
Will help thee turn to God and live.

44 SHALL WE KNOW EACH OTHER?

Music by Rev. R. Lowry.

1. When we hear the music ring-ing In the bright celestial dome,
2. When the ho-ly angels meet us As we go to join their band;

When sweet an-gel voic-es sing-ing, Glad-ly bid us welcome home.
Shall we know the friends that greet us, In the glorious spir-it land?

To the land of ancient sto-ry, Where the spirit knows no care;
Shall we see the same eyes shining On us, as in days of yore?

In that land of light and glo-ry, Shall we know each oth-er there?
Shall we feel their dear arms twining Fondly round us, as be-fore?

Chorus.

Shall we know . . . . each other? Shall we know . . . each oth-er?
Shall we know each oth-er? Shall we know each oth-er?

SHALL WE KNOW EACH OTHER?   45

3.
Yes, my earth-worn soul rejoices,
 And my weary heart grows light,
For the thrilling angel voices
 And the angel faces bright
That shall welcome us in heaven,
 Are the lov'd of long ago,
And to them is kindly given,
  Thus their mortal friends to know.
  Shall we know, etc.

4.
Oh! ye weary, sad, and toss'd ones,
 Droop not, faint not, by the way;
Ye shall join the lov'd and just ones
 In the land of perfect day!
Harp-strings touched by angel fingers,
 Murmured in my raptured ear,
Evermore their sweet song lingers,
 "We shall know each other there!"
 We shall know, etc.

LOVE'S ATTRIBUTES.

Words by A. W. LEVY.   Music by ASA HULL.

2. Love has a feeling heart:
    It loves to sympathize;
   And hastes to bear a part
    Wherever trouble tries.

3. Love has an open eye:
    It slumbers not nor sleeps;
   Grief never passes by,
    But with the suff'rer weeps.

4. Love has a liberal hand,
    And giveth of its store;
   Waits not for a demand,
    But gladly aids the poor.

5. Love has a patient soul:
    It waiteth oft too long;
   Looks steadfast to the goal,
    And cheers the way with song.

CLINGING TO THE ROCK.

Prof. C. S. HARRINGTON.

1. When the tempest rages high, Sailing on life's boist'rous sea,
Stormy billows I de-fy, If I then may on-ly (*Omit*) be

Chorus.
Anchor'd to the Rock, Anchor'd to the Rock, Shelter for me ev-er, Strength that fail-eth nev-er; When the storms of life are o'er, Look for me on Canaan's shore; Cling-ing to the Rock.

2.
When 'mid drifting wrecks I'm cast,
Darkness settling thickly round,—
Hope shall lift her light at last,
If I then be only found
Clinging to the rock,
Clinging to the rock,
Shelter for me ever, etc.

3.
When the conq'ring waves shall close
Proudly o'er me as I die,—
Over these brief victor foes
I shall triumph, while I cry,
Clinging to the rock,
Clinging to the rock,
Shelter for me ever. etc.

LORD, LEAD ME TO THEE.

Music by Asa Hull.

1. Beau-ti-ful mansions, home of the blest, Land where the faithful ev-er shall rest; There is my treasure, there shall I be;
2. Here in a des-ert, cheerless I roam; La-den with sorrow, far from my home: Clouds on my path-way darkly I see;

Chorus.

Lord, I am wea-ry, lead me to thee. Lead me to thee, — — — — Lead me to thee, — — — — Lord, I am weary, lead me to thee.

3.
Thou wilt not leave me comfortless here,
Why should I doubt thee? what do I fear?
Light in the distance breaking I see;
Yet I am weary, lead me to thee.
  Lead me to thee, etc.

4.
Jesus I love thee, dwell in my heart,
Never, O never from me depart!
Hope, like a rainbow shining, I see,
Yet I am weary, lead me thee.
  :||: Lead me to thee :||:
  Lord, I am weary, lead me to thee.

I'M NEARER MY HOME.

Words by PHOEBE CAREY.   (Arranged for this work.)   Music by JOHN M. EVANS.

1. One sweetly sol-emn thought Comes to me o'er and o'er;
2. Near-er my Father's house, Where man-y mansions be;

I'm nearer my home to day, Than ev-er I've been be-fore.
I'm nearer the great white throne, And nearer the Jas-per sea.

Chorus.

I'm nearer my home, nearer my home, Nearer my home to day;

Yes, nearer my home in heav'n to day, Than ev-er I've been before.

3. Nearer the bound of life,
   Where we lay our burdens down;
   I'm nearer leaving the cross,
   And nearer wearing the crown.
       I'm nearing my home, etc.

4. But lying dark between,
   And winding through the night,
   In silence that unknown stream
   Is bearing us to the light.
       I'm nearing my home, etc.

5. Perhaps my weary feet,
   Now tread upon its brink;
   And I may be nearer my home
   Than even I now may think.
       I'm nearer my home, etc.

6. Father, perfect my trust;
   Strengthen my feeble faith;
   Oh, bear me triumphantly o'er,
   Though crossing the river death.
       I'm nearer my home, etc.

THE ONLY PLEA.

Music by ASA HULL.

3.
Just as I am, poor, wretched, blind,
Sight, riches, healing of the mind,
Yea, all I need in thee I find;
 O Lamb of God, I come.—*Cho.*

4.
Just as I am, though toss'd about,
With many a conflict, many a doubt,
Fightings, within and fears without,—
 O Lamb of God, I come.—*Cho.*

5.
Just as I am thou wilt receive,
Wilt welcome, pardon, cleanse, relieve;
Because thy promise I believe,
 O Lamb of God, I come.—*Cho.*

6.
Just as I am, thy love unknown
Has broken every barrier down;
Now to be thine, yea, thine alone,
 O Lamb of God, I come.—*Cho.*

3. For nothing good have I,
    Where-by thy grace to claim—
  I'll wash my garments white
    In the blood of Calvary's Lamb.
  Jesus paid it all, etc.

4. And then complete in him,
    My robe his righteousness,
  Close shelter'd 'neath his side,
    I am divinely blest.
  Jesus paid it all, etc.

5. When from my dying bed
    My ransom'd soul shall rise,
  Then "Jesus paid it all!"
    Shall rend the vaulted skies.
  Jesus paid it all, etc.

6. And when before the throne
    I stand, in him complete,
  I'll lay my trophies down,
    All down at Jesus' feet.
  Jesus paid it all, etc.

THE CHRISTIAN HERO.

Rev. E. H. Nevin, D.D.

1. *Live* on the field of bat-tle! Be earnest in the fight;
   Stand forth with manly courage, And struggle for the right.
2. *Watch* on the field of bat-tle! The foe is ev'-ry-where,
   His fi-ery darts fly thickly, Like lightning, thro' the air.

Chorus.

Live, live, live! Live on the field of bat-tle.
Watch, watch, watch! Watch on the field of bat-tle.

3. *Pray* on the field of battle!
   God works with those who pray;
   His mighty arm can nerve us,
   And make us win the day.
   Pray, pray, pray!
   Pray on the field of battle.

4. *Die* on the field of battle!
   'Tis noble thus to die;
   God smiles on valiant soldiers,—
   Their record is on high.
   Die, die, die!
   Die on the field of battle.

SECOND HYMN for "All to Christ I Owe."

1. God's holy law, transgressed,
   Speaks nothing but despair;
   Burdened, with guilt oppressed
   We find no comfort there.
   Jesus paid it all, etc.

2. Not all our groans and tears,
   Nor works which we have done,
   Nor vows nor promises,
   Can e'er for sin atone.
   Jesus paid it all, etc.

3. Relief alone is found
   In Jesus precious blood:
   'Tis this that heals the wound,
   And reconciles to God.
   Jesus paid it all, etc.

4. High lifted on the cross,
   The spotless victim dies:
   This is salvation's source,
   On which our hope relies.
   Jesus paid it all, etc.

"LET THERE BE LIGHT."

Words by WILLIE WILDER. (Gen. i. 3.) Music by ASA HULL.

3.
The sons of morn with lasting song,
Will ever pass the word along;
  And waking men with rapture thrill,
  For, breaking o'er each eastern hill,
  The early dawn is shouting still,
    "Let there be light!"

4.
The soul may feel the heavy blight
Of deepest ignorance and night;
  Yet may the densest cloud be riven,
  And back the darkness may be driven,
  By that command which God has giv'n,
    "Let there be light!"

SEEKING JOYS IMMORTAL.

Music by Asa Hull.

1. My soul is now u-ni-ted To Christ the liv-ing vine;
   His grace I long have slight-ed, But now I feel Him mine.
2. Soon as my all I ventur'd On the a-ton-ing blood,
   The Ho-ly Spir-it en-ter'd, And I was born of God.

Chorus.

There's glo-ry in my soul; And glo-ry all a-round:
I am seek-ing joys im-mor-tal, A bright,—a star-ry crown.

coda.

I am seeking, I am seeking, I am seeking joys im-mortal.
Seek-ing, seek-ing, seek-ing joys im-mor-tal.

SEEKING JOYS IMMORTAL.

3. Now Christ is my salvation,
   What can I covet more?
   I have no condemnation;
   My Father's wrath is o'er.—*Cho.*

4. I taste a heavenly pleasure,
   And need not fear a frown;
   Christ is my joy and treasure,
   My glory and my crown.—*Cho.*

5. When I reach the world of glory,
   And take my seat above;
   I'll repeat the wondrous story,
   Of Jesus' dying love.

   Chorus.
   With glory in my soul,
   And glory all around;
   I will sing forever glory!
   And wear the conqueror's crown.

I LOVE THEE.

2. I'm happy, I'm happy, oh, wondrous account!
   My joys are immortal, I stand on the mount!
   I gaze on my treasure, and long to be there,
   With Jesus and angels, my kindred so dear.

3. O Jesus, my Saviour, with thee I am blest!
   My Life and Salvation, my Joy and my Rest!
   Thy name be my theme, and thy love be my song,
   Thy grace shall inspire both my heart and my tongue.

THE BEAUTIFUL VALE.

3.
The joys of earth, how soon they fade,
  Beautiful vale of rest;
Like morning dew or evening shade,
  Beautiful vale of rest;
Yet, when we reach thy golden strand,
Our gentle Saviour's promised land,
We'll sing with all the angel band,
  Beautiful vale of rest.
    Beautiful vale, etc.

4.
Oh, who would dwell for ever here,
  Beautiful vale of rest;
With joy, unfading joy so near,
  Beautiful vale of rest;
Oh, may I live, that I may wear
A starry crown for ever there,
And breathe thy sweet and balmy air,
  Beautiful vale of rest.
    Beautiful vale, etc.

DEPTH OF MERCY. Arranged by ASA HULL.

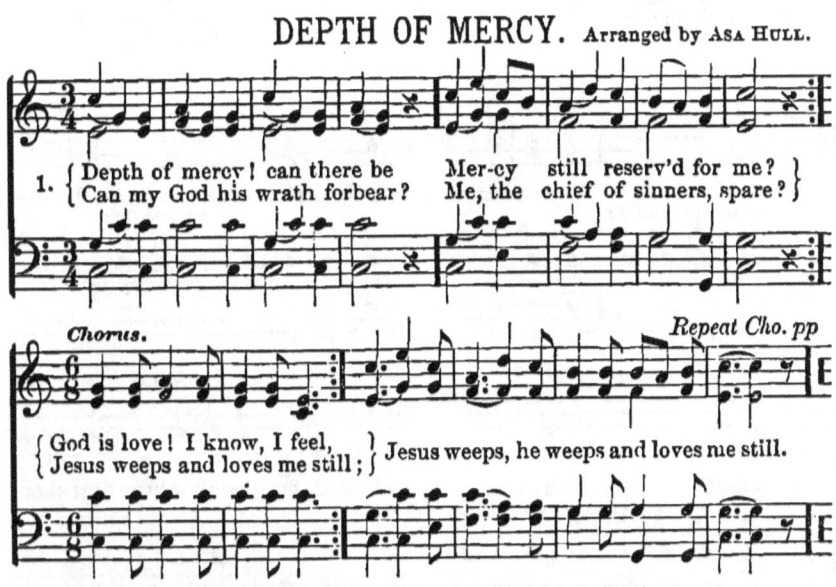

2. I have long withstood his grace;
   Long provoked him to his face;
   Would not hearken to his calls;
   Grieved him by a thousand falls.—*Cho.*

3. Now incline me to repent;
   Let me now my sins lament;
   Now my foul revolt deplore,
   Weep, believe, and sin no more.—*Cho.*

4. Kindled his relentings are;
   Me, he now delights to spare;
   Cries, How shall I give thee up?—
   Lets the lifted thunder drop.—*Cho.*

5. There for me the Saviour stands,
   Shows his wounds, and spreads his
   God is love! I know, I feel, [hands;
   Jesus weeps, and loves me still.—*Cho.*

58 SWEET BY AND BY.

Words by S. F. Bennett.   Music by J. P. Webster.

2.
We shall sing on that beautiful shore
  The melodious songs of the blest,
And our spirits shall sorrow no more,
  Not a sigh for the blessing of rest.
    In the sweet, etc.

3.
To our bountiful Father above,
  We will offer the tribute of praise,
For the glorious gift of his love,
  And the blessings that hallow our
    In the sweet, etc. [days!

TRUSTING IN THE LORD. 59

Words by REV. WM. McDONALD. (From "Tribute of Praise.")   Music by WM. G. FISCHER.

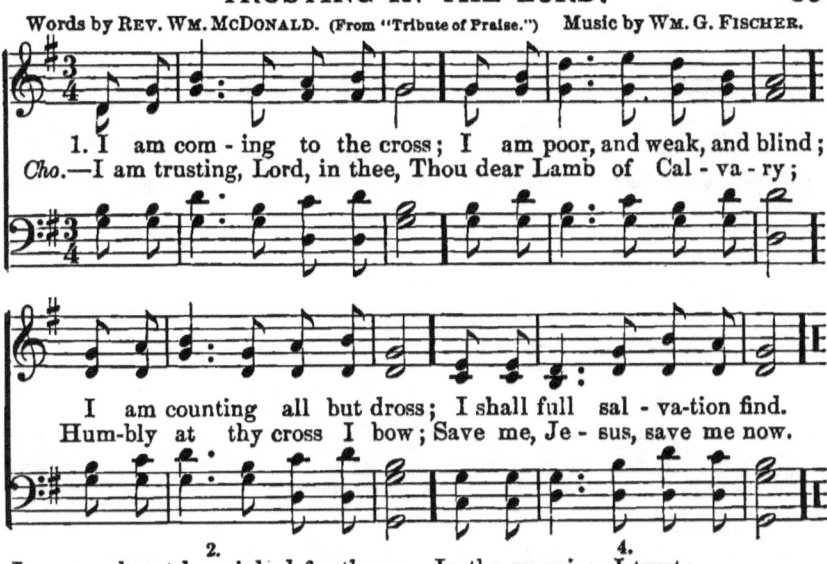

1. I am coming to the cross; I am poor, and weak, and blind;
I am counting all but dross; I shall full salvation find.

Cho.—I am trusting, Lord, in thee, Thou dear Lamb of Calvary;
Humbly at thy cross I bow; Save me, Jesus, save me now.

2.
Long my heart has sighed for thee;
 Long has evil reigned within;
Jesus sweetly speaks to me,
 I will cleanse you from all sin.
  I am trusting, etc.

3.
Here I give my all to thee,—
 Friends, and time, and earthly store;
Soul and body thine to be—
 Wholly thine—forever more.
  I am trusting, etc.

4.
In the promises I trust;
 Now I feel the blood applied;
I am prostrate in the dust;
 I with Christ am crucified.
  I am trusting, etc.

5.
Jesus comes! he fills my soul!
 Perfected in love I am;
I am every whit made whole;
 Glory, glory to the Lamb.
  I am trusting, etc.

SECOND HYMN.

1. Saviour of the sin-sick soul,
 Give me faith to make me whole;
 Finish thy great work of grace;
 Cut it short in righteousness.

2. Speak the second time,—Be clean!
 Take away my inbred sin;
 Every stumbling-block remove;
 Cast it out by perfect love.

3. Nothing less will I require;
 Nothing more can I desire;
 None but Christ to me be given;
 None but Christ in earth or heaven.

4. O that I might now decrease!
 O that all I am might cease!
 Let me into nothing fall;
 Let my Lord be all in all.

SWEET BY AND BY.—Concluded.

4.
We shall rest on that beautiful shore,
 In the joys of the saved we shall share;
All our pilgrimage toil will be o'er,
 And the conqueror's crown we shall wear.—In the sweet, etc.

5.
We shall meet, we shall sing, we shall reign,
 In the land where the saved never die;
We shall rest free from sorrow and pain,
 Safe at home in the sweet by and by.
  In the sweet, etc.

STAND UP FOR JESUS.

Words by R. TORREY, JR. Music by ASA HULL.

2.
Stand up for Jesus, Christian, stand!
Sound forth his name o'er sea and land!
Spread ye his glorious word abroad,
Till all the world shall own him Lord.
    Stand up for Jesus, &c.

3.
Stand up for Jesus, Christian, stand!
Lift high the cross with steadfast hand,
Till heathen lands, with wond'ring eye,
Its rising glory shall descry.
    Stand up for Jesus, &c.

4.
Stand up for Jesus, Christian, stand!
Soon with the blest immortal band
We'll dwell for aye, life's journey o'er,
In realms of light, on heav'n's bright
    shore.—Stand up &c.

THE PEARLY GATE.

Words by E. H. NEVIN, D. D.   *Music by* ASA HULL.

1. The night is dark, the storm is loud; Beneath its force the trees are bow'd;
2. My heart is sad, deep sorrows roll, Like streams of fire across my soul;

Yet still the pearly gate I see, Where angels stand to welcome me.
And yet the pearly gate I see, Where angels stand to welcome me.

Chorus.

To welcome me, to welcome me; The angels stand to welcome me.

3.
With fears without, and foes within,
  I seem almost subdued by sin;
And yet the pearly gate I see,
  Where angels stand, etc.

4.
The road is rough, my feet are sore,
  I long to have the journey o'er;
And yet the pearly gate I see,
  Where angels stand, etc.

5.
My eyes are dim, and faint my breath,
  Within me are the seeds of death;
But still the pearly gate I see,
  Where angels stand, etc.

6.
When life is gone, and in my breast
  All grief and fears are hushed to rest,
I hope the pearly gate to see,
  Where angels stand, etc.

SECOND HYMN.

1. My hope is built on nothing less
  Than Jesus' blood and righteousness;
  I dare not trust the sweetest frame,
  But wholly lean on Jesus' name
  On Christ, the solid Rock, I stand,
  All other ground is sinking sand.

2. When darkness seems to vail his face,
  I rest on his unchanging grace;
  In every high and stormy gale,
  My anchor holds within the vail;
  On Christ, the solid Rock, &c.

3. His oath, his covenant, and blood,
  Support me in the whelming flood;
  When all around my soul gives way,
  He then is all my hope and stay:
  On Christ, the solid Rock, &c.

I WILL SING FOR JESUS.

PHILIP PHILLIPS.

1. I will sing for Je - sus! With his love he bought me,
And all a - long my pilgrim way His lov-ing hand has bro't me.

2. Can there o - ver-take me An - y dark dis - as - ter
While I sing for Je - sus, My blessed, blessed Mas-ter?

Chorus.
Oh! help me sing for Je - sus; Help me tell the sto - ry
Of him who did redeem us, The Lord of life and glo - ry.

3.
I will sing for Jesus!
  His name alone, prevailing,
Shall be my sweetest music,
  When heart and flesh are failing.
    Oh, help me sing etc.

4.
Still I'll sing for Jesus!
  Oh, how will I adore him!
Among the cloud of witnesses
  Who cast their crowns before him.
    Oh, help me sing, etc.

THE HOME OF THE SOUL.

Arranged from PHILIP PHILLIPS.

3. That unchangeable home is for you and for me,
Where Jesus of Nazareth stands;
The King of all kingdoms forever is he,
:||: And he holdeth our crowns in his hands. :||:
The King of all kingdoms, etc.

4. O, how sweet it will be in that beautiful land,
So free from all sorrow and pain;
With songs on our lips, and with harps in our hands,
:||: To meet one another again. :||:
With songs on our lips, etc.

3. Nearer home! yes, one day nearer
   To our Father's house on high,
   To the green fields and the fountains
   Of the land beyond the sky;
   For the heav'ns grow brighter o'er us,
   And the lamps hang in the dome,
   And our tents are pitched still closer,
   For we're one day nearer home.

4. "One day nearer," sings the mariner,
   As he glides the waters o'er,
   While the light is softly dying
   On his distant native shore;
   Thus the Christian on life's ocean,
   As his light-boat cuts the foam,
   In the evening cries with rapture,
   "I am one day nearer home."

FUGITIVE MOMENTS.

Asa Hull. 65

1. Come, let us a-new Our journey pursue; Roll round with the year, Roll round with the year, And nev-er stand still Till the Master ap-pear, And never stand still Till the Mas-ter ap-pear.
2. His a-dor-a-ble will Let us glad-ly ful-fil; And our talents im-prove, And our tal-ents improve, By the patience of hope, And the labor of love, By the patience of hope, And the la-bor of love.

3. Our life is a dream;
   Our time, as a stream,
   :||: Glides swiftly away,:||:
   :||: And the fugitive moment
   Refuses to stay.:||:

4. The arrow is flown,
   The moment is gone;
   :||: The millenial year:||:
   :||: Rushes on to our view,
   And eternity's here. :||:

5. Oh, that each in the day
   Of his coming may say,—
   :||: "I have fought my way thro';:||:
   :||: I have finished the work
   Thou didst give me to do. :||:

6. Oh, that each from his Lord
   May receive the glad word,—
   :||:Well and faithfully done!:||:
   :||: Enter into my joy,
   And sit down on my throne. :||:

1. SECOND HYMN for "Nearer Home." 2.

Praise the Lord; ye heavens, adore him; Praise the Lord, for he is glorious;
  Praise him, angels, in the height;   Never shall his promise fail;
Sun and moon, rejoice before him; God hath made his saints victorious,
  Praise him, all ye stars of light.   Sin and death shall not prevail.
Praise the Lord, for he hath spoken; Praise the God of our salvation;
  Worlds his mighty voice obeyed;   Hosts on high, his power proclaim;
Laws, which never can be broken, Heaven and earth, and all creation,
  For their guidance he hath made.   Praise and magnify his name.

CHRIST OUR INTERCESSOR.

Words arranged by D. F. WOOD.
Music by ASA HULL.

1. Oh, bless-ed feet of Je-sus, Wea-ry with seeking me!
Stand at God's bar of judgment And in-ter-cede for me.
In-ter-cede for me, my Sa-viour, Oh, in-ter-cede for me;
Stand at God's bar of judgment, And in-ter-cede for me.

2. Oh, knees which bent in an-guish, In dark Gethsem-a-ne!
Kneel at the throne of glo-ry, And in-ter-cede for me.
In-ter-cede for me, my Sa-viour, Oh, in-ter-cede for me;
Kneel at the throne of glo-ry, And in-ter-cede for me.

3. O hands that were extended
  Upon that hallow'd tree!
:||: Hold up those precious nail prints
  Which intercede for me. :||:

4. O side from whence the spear point
  Brought blood and water free,
:||: For healing and for cleansing!
  Still intercede for me. :||:

5. O holy, scarred, and wounded,
  My sacrifice to be!
:||: Present thy perfect off'ring
  And intercede for me. :||:

6. O loving, risen Saviour,
  From death and sorrow free!
:||: Enthroned in endless glory,
  Still intercede for me. :||:

68. MY TITLE CLEAR.

Chorus by T. C. O'Kane.

2.
Should earth against my soul engage,
  And fiery darts be hurled;
Then I can smile at Satan's rage,
  And face a frowning world.
    Cho.—We will stand, etc.

3.
There I shall bathe my weary soul
  In seas of heavenly rest;
And not a wave of trouble roll
  Across my peaceful breast.
    Cho.—We will stand, etc.

BEAR THY CROSS.

Music by ASA HULL.

1. Bear thy cross cheerful-ly, Brother, the night Pass-eth, tho' tear-ful-ly; Dim is thy sight: Car-ry it du-teous-ly, Looking a-far, Where gleameth beauteously The morning star.

2. Bear thy cross meekly up, Sis-ter in pain, Drinking life's bit-ter cup, Ne'er think it vain: Hope-ful-ly, pray'r-ful-ly, Light then 'twill be, For the Lord careful-ly Thus leadeth thee.

3. Through surging sorrow's tides,
   Vales dark and lone,
Up rugged mountain sides,
   Making no moan:
Though shrinking wearily
   Beneath the load,
Take it up cheerily,
   'Tis from thy God.

4. Bear thy cross trustingly,
   Whate'er it be;
Then will it tenderly
   Rest upon thee:
Think not to lay it down
   Till life is done;
Beneath the cross the crown,
   When heav'n is won.

---

1. SECOND HYMN, for "My Title Clear." 3.

THERE is a land of pure delight,
   Where saints immortal reign;
Infinite day excludes the night,
   And pleasures banish pain.—*Cho.*

2.
There everlasting spring abides,
   And never-with'ring flowers;
Death, like a narrow sea, divides
   This heavenly land from ours.—*Cho.*

Sweet fields beyond the swelling flood
   Stand dressed in living green;
So to the Jews old Canaan stood,
   While Jordan roll'd between.—*Cho.*

4.
Could we but climb where Moses stood,
   And view the landscape o'er, [flood,
Not Jordan's stream, nor Death's cold
   Should fright us from the shore. *Cho.*

THE ROCK ON WHICH I BUILD.

Music by Asa Hull.

2.
While the fool is building upon the sand,
And scoffing at his neighbor, [wind,
Comes the roaring torrent and raging
And sweeps away all his labor;
But my Rock is firm, etc.

3.
What a glorious prospect! what joys I
While waiting by the river! [taste
On the Rock I rest, far above the blast;
Beyond, fair Eden discover:
For my Rock is firm, etc.

2.
When cares of earth, like burdens rest,
  Upon a life, by toil oppressed;
When all alone with God in prayer,
  You ask His aid, His grace, His care.

3.
When all is bright, and joys abound,
  And happiness is sought and found;
When earth recedes, and Death draws near
  And fills the heart with hope or fear.

3. 'Tis a note that is wafted across the troubled wave
   'Tis a song I've heard upon the shore;
   'Tis a sweet-thrilling murmur around the Christian's grave:
   "Oh, sorrow shall come again no more."—'Tis a song, etc.

4. 'Tis the loud-pealing anthem, the victor's holy song,
   Where the conflict and the strife are o'er;
   When the saved ones forever in joyous notes prolong:
   "Oh, sorrow shall come again no more."—'Tis a song, etc.

THE PRAISE OF JESUS.

Music by R. K. CARTER.

1. Come, sing the praise of Je-sus, And bless his ho-ly name;
He from our sins relieves us, He bore the cross and shame.

Chorus.
O, sing the praise of Je-sus, O, sing the praise of Je-sus,
O, sing the praise of Je-sus, For-ev-er, ev-er more.

2.
We'll shout with loud hosanna,
 His cross we'll glory in;
And bear the gospel banner,
 To all who live in sin.
 O, sing the praise, etc.

3.
Then praise him, praise him, praise him,
 And let the chorus swell,
For Christ, our Lord and Saviour,
 Hath conquered death and hell.
 O, sing the praise, etc.

4.
Then lift your heads ye portals!
 Ye everlasting doors
Lift up! that ransomed mortals
 May reach the heavenly shore.
 O, sing the praise, etc.

5.
And then before him ever,
 With all the white-robed throng,
Forever, and forever,
 We'll sing the *new, new song.*
 O, sing the praise, etc.

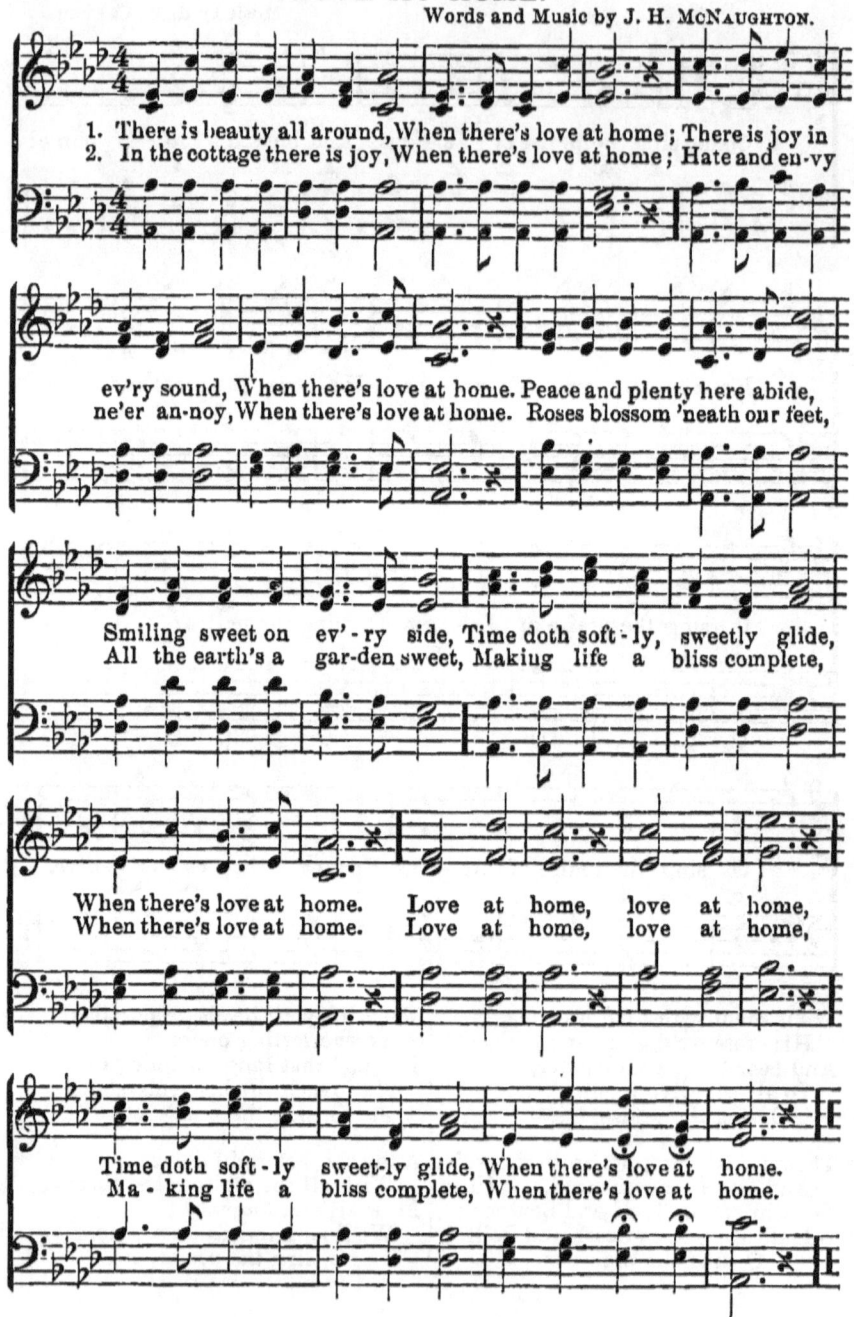

3. O, bliss of the purified! bliss of the pure!
No wound hath the soul that his blood cannot cure;
No sorrow-bowed head but may sweetly find rest,
No tears—but may dry them on Jesus's breast.—*Chorus.*

4. O, Jesus the crucified! Thee will I sing!
My blessed Redeemer! my God, and my King!
My soul filled with rapture shall shout o'er the grave,
And triumph in death in the mighty to save!—*Chorus.*

LOVE AT HOME.—Concluded.

3. Kindly heaven smiles above,
   When there's love at home;
All the earth is filled with love,
   When there's love at home.
Sweeter sings the brooklet by,
Brighter beams the azure sky;
Oh, there's One who smiles on high,
   When there's love at home.

4. Jesus, show thy mercy mine,
   Then there's love at home;
Sweetly whisper, I am thine,
   Then there's love at home.
Source of love, thy cheering light
Far exceeds the sun so bright—
Can dispel the gloom of night;
   Then there's love at home.

3.
These, these are they who in the
　conflict dire
Boldly have stood amid the hottest fire,
Jesus now says, "Come up higher,"
　"Wash'd in the blood of the Lamb."
　　"Sweeping thro' the gates," etc.

4.
Safe, safe upon the ever-shining shore,
Sin, pain, and death, and sorrow all
　are o'er;
Happy now and evermore,
"Wash'd in the blood of the Lamb."
Sweeping thro' the streets of the, etc.

* Suggested by the last words of Rev. Alfred Cookman.

LIFE'S BATTLE-FIELD.

Words by R. TORREY, Jr. Music by ASA HULL.

1. Soldiers on life's bat-tle-field, Be ye valiant, bold, and strong;
  In the strife, with cheerful zeal, Urge the Saviour's cause a-long.
2. Hark! the battle is be-gun! Rally, Christians, for your King;
  Forward, till the vict'ry's won, Till the shouts of triumph ring!

Chorus.
On-ward, on-ward to glo-ry! Yield not to the wi-ly foe;
Vict'ry and heav'n are before thee; Shout your triumph as you go.

3. Jesus calls us to the field!
  He will lead us evermore;
  'Neath his banner ne'er to yield,
  Till the mighty conflict's o'er.

4. Then, in yonder world of light
  We will lay our armor down,
  And 'mid throngs of angels bright,
  Each receive a starry crown.

SECOND HYMN.

1. Hasten, sinner, to be wise!
  Stay not for the morrow's sun:
  Wisdom, if you still despise,
  Harder is it to be won.

2. Hasten mercy to implore!
  Stay not for the morrow's sun,
  Lest thy season should be o'er,
  Ere this evening's stage be run.

3. Hasten, sinner, to return!
  Stay not for the morrow's sun,
  Lest thy lamp should fail to burn
  Ere salvation's work be done.

4. Hasten, sinner, to be blest!
  Stay not for the morrow's sun,
  Lest perdition thee arrest
  Ere the morrow is begun.

# WATCH AND PRAY.

Music by ASA HULL.

1. Watch, for the time is short; Watch, while 'tis call'd to-day; Watch, lest temptations overcome; Watch, Christian, watch and pray. Watch, for the flesh is weak, Watch, for the foe is strong; Watch, lest the bridegroom knock in vain, Watch, tho' he tarry long.

2.
Chase slumber from thine eyes,
  Chase doubting from thy breast;
Claim now as thine the promis'd prize,
  Of heaven's eternal rest.
Watch, Christian, watch and pray,
  Thy Saviour watch'd for thee;
Till from his brow, the blood-sweat
  In drops of agony. [pour'd,

3.
Take Jesus for thy trust;
  Watch, watch forever more;
Watch, for in death thou soon must
  With all who've gone before.[sleep,
Now, when thy sun is up,—
  Now, while 'tis called to-day;
O, now, in thine accepted time,
  Watch, Christian, watch and pray.

THE SWEETEST NAME.

Melody by GODFREY.
Arr. and Harm'd by A. HULL.

1. The great Phy-si-cian now is near, The sym-pa-thiz ing Je-sus,
2. Your ma-ny sins are all forgiven, Oh! hear the voice of Je-sus.

He speaks the drooping heart to cheer, Oh, hear the voice of Je-sus.
Go on your way in peace to heav'n, And wear a crown with Jesus.

Chorus.
Sweetest note in ser-aph song, Sweetest name on mor-tal tongue,
Sweet-est car-ol ev-er sung, Je-sus, Je-sus, Je-sus.

3.
All glory to the dying Lamb,
I now believe in Jesus:
I love the blessed Saviour's name.
I love the name of Jesus.—*Cho.*

4.
His name dispels my guilt and fear.
No other name but Jesus:
Oh! how my soul delights to hear
The charming name of Jesus.—*Cho.*

5.
Come, brethren, help me sing his praise,
Oh! praise the name of Jesus;
And, sisters, all your voices raise.
Oh! bless the name of Jesus.—*Cho.*

6.
And when to that bright world above,
We rise to see our Jesus,
We'll sing around the throne of love,
The name, the name of Jesus.—*Cho.*

THE BEAUTIFUL CITY.

Music by T. J. Cook.

1. Beauti-ful Zi-on, built above, Beau-ti-ful ci-ty that I love!
Beauti-ful gates of pearly white, Beautiful temple—God its light!

Chorus.
He who was slain on Cal-va-ry,
O-pens those pearl-y gates to me.
Zi-on, Zi-on, Zi-on, etc.

love-ly Zi-on, Beau-ti-ful Zi-on, ci-ty of our God.

2.
Beautiful heav'n where all is light,
Beautiful angels, clothed in white;
Beautiful strains that never tire,
Beautiful harps thro' all the choir;
There shall I join the chorus sweet,
Worshipping at the Saviour's feet.
　　Zion, Zion, etc.

3.
Beautiful crowns on every brow,
Beautiful palms the conquerors' show;
Beautiful robes the ransomed wear,
Beautiful all who enter there;
Thither I press with eager feet,
There shall my rest be long and sweet.
　　Zion, Zion, etc.

4.
Beautiful throne for Christ our King,
Beautiful songs the angels sing;
Beautiful rest—all wanderings cease,
Beautiful home of perfect peace;
There shall my eyes the Saviour see;
Haste to this heavenly home with me.
　　Zion, Zion, etc.

3. That land far away, yet ever is nigh,
   Where the weary rest, free from tears or sigh;
   There waters of life are abundant, full and free,
   And flowing forever for you and for me.—*Chorus.*

4. The dear ones of earth have pass'd on before,
   Where the ills of life enter nevermore;
   They dwell in the land of the glorified above,
   And drink of the flowing of Jesus' love.—*Chorus.*

82. TREASURES OF HEAVEN.

T. C. O'KANE.

1. There's a crown in heav'n for the striving soul, Which the blessed Jesus himself will place On the head of each who shall faithful prove, Even unto death, in the heav'nly race.
2. There is Rest in heav'n for the weary soul,—'Tis for all by care and by sin oppress'd; To the sons of God it remaineth sure, And the prophet says, 'tis a "glorious rest."

Chorus.

Oh, may that crown, in heav'n be mine, And I among the angels shine; Be thou, O Lord, my daily guide, Let me ever in thy love abide.

Oh, may that rest, etc.

WE'LL STAND THE STORM.

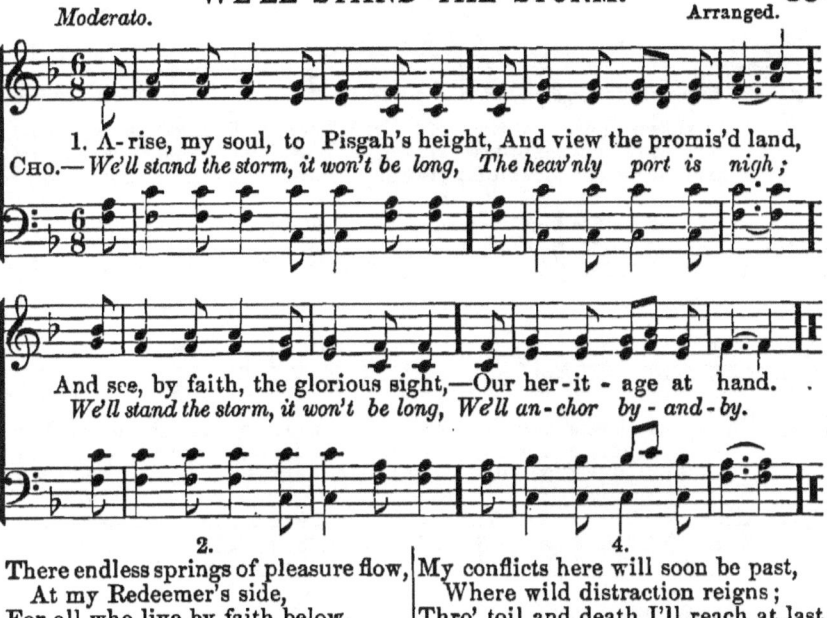

Moderato.   Arranged.

1. A-rise, my soul, to Pisgah's height, And view the promis'd land,
And see, by faith, the glorious sight,—Our her-it-age at hand.

CHO.—*We'll stand the storm, it won't be long, The heav'nly port is nigh;*
We'll stand the storm, it won't be long, We'll an-chor by-and-by.

2.
There endless springs of pleasure flow,
   At my Redeemer's side,
For all who live by faith below,
   And in their Lord confide.
    We'll stand the storm, etc.

3.
Fair Salem's dazzling gates are seen,
   Just o'er the narrow flood,
And fields adorned in living green,—
   The residence of God.
    We'll stand the storm, etc.

4.
My conflicts here will soon be past,
   Where wild distraction reigns;
Thro' toil and death I'll reach at last
   Fair Canaan's happy plains.
    We'll stand the storm, etc.

5.
Oh, could I cross rough Jordan's wave,
   No danger would I fear;
My bark would every tempest brave,
   For oh! my Captain's near.
    We'll stand the storm, etc.

TREASURES OF HEAVEN.—Concluded.

3. There is Joy in heaven for the mourning soul;
   Though the tears my fall all the earthly night;
  Yet the clouds of sadness will break away,
   And rejoicing come with the morning light.
    Oh, may that Joy in heaven me mine, etc.

4. There is Peace in heaven for the troubled soul,
   Where the wicked shall from their troubling cease,
  And to all the saints like a river flow,
   Through the endless ages the stream of peace.
    Oh, may that Peace in heaven be mine, etc.

5. There's a Home in heaven for the faithful soul,
   In the many mansions prepared above,
  Where the glorified shall forever sing,
   Of a Saviour's free and unbounded love.
    Oh, may that Home in heaven be mine, etc.

4.
At the smiling of the river,
  Mirror of the Saviour's face,
Saints whom death will never sever,
  Lift their songs of saving grace.
    Yes, we'll gather, etc.

5.
Soon we'll reach the silver river;
  Soon our pilgrimage will cease;
Soon our happy hearts will quiver
  With the melody of peace.
    Yes, we'll gather, etc.

OUR MISSION.

Words by D. D. BUCK. D. D.
Music by ASA HULL.

1. If we can not plant our cottage 'Mid an Eden's blooming bow'rs,
2. If we can not win a title To enwreath our humble name;

Whiling life's delightful summer Gaily 'mid unfading flow'rs,
D.S. We can consecrate to duty Willing hearts and ready hands.
   If we boast not birth nor beauty, Wealth nor wisdom, might nor fame,
D.S. And, tho' men may be ungrateful, God will prize the humble heart.

We with holy love can labor, Tilling Zion's fertile lands;
We can still be kindly hearted, Acting well our lowly part;

3.
If we can not cease from sorrow,
  Mingling pray'r with sighing breath;
If we can not keep our loved ones
  From the greedy grasp of death,—
We can smile amid the weeping,
  As we fully trust in God,
And still leaning on the Saviour,
  Meekly kiss the chast'ning rod.

4.
If we cannot mount the heavens,
  Where no cloud its shadow flings,
Ranging through the bright Elysian,
  Soaring on angelic wings,—
We with pilgrim-steps can journey,
  Onward pressing day by day,
Looking for our Leader's footprints
  All along the toilsome way.

5.
If we can not read the future,
  Whether weal or woe betide;
If within the veil of darkness
  Mercy from our vision hide,—
We can understand our mission,
  What is here to do or bear;
We can love and help each other,
  And the cross with Jesus share.

6.
Let us, then, be ever doing;
  Day declineth, night is near;
Short the time of toil and suff'ring;
  Jesus numbers every tear.
See! the pearly gates are opening;
  Lo! the splendor from above;
List to lov'd ones yonder singing;
  Welcome to the land of love.

THE POLAR STAR.

Words by FANNY CROSBY.   From "Sabbath Carols."   Music by T. E. PERKINS.

1. Weary wanderer o'er the main, Seeking for thy home again,
Thro' the gath'ring mists that rise, Veiling thy natal skies;
Look beyond, there's light for thee, Streaming o'er the turbid sea:
Softly it smiles, tho' distant far, The beautiful polar star.

2.
Stranger on a rocky strand,
Longing for thy fatherland,
Thro' the gathering clouds that rise,
Veiling thy natal skies;
Look beyond, there's hope for thee,
Dawning o'er a tranquil sea:
Softly it smiles, though distant far,
The beautiful polar star.

3.
Lonely watcher, pale with grief,
Thou shalt find a sweet relief,
Though thy tears unheeded fall,
Jesus will count them all;
Look beyond, there's joy for thee,
Breaking o'er a troubled sea;
Softly it smiles, though distant far
The beautiful polar star.

2.
I know I'm nearing the holy ranks
  Of friends and kindred dear;
For I brush the dews on Jordan's banks;
  The crossing must be near.
    Oh, come, etc.

3.
I've almost gain'd my heav'nly home;
  My spirit loudly sings;
The holy ones, behold, they come!
  I hear the noise of wings.
    Oh, come, etc.

4.
Oh, bear my longing heart to Him
  Who bled and died for me,—
Whose blood now cleanses from all sin,
  And gives me victory.
    Oh, come, etc.

MY SPIRIT NAME IN HEAVEN.

Words by FANNY CROSBY. Music by ASA HULL.

1. There is a radiant, sunny clime, Where those who lov'd me here
Are waiting on the ro-sy banks, Be-side the riv-er clear;
D. S.—Yet oft I won-der what shall be My spir-it name in heav'n.
And if I well have borne the cross, A crown will there be giv'n,—

2.
Sweet tho'ts came o'er me, in a dream,
Of pure, unclouded skies,
Of joy my Father's hand bestows,
And love that never dies.
I seemed to hear a still, small voice,
Like whispered tones at ev'n,
And paused to ask,—Oh, what shall be
My spirit name in heav'n?

3.
I know there is a better land—
By faith I see it now;
I almost reach the clust'ring vines
That grace the mountain's brow:
A robe of white, a harp of gold,
To me will there be giv'n,
And then, oh, then my soul shall know
Its spirit name in heav'n.

SECOND HYMN.

1.
And let this feeble body fail,
And let it faint or die:
My soul shall quit the mournful vale,
And soar to worlds on high:
Shall join the disembodied saints,
And find its long-sought rest,—
That only bliss for which it pants,
In the Redeemer's breast.

2.
In hope of that immortal crown
I now the cross sustain,
And gladly wander up and down,
And smile at toil and pain:
I suffer on my three score years,
Till my deliv'rer come,
And wipe away his servant's tears,
And take his exile home.

"OH, DON'T STAY AWAY." 91
Words and Music by O. Snow.

1. We're going home to glory, We're going home to glory,
Dear friends, come and join us, Oh, don't stay away.
2. We'll sing among the angels, We'll sing among the angels,
We'll swell th' joyful chorus, We'll not stay away.

Chorus.
Oh, don't stay away, Oh, My brother, don't stay away; 'Tis Jesus invites you, Oh, don't stay away.

3. There is joy in religion,
   Dear friends, come and seek it,
   Oh, don't stay away.—*Cho.*
4. Our heavy hearts were burdened,
   But now they are are happy,
   We did not stay away.—*Cho.*
5. Oh, come and seek the Saviour,
   And feel you are pardoned,
   Oh, don't stay away.—*Cho.*

6. I'm glad I'm in this army,
   And Jesus is our Captain,
   And leads us on the way.—*Cho.*
7. We'll wash in the fountain,
   We'll find full salvation,
   We will not stay away.—*Cho.*
8. In heaven we'll sing forever;
   Dear sinner, will you join us,
   Oh, why will you delay.—*Cho.*

Concluded from opposite page.

3.
Oh, what hath Jesus brought for me!
  Before my ravished eyes
Rivers of life divine I see,
  And trees of Paradise:
I see a word of spirits bright,
  Who taste the pleasures there;
They all are robed in spotless white,
  And conq'ring palms they bear.

4.
Oh, what are all my suff'rings here,
  If, Lord, thou count me meet
With that enraptured host t'appear,
  And worship at thy feet;
Give joy or grief, give ease or pain,
  Take life or friends away,
But let me find them all again
  In that eternal day

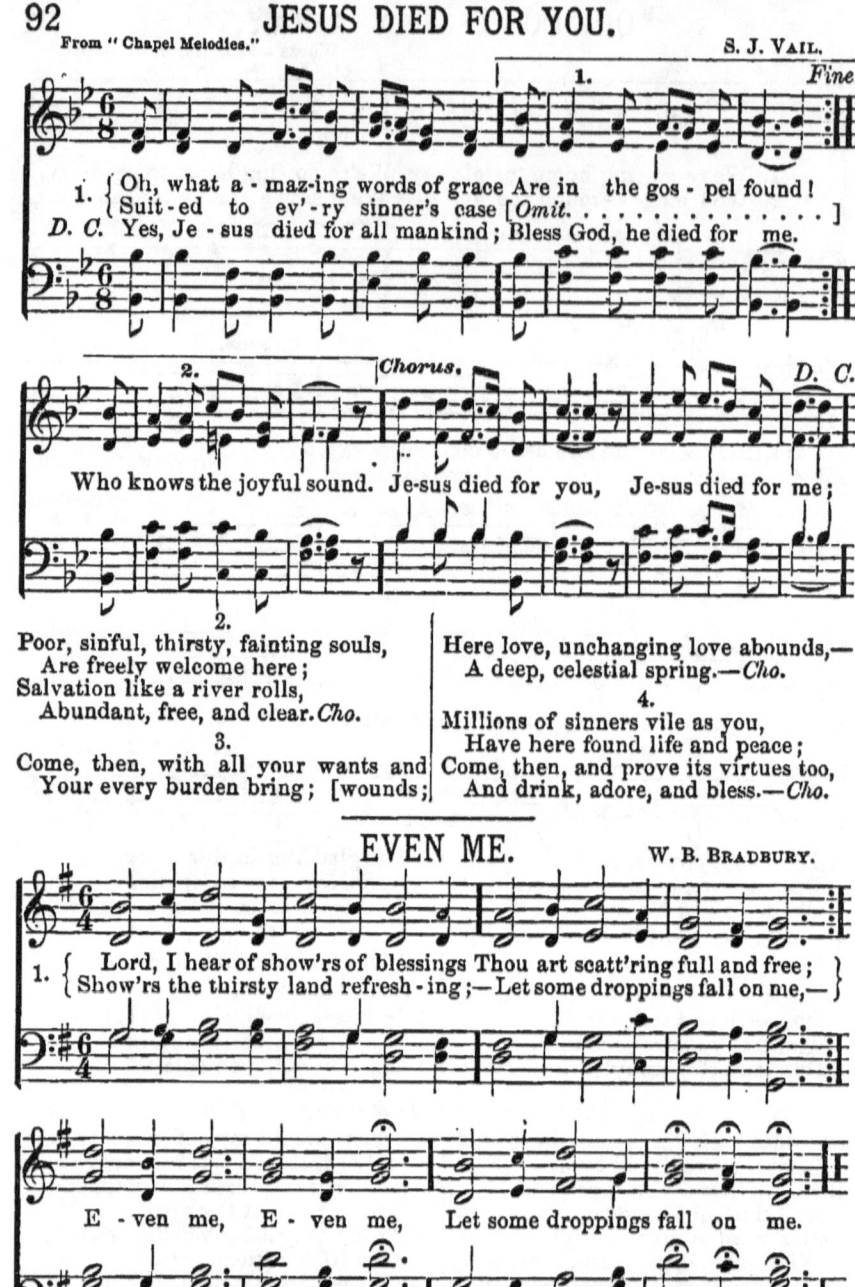

THERE, THERE IS REST.

From MS. of Rev. G. D. BROWNE.

1. Come, poor pilgrim, sad and weary, Why heaves thy breast?
Roaming this wide world so dreary, (*Omit*.........) Sighing for rest.

Chorus, ad lib. *a tempo.*
Rest, rest, sweet rest; Where the wicked cease from troubling, And the wea-ry are at rest.

2.
There is rest for thee in glory,
  Among the blest;
Listen to the joyful story,—
  There, there is rest. Rest, etc.

3.
There are those who've gone before us,
  All who are blest,
Singing now the happy chorus,
  There, there is rest. Rest, etc.

4.
There the golden harps are ringing,
  Harps of the blest;
And the angels bands are singing,
  There, there is rest. Rest, etc.

5.
We shall meet where parting never
  Comes to the blest;
And we'll safely dwell for ever
  In heavenly rest. Rest, etc.

EVEN ME, Concluded.

2.
Pass me not, O gracious Saviour,
  Let me live and cling to thee;
Fain I'm longing for thy favor;
  Whilst thou'rt calling, call for me.
    Even me, even me,
  Whilst thou'rt calling, call for me.

3.
Pass me not, O mighty Spirit,
  Thou canst make the blind to see;
Witnesses of Jesus' merit,
  Speak some word of pow'r to me.
    Even me, even me,
  Speak some word of pow'r to me.

4.
Love of God, so pure and changeless,
  Blood of Christ, so rich and free;
Grace of God, so rich and boundless,
  Magnify it all in me.
    Even me, even me,
  Magnify it all in me.

5.
Pass me not, thy lost one bringing,
  Bind my heart, O Lord, to thee;
Whilst the streams of life are springing,
  Blessing others, oh, bless me.
    Even me, even me,
  Blessing others, oh, bless me.

THE RESTING PLACE.

Music by ASA HULL.

2. I heard the voice of Jesus say,
   "Behold, I freely give
   The living water: thirsty one,
   Stoop down and drink, and live."
   I came to Jesus, and I drank
   Of that life-giving stream ;
   My thirst was quench'd, my soul re-
   And now I live in him. [vived,

3. I heard the voice of Jesus say,
   "I am this dark world's light;
   Look unto me, thy morn shall rise,
   And all thy day be bright."
   I looked to Jesus, and I found
   In him my Star, my Sun ;
   And in that light of life I'll walk,
   Till trav'lling days are done.

THE SUNNY SHORE.—Concluded.

2. Now they feel no chilling blast,
   For their winter time is past,
   And their summers always last,
   Over there :
   :||:They can never know a fear,
   For the Saviour's always near,
   And with them is endless cheer,
   Over there. :||:

3. They have fought the weary fight,
   Jesus saved them by his might,
   Now they dwell with him in light;
   Over there :
   :||:Soon we'll reach the shining strand,
   But we'll wait our Lord's command,
   Till we see his beck'ning hand,
   Over there. :||:

GLORY TO THE LAMB!

B. W. Gorham.

1. The world is o-ver-come, By the blood of the Lamb!
2. My sins are washed a-way In the blood of the Lamb!

Glory to the Lamb! Glory to the Lamb! Glory to the Lamb!

3. The Mar-tyr's overcame,
By the blood of the Lamb!

4. I soon shall gain the skies,
Through the blood of the Lamb!

HENLEY.

Dr. L. Mason.

1. Come un-to me when shadows dark-ly gath-er, When the sad heart is weary and distress'd, Seeking for comfort from your heav'nly Fa-ther, Come un-to me, and I will give you rest.

WAITING BY THE RIVER.

Words by MARY P. GRIFFIN.   Music by ASA HULL.

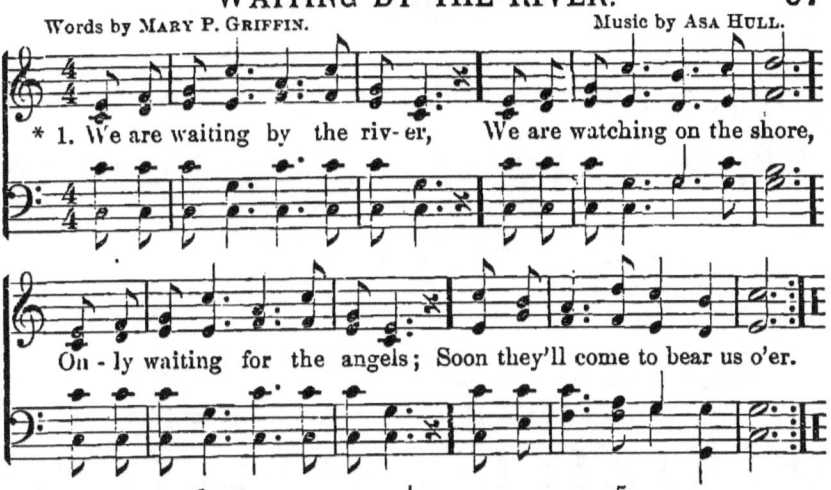

*1. We are waiting by the river, We are watching on the shore,
On-ly waiting for the angels; Soon they'll come to bear us o'er.

2.
Tho' the mist hang o'er the river,
 And its billows loudly roar,
Yet we hear the song of angels,
 Wafted from the other shore.
  We are waiting, etc.

3.
And the bright celestial city,
 We have caught such radiant gleams
Of its towr's, like dazzling sunlight,
 With its sweet and peaceful streams.
  We are waiting, etc.

4.
He has called for many a loved one;
 We have seen them leave our side;
With our Saviour we shall meet them,
 When we too have crossed the tide.
  We are waiting, etc.

5.
When we've pass'd that vale of shad-
 With its dark and chilling tide, [ows,
In that bright and glorious city
 We shall evermore abide.
  We are waiting, etc.

6.
Pain nor sickness ne'er shall enter;
 Grief nor woe my lot shall share;
But, in that celestial center
 I a crown of life shall wear.
  We are waiting, etc.

7.
Oh, that hope, how bright, how glor-
 'Tis his people's blest reward; [ious,
In the Saviour's strength victorious,
 They at length behold their Lord.
  We are waiting, etc.

HENLEY.—Concluded.

2. Ye who have mourned when the spring flowers were taken,
  When the ripe fruit fell richly to the ground,
 When the loved slept, in brighter homes to waken,
  Where their pale brows with spirit wreaths are crowned.

3. Large are the mansions in thy Father's dwelling;
  Glad are the homes that sorrows never dim;
 Sweet are the harps in holy music swelling;
  Soft are the tones which raise the heavenly hymn.

4. There, like an Eden blossoming in gladness,
  Bloom the fair flowers the earth too rudely press'd:
 Come unto me, all ye who droop in sadness,
  Come unto me, and I will give you rest!

* May be sung as duet first time, repeating 1st verse as Chorus after each verse.

THE GOLDEN SHORE.

Words and Melody by Rev. R. H. McCray.

FAITH IN GOD.

Words by D. F. WOOD.   Music by ASA HULL.

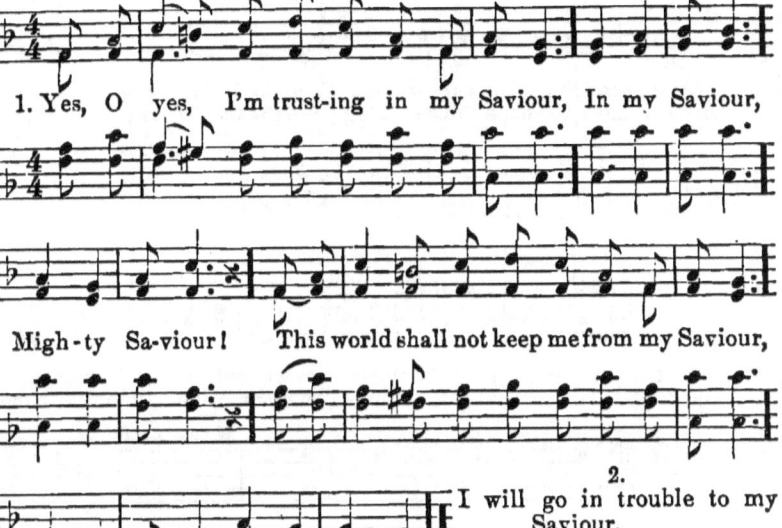

1. Yes, O yes, I'm trusting in my Saviour, In my Saviour, Mighty Saviour! This world shall not keep me from my Saviour, From my Saviour, Loving Saviour!

2. I will go in trouble to my Saviour, To my Saviour, Helping Saviour! To thee will I live, oh, blessed Saviour, Blessed Saviour, Living Saviour!

3. Peace and love receive I from my Saviour, From my Saviour, Gentle Saviour! From thee, full salvation comes, dear Saviour, Comes, dear Saviour, Giving Saviour!

4. Now I'm trusting in my God and Saviour, In my Saviour, God, and Saviour! Oh, ye doubting ones, trust now your Saviour, Trust your Saviour, Lord, and Saviour!

THE GOLDEN SHORE.—Concluded.

2. Over there on the bright azure plains,
   The river of life sweetly flows;
For the Saviour eternally reigns,
   And the beautiful gates never close.
       In a bright happy home, etc.

3. Blessed Jesus has gone to prepare
   Us a crown that is brighter than day,
Then forever he'll dwell with us there,
   His own hand shall wipe all tears away.—In a bright, etc.

4. No sorrow shall e'er taint the air,
   Where God dwells evil never can come;
No weeping will break on the ear,
   When the day of life's turmoil is done.—In a bright, etc.

5. We will meet in the land ever fair,
   Where the weary forever shall rest,
The crown of redemption we'll wear,
   And triumphantly chant with the blest.—In a bright, etc.

SAFE WITHIN THE VAIL.

JOHN M. EVANS.

1. "Land ahead!" its fruits are waving O'er the hills of fadeless green;
2. Onward, bark, the cape I'm rounding; See the blessed wave their hands;

And the liv-ing waters laving Shores where heav'nly forms are seen.
Hear the harps of God resounding From the bright, immortal bands.

Chorus.

Rocks and storms I'll fear no more, When on that e-ter-nal shore;

Drop the anchor! furl the sail! I am safe within the vail!

3.
There, let go the anchor, riding
On this calm and silv'ry bay;
Seaward fast the tide is gliding;
Shores in sunlight stretch away.
Rocks and storms, etc.

4.
Now we're safe from all temptation;
All the storms of life are past;
Praise the Rock of our salvation!
We are safe at home at last!
Rocks and storms, etc.

NOTE.—Any appropriate hymn of 8s & 7s meter may be used with this tune.

"JESUS IS MINE."

Words by BONAR. Arranged. The original by ASA HULL.

1. Fade, fade, each earthly joy, Jesus is mine! Break ev'ry tender tie, Jesus is mine! Dark is the wilderness; Earth has no resting place; Jesus alone can bless; Jesus is mine!

2. Tempt not my soul away; Jesus is mine! Here would I ever stay; Jesus is mine! Perishing things of clay, Born but for one brief day, Pass from my heart away; Jesus is mine!

3. Farewell, ye dreams of night,
   Jesus is mine!
   Lost in this dawning bright,
   Jesus is mine!
   All that my soul has tried
   Left but a dismal void;
   Jesus has satisfied;
   Jesus is mine!

4. Farewell, mortality,
   Jesus is mine!
   Welcome, eternity,
   Jesus is mine!
   Welcome, O loved and blest;
   Welcome, sweet scenes of rest;
   Welcome, my Saviour's breast;
   Jesus is mine.

SECOND HYMN, for "Safe Within the Vail."

1. THIS is not my place of resting—
   Mine's a city yet to come;
   Onward to it I am hasting—
   On to my eternal home.
   Rocks and storms, etc.

2. In it all is light and glory;
   O'er it shines a nightless day;
   Every trace of sin's sad story,
   All the curse hath passed away.
   Rocks and storms, etc.

3. There the Lamb, our Shepherd, leads us
   By the streams of life along;
   On the freshest pastures feeds us,
   Turns our sighing into song.
   Rocks and storms, etc.

4. Soon we pass this desert dreary,
   Soon we bid farewell to pain;
   Never more are sad and weary,
   Never, never sin again.
   Rocks and storms, etc.

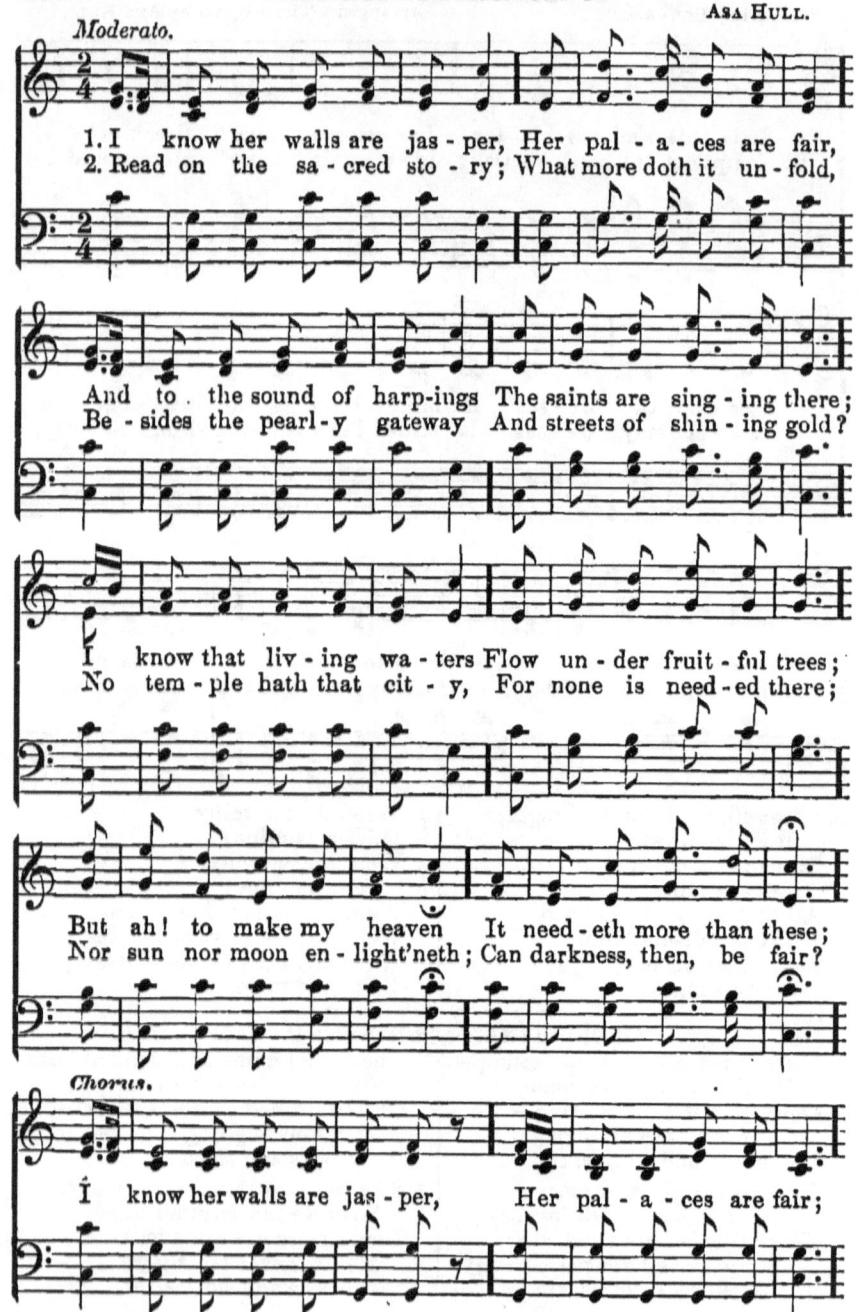

THE CELESTIAL CITY.

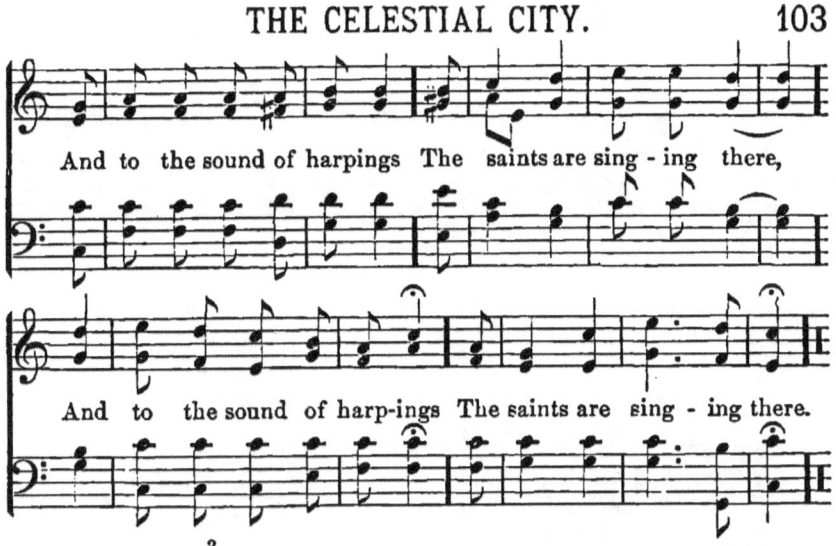

And to the sound of harpings The saints are sing-ing there,

And to the sound of harp-ings The saints are sing-ing there.

3.
Ah! now the glad revealing,
  The crowning joy of all;
What need of other sunlight,
  Where God is all in all!
He fills the wide ethereal
  With glory all his own,
He whom my soul adoreth—
  The Lamb amid the throne.—*Cho.*

4.
Oh, heaven without my Saviour
  Would be no heaven to me;
Dark were the walls of jasper,
  Rayless the crystal sea;

He gilds earth's darkest valley
  With light, and joy, and peace;
What, then, must be the radiance
  When night and death shall cease?

5.
Speed on, O lagging moments!
  Come, birthday of the soul!
How long the night appeareth;
  The hours, how slow they roll!
How sweet the welcome summons
  That greets the willing bride!
And when my eyes behold him,
  I shall be satisfied.—*Cho.*

SECOND HYMN.

1.
OH, when shall I see Jesus,
  And reign with him above,
And from that flowing fountain
  Drink everlasting love?
When shall I be delivered
  From this vain world of sin,
And with my blessed Jesus,
  Drink endless pleasures in?

2.
But now I am a soldier,
  My Captain's gone before;
He's given me my orders,
  And bids me not give o'er;
And since he has proved faithful,
  A righteous crown he'll give,
And all his valiant soldiers
  Eternal life shall have.

3.
Through grace I am determined,
  To conquer, though I die,
And then away to Jesus
  On wings of love I'll fly:
Farewell to sin and sorrow,
  I'll bid you all adieu;
Then, O my friends, prove faithful,
  And on your way pursue.

4.
Whene'er you meet with troubles
  And trials on your way,
Oh, cast your care on Jesus,
  And don't forget to pray;
Gird on the heavenly armor
  Of faith, and hope, and love;
Then, when the combat's ended,
  He'll carry you above.

REST FOR THE WEARY.

Arr. from Rev. W. M'Donald.

1. In the Christian's home in glory There remains a land of rest;
There my Saviour's gone before me, To fulfill my soul's request.

Chorus.

{ There is rest for the weary, There is rest for the weary,
On the other side of Jordan, In the sweet fields of Eden,
There is rest for the weary, There is rest for you.
Where the tree of life is blooming, There is rest for you. }

2.
He is fitting up my mansion,
  Which eternally shall stand,—
For my stay shall not be transient
  In that holy, happy land.—*Cho.*

3.
Pain nor sickness ne'er shall enter,
  Grief nor woe my lot shall share;
But in that celestial center
  I a crown of life shall wear.—*Cho.*

4.
Death itself shall then be vanquish'd,
  And his sting shall be withdrawn;
Shout for gladness, O ye ransomed;
  Hail with joy the rising morn. *Cho.*

5.
Sing, oh, sing, ye heirs of glory,
  Shout your triumph as you go!
Zion's gates shall open for you;
  You shall find an entrance thro'.

"JESUS SAVES ME." Words by Jas. Nicholson. Music by J. A. Duncan. Arranged for this work.

1. Je-sus saves me eve-ry day, Je-sus saves me eve-ry night;
Je-sus saves me all the way, Thro the darkness, thro' the light.

Chorus.
Je-sus saves, O bliss sublime, Je-sus saves me all the time

2.
Jesus saves when I repine,
  Jesus saves when I rejoice;
Jesus saves when hopes decline—
  Faith can always hear his voice.
    Chorus.—Jesus saves, etc.

3.
Jesus saves when sorrows come,
  Jesus saves when death appears;
Jesus saves and leads me home—
  When shall end my doubts and fears.
    Chorus.—Jesus saves, etc.

4.
Jesus saves me, He is mine;
  Jesus saves me, I am His;
Jesus saves while I recline—
  On his precious promises.
    Chorus.—Jesus saves, etc.

5.
Jesus saves, He saves from sin,
  Jesus saves, I feel him nigh;
Jesus saves, He dwells within,
  Gladly do I testify.
    Chorus.—Jesus saves, etc.

SECOND HYMN.

1. Now, O God, thine own I am!
    Now I give thee back thine own:
  Freedom, friends, and health, and fame,
    Consecrate to thee alone:
  Thine I live, thrice happy I!
  Happier still, if thine I die.

2. Take me, Lord, and all my powers;
    Take my mind, and heart, and will;
  All my goods, and all my hours.

  All I know, and all I feel,
  All I think, or speak, or do—
  Take my soul and make it new!

3. Father, Son, and Holy Ghost,
    One in Three, and Three in One,
  As by the celestial host,
    Let thy will on earth be done:
  Praise by all to thee be given,
  Glorious Lord of earth and heaven!

HEAVENLY VISION.

1. These are the crowns that we shall wear When all the saints are crown'd;
   These are the palms that we shall bear On yonder holy ground.
2. Far off, as yet, reserved in heav'n, Above the veiling sky,
   They sparkle like the stars of ev'n To Hope's far-piercing eye.

Chorus.
We will walk thro' the valley in peace, We will walk thro' the valley in peace,
If Jesus himself will be our Leader, We will walk thro' the valley in peace.

3.
These are the robes, unsoiled and white,
 Which there we shall put on,
When, foremost 'mong the sons of light,
 We sit on yonder throne.—*Cho.*

4.
With these in view, how poor appear
 The world's most winning smiles!
Vain is the tempter's subtlest snare,
 And weak his varied wiles.—*Cho.*

5.
Then welcome, toil, and care, and pain!
 And welcome sorrow, too!
All toil is rest, all grief is gain,
 With such a prize in view.—*Cho.*

6. [palm!
Come, crown and throne and robe and
 Burst forth, glad streams of peace!
Come, holy city of the Lamb!
 Rise, Sun of righteousness.—*Cho.*

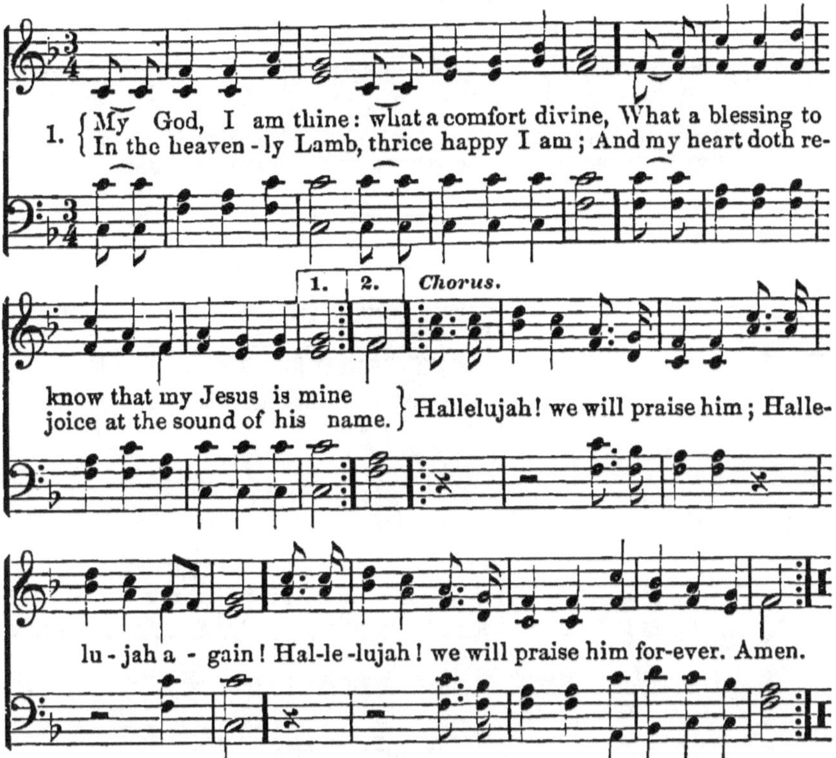

THE HEAVENLY FEAST.

1. My God, I am thine: what a comfort divine, What a blessing to know that my Jesus is mine
   In the heavenly Lamb, thrice happy I am; And my heart doth rejoice at the sound of his name.

Chorus.
Hallelujah! we will praise him; Hallelujah again! Hallelujah! we will praise him for-ever. Amen.

2. True pleasures abound in the rapturous sound,
   And whoever hath found it, hath paradise found;
   My Redeemer to know, to feel his blood flow,—
   This is life everlasting; 'tis heaven below.—*Chorus.*

3. Yet onward I haste, to the heavenly feast:
   That indeed is the fullness, but this is the taste;
   And this I shall prove till with joy I remove
   To the heaven of heavens, in Jesus's love.—*Chorus.*

---

1. SECOND HYMN for "Heavenly Vision." 3.

Oh, what hath Jesus bought for me!
  Before my ravished eyes
Rivers of life divine I see,
  And trees of Paradise:—*Cho.*

2.
I see a world of spirits bright,
  Who taste the pleasures there;
They all are robed in spotless white,
  And conq'ring palms they bear.—*Cho.*

Oh, what are all my suff'rings here,
  If, Lord, thou count me meet
With that enraptured host t'appear,
  And worship at thy feet!—*Cho.*

4.
Give joy or grief, give ease or pain,
  Take life or friends away,
But let me find them all again
  In that eternal day.—*Cho.*

THE GLORIOUS TREASURE.

3.
Yes, I'll to my bosom press thee;
  Precious Word, I'll hide thee here!
Sure my very heart will bless thee,
  For thou ever says't, "Good cheer!"

4.
Speak, spoor heart, and tell thy pon- [d'rings:
  Tell how far thy rovings led, [d'rings,
When this book bro't back thy wan-
  Speaking life as from the dead.

5.
Yes, sweet Bible! I will hide thee
  Deep, yes, deeper in this heart!
Thou through all my life wilt guide me,
  And in death we will not part.

6.
Part in death? No, never, never!
  Through death's vale I'll lean on thee;
Then, in worlds above forever,
  Sweeter still thy truths shall be.

THE SABBATIC YEAR.

109

Music by ASA HULL.

1. When shall I see the day That ends my woes?
   When shall I vict'ry gain O'er all my foes? When will the trumpet sound
2. A crown of glo-ry bright, By faith I see,
   In yonder realms of light, Prepared for me; Oh, may I faithful prove,

That calls the ex-ile home? The grand Sabbatic year, When will it come?
And keep the prize in view, And thro' the storms of life My way pur-sue.

3. Jesus, be thou my Guide!
   My steps attend;
   Oh, keep me near thy side;
   Be thou my Friend;
   Be thou my Shield and Sun,
   My Saviour and my Guard,
   And, when my work is done,
   My great Reward.

4. Oh, how I long to see
   That happy day,
   When sorrow, sin, and pain
   Shall flee away;
   When all the heavenly tribes
   Shall find their long-sought home;
   The jubilee of heaven,—
   When will it come?

COME TO JESUS.

1. Come to Je-sus, come to Je-sus, come to Je-sus just now,

Just now come to Je-sus, Come to Je-sus just now.

2. He will save you, etc.
3. Oh, believe him, etc.
4. He'll receive you, etc.
5. Flee to Jesus, etc.
6. He will hear you, etc.
7. He'll have mercy, etc.
8. He'll forgive you, etc.
9. He will cleanse you, etc.
10. Jesus loves you, etc.

110 LIGHTS ALONG THE SHORE.

Words by Rev. J. H. Stockton.   (Arranged for this work.)   Music by E. Roberts.

1. I'm a 'pilgrim and a stranger passing o-ver, The road may be rough, but 'tis clear; And a starry crown awaits me o'er the riv-er, And Jesus bids me welcome there.

Chorus.

There are lights along the shore that never grow dim, That never, never grow dim; These souls are all aflame, With the love of Jesus' name, They guide us, yes, they guide us unto Him.

ON THE CROSS.

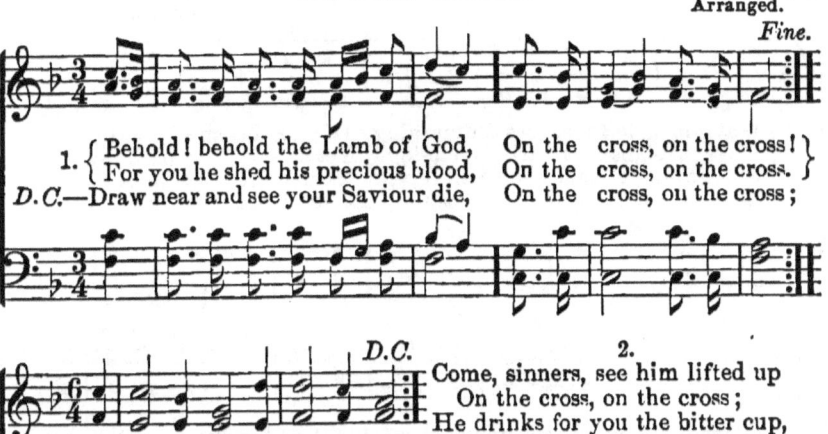

3.
'Tis done, the mighty deed is done,
  On the cross, on the cross;
The battle fought, the vict'ry won,
  On the cross, on the cross. [quake
The rocks do rend, the mountains
While Jesus doth atonement make,
While Jesus suffers for your sake,
  On the cross, on the cross.

4.
Where'er I go I'll tell the story
  Of the cross, of the cross;
In nothing else my soul shall glory,
  Save the cross, save the cross.
Yes, this my constant theme shall be
Through time and in eternity,—
That Jesus suffered death for me,
  On the cross, on the cross.

LIGHTS ALONG THE SHORE.—Concluded.

2. Many times I meet with trials on my journey,
     Temptation and grief by the way;
   But, then Jesus speaks, and says, I'm ever near thee,
   To guide to realms of endless day.
       There are lights along the shore, etc.

3. Friends of Jesus! may your lamps be trimm'd and burning,
     Illuming the pathway of love;
   Soon you'll gain the heights of glory, and be singing,
     The happy songs of saints above.
       There are lights along the shore, etc.

4. We're a happy band of Christians, bound for Canaan
     The land is in view; all is fair;
   We will sing redeeming love beyond the Jordan,
     And dwell with Christ forever there.
       There are lights along the shore, etc,

WATCHMAN.

Arr'd by ASA HULL.

1. { Watchman, tell me, does the morning Of fair Zi-on's glo-ry dawn?
   { Have the signs that mark its com-ing Yet up-on my pathway shone?
2. { Pil-grim, in that golden cit-y, Seated on his jas-per throne,
   { Zi-on's King, array'd in beau-ty, Reigns in peace from zone to zone,

Pilgrim, yes, arise, look round thee! Light is breaking in the skies;
There, on verdant hills and mountains, Where the golden sunbeams play,

Spurn the un-belief that bound thee: Morning dawns, a-rise, a-rise!
Purling streams and crystal fountains Sparkle in th' e-ter-nal day

3.
Pilgrim, see! the light is beaming
  Brighter still upon thy way;
Signs thro' all the earth are gleaming,
  Omens of the coming day.
When the last loud trumpet, sounding,
  Shall awake from earth and sea
All the saints of God now sleeping,
  Clad in immortality.

4.
Watchman, lo! the land we're nearing,
  With its vernal fruits and flowers,
On just yonder; oh, how cheering
  Bloom for ever Eden's bowers!
Hark! the choral strains there ringing,
  Wafted on the balmy air;
See the millions! hear them singing!
  Soon the pilgrims will be there.

SECOND HYMN.

1.
Ye who know your sins forgiven,
  And are happy in the Lord,
Have you read that gracious promise
  Which is left you in his word?
"I will sprinkle you with water,
  I will cleanse you from all sin,
Sanctify and make you holy;
  I will dwell and reign within."

2.
Tho' you have much peace and comfort,
  Greater things you yet shall find:
Freedom from unholy tempers,
  Freedom from the carnal mind;
To procure you full salvation
  Jesus suffered, groaned, and died;
Oh, behold the cleansing fountain
  Gushing from his bleeding side!

THE HALLOWED SPOT.

Words by Rev. W. Hunter. Music by Asa Hull.

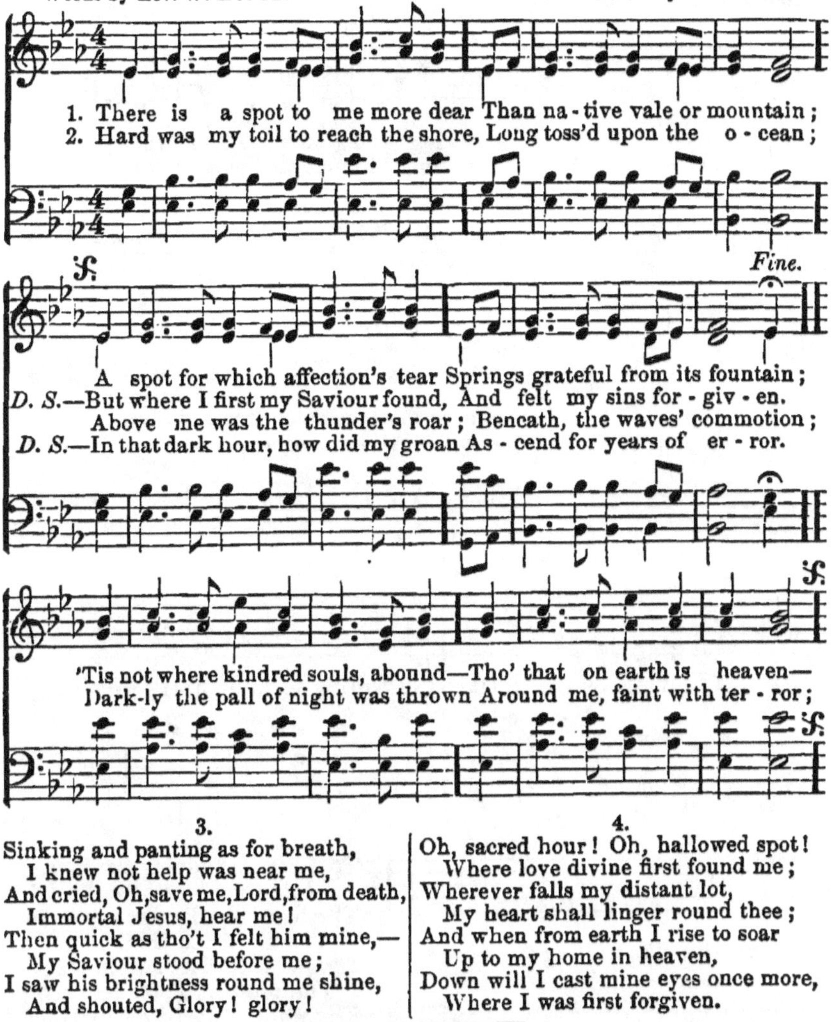

1. There is a spot to me more dear Than native vale or mountain;
2. Hard was my toil to reach the shore, Long toss'd upon the ocean;

A spot for which affection's tear Springs grateful from its fountain;
D. S.—But where I first my Saviour found, And felt my sins forgiven.
Above me was the thunder's roar; Beneath, the waves' commotion;
D. S.—In that dark hour, how did my groan Ascend for years of error.

'Tis not where kindred souls, abound—Tho' that on earth is heaven—
Darkly the pall of night was thrown Around me, faint with terror;

3.
Sinking and panting as for breath,
I knew not help was near me,
And cried, Oh, save me, Lord, from death,
Immortal Jesus, hear me!
Then quick as tho't I felt him mine,—
My Saviour stood before me;
I saw his brightness round me shine,
And shouted, Glory! glory!

4.
Oh, sacred hour! Oh, hallowed spot!
Where love divine first found me;
Wherever falls my distant lot,
My heart shall linger round thee;
And when from earth I rise to soar
Up to my home in heaven,
Down will I cast mine eyes once more,
Where I was first forgiven.

Concluded from opposite page.

3.
Come, my brother; come, my sister,
Seek, oh, seek this holy state;
None but holy ones can enter
Through the pure, celestial gate;
Can you bear the thought of losing
All the joys that are above?
No, my brother; no, my sister,
God will perfect you in love.

4.
May a mighty sound from heaven
Suddenly come rushing down;
Cloven tongues, like as of fire,—
May they sit on all around;
On the soul of each believer
May the Holy Ghost come down;
It is coming, it is coming;
Glory, glory to the Lamb.

3. My trust, my consecration,
   My all, I bring to Thee;
   But to consume oblation,
   The power is not in me.
   The Holy Ghost's illuming,
   Thou must Thyself inspire—
   The holy, pure, consuming,
   The sanctifying fire.—*Cho.*

4. Lord, send the blest anointing,
   The Holy Ghost impart—
   Baptismal fire outpouring
   To melt and mould my heart.
   Oh, let the flame, from heaven,
   Sweep through my longing soul,
   My dross and sin consuming—
   And purify the whole.—*Cho.*

"I WILL FOLLOW THEE."

JAS. L. ELGINBURG.

1. I will follow thee, my Saviour, Where-so-e'er my lot may be;
Where thou go-est, I will fol-low, Yes, my Lord, I'll follow thee.

2. Tho' the road be rough and thorny, Trackless as the foaming sea,
Thou hast trod this way before me, And I glad-ly follow thee.

Chorus.

I will follow thee, my Saviour, Thou didst shed thy blood for me;
And tho' all men should forsake thee, By thy grace I'll follow thee.

3.
Though 'tis lone, and dark, and dreary,
  Cheerless though my path may be,
If thy voice I hear before me,
  Fearlessly I'll follow thee.
    I will follow thee, etc.

4.
Though I meet with tribulations,
  Sorely tempted though I be,
I remember thou wast tempted,
  And rejoice to follow thee.
    I will follow thee, etc.

5.
Though thou lead'st me thro' affliction,
  Poor, forsaken, though I be,
Thou wast destitute, afflicted,
  And I only follow thee.
    I will follow thee, etc.

6.
Though to Jordan's rolling billows,
  Cold and deep, thou leadest me,
Thou hast crossed its waves before me,
  And I still will follow thee.
    I will follow thee, etc.

SWEET REST IN HEAVEN.

W. B. BRADBURY.

1. Come, brethren, don't grow wea-ry, But let us jour-ney on;
   The passing scenes all tell us That death will sure-ly come;
   The moments will not tar-ry— This life will soon be gone;
   These bod-ies soon will moulder In the dark and dreary tomb;

Chorus.
There is sweet rest in heav'n, There is sweet rest in heaven,

Repeat chorus softly.
There is sweet rest, there is sweet rest, There is sweet rest in heav'n.

2.
Loved ones have gone before us;
  They beckon us away;
O'er aerial plains they're soaring,
  Blest in eternal day;
But we are in the army,
  And dare not leave our post;
We'll fight until we conquer
  The foe's most mighty host.—*Cho.*

3.
Our Captain's gone before us;
  He kindly calls us home
To yonder world of glory,
  And sweetly bids us come;
The world, the flesh, and Satan,
  Will strive to hedge our way,
But we'll o'ercome these powers,
  And hourly watch and pray.—*Cho.*

4.
And Jesus will be with us,
  E'en to our journey's end,
In every sore affliction
  His present help to lend;
He never will grow weary;
  Though often we request,
He'll give us grace to conquer,
  And take us home to rest.—*Cho.*

OH, HOW I LOVE JESUS.

1. Jesus, the name high over all In hell, or earth, or sky; Angels and men before it fall, And devils fear and fly.

2. Jesus, the name to sinners dear, The name to sinners given; It scatters all their guilty fear; It turns their hell to heav'n.

Cho. Oh, how I love Jesus! Oh, how I love Jesus! Oh, how I love Jesus! Because he first lov'd me.
How can I forget thee? How can I forget my Lord? How can I forget thee? Dear Lord, remember me.

3.
Jesus the pris'ner's fetters breaks,
  And bruises Satan's head;
Pow'r into strengthless souls he speaks,
  And life into the dead.—*Cho.*

4.
Oh, that the world might taste and see
  The riches of his grace;
The arms of love that compass me
  Would all mankind embrace.—*Cho.*

5.
His only righteousness I show;
  His saving truth proclaim;
'Tis all my business, here below,
  To cry, Behold the Lamb!—*Cho.*

6.
Happy, if with my latest breath
  I may but gasp his name;
Preach him to all, and cry, in death,
  Behold, behold the Lamb!—*Cho.*

FLEE TO YOUR MOUNTAIN.

Words by Mrs. S. B. Dana.
Music by Asa Hull.

1. Flee as a bird to your mountain, Thou who art weary of sin;
Go to the clear flowing fountain, Where you may wash and be clean;
Fly, for th' avenger is near thee;
Call, and the Saviour will hear thee;
He on his bo-som will bear thee;
O thou who art weary of sin, O thou who art wea-ry of sin.

2.
He will protect thee forever,
Wipe ev'ry sad falling tear;
He will forsake thee, oh, never,
Cherish'd so tenderly there:
Haste, then, the hours now are flying;
Spend not the moments in sighing;
Cease from your sorrow and crying;
:||:The Saviour will wipe ev'ry tear.:||:

3.
Come, then, to Jesus, thy Saviour;
He will redeem thee from sin,
Bless with a sense of his favor,
Make thee all-glorious within;
Call, for the Saviour is near thee,
Waiting in mercy to hear thee,
And by his presence to cheer thee,
:||: O thou who art weary of sin. :||:

WORK, FOR THE NIGHT IS COMING.

Dr. L. Mason.

3.
Work, for the night is coming,
  Under the sunset skies;
While their bright tints are glowing,
  Work, for the daylight flies;
Work, till the last beam fadeth,
  Fadeth to shine no more;
Work, while the night is dark'ning,
  When man's work is o'er.

4.
Work, for the night is coming,
  Work, while the fields are white;
Work, for thy sands are running,
  Work, while hopes are bright;
Gather thy sheaves at morning;
  Rest not thy hand at noon;
Labor and strive till ev'ning;
  Rest when daylight's gone.

120. THE FOUNTAIN OF MERCY.

Words by H. Q. WILSON. Music by ASA HULL.

1. 'Twas Jesus, my Saviour, who died on a tree,
To open a fountain for sinners like me;
His blood is that fountain, which pardon bestows,
And cleanses the foulest wherever it flows.

CHO.—For the Lion of Judah shall break ev'ry chain,
[has broken]
And give us the vict'ry again and again,
[gives]
For the Lion of Judah shall break ev'ry chain,
[has broken]
And give us the vict'ry again and again.
[gives]

2.
And when I was willing with all things to part,
He gave me my bounty,—his love in my heart;
So now I am joined with the conquering band
Who are marching to glory at Jesus' command.
For the Lion of Judah, etc.

3.
Though round me the storms of adversity roll,
And the waves of destruction encompass my soul,
In vain this frail vessel the tempest shall toss;
My hopes rest secure on the blood of the cross.
For the Lion of Judah, etc.

4.
And when the last trumpet of judgment shall sound,
And wake all the nations that sleep in the ground,
Then, when heaven and earth shall be melting away,
I'll sing of the blood of the cross in that day.
For the Lion of Judah, etc.

5.
And when with the ransomed by Jesus, my head,
From fountain to fountain I then shall be led;
I'll fall at his feet and his mercy adore,
And sing of the blood of the cross evermore.
For the Lion of Judah, etc.

SALVATION'S FREE. 121
Arranged.

1. Come, ye that love the Lord, And let your joys be known;
Join in a song with sweet ac-cord, While ye surround his throne.

Cho.—I'm glad sal-va-tion's free, I'm glad sal-va-tion's free;
Sal-va-tion's free for you and me; I'm glad sal-va-tion's free.

2.
Let those refuse to sing
 Who never knew our God,
But servants of the heav'nly King
 May speak his praise abroad.
  I'm glad, etc.

3.
There we shall see his face,
 And never, never sin;
There, from the rivers of his grace,
 Drink endless pleasures in.
  I'm glad, etc.

4.
Yea, and before we rise
 To that immortal state,
The thoughts of such amazing bliss
 Should constant joys create.
  I'm glad, etc.

5.
The men of grace have found
 Glory begun below:
Celestial fruit on earthly ground
 From faith and hope may grow.
  I'm glad, etc.

6.
Then let our songs abound,
 And every tear be dry;
We're marching through Immanuel's [ground,
 To fairer worlds on high.
  I'm glad, etc.

SECOND HYMN.
No Sorrow there.

Come, sing to me of heaven,
 When I'm about to die;
Sing songs of holy ecstasy,
 To waft my soul on high!
  CHORUS.
There'll be no sorrow there,
 There'll be no sorrow there,
In heaven above, where all is love,
 There'll be no sorrow there.

2.
When the last moments come,
 Oh, watch my dying face,
To catch the bright, seraphic glow
 Which in each feature plays.—*Cho.*

3.
Then to my raptured ear
 Let one sweet song be given;
Let music charm me last on earth,
 And greet me first in heaven.—*Cho.*

4.
Then close my sightless eyes,
 And lay me down to rest,
And clasp my cold and icy hands
 Upon my lifeless breast.—*Cho.*

5.
When round my senseless clay
 Assemble those I love,
Then sing of heav'n, delightful heav'n,
 My glorious home above.—*Cho.*

122. THE WELCOME HOME.

Arranged from Rev. R. Lowry.

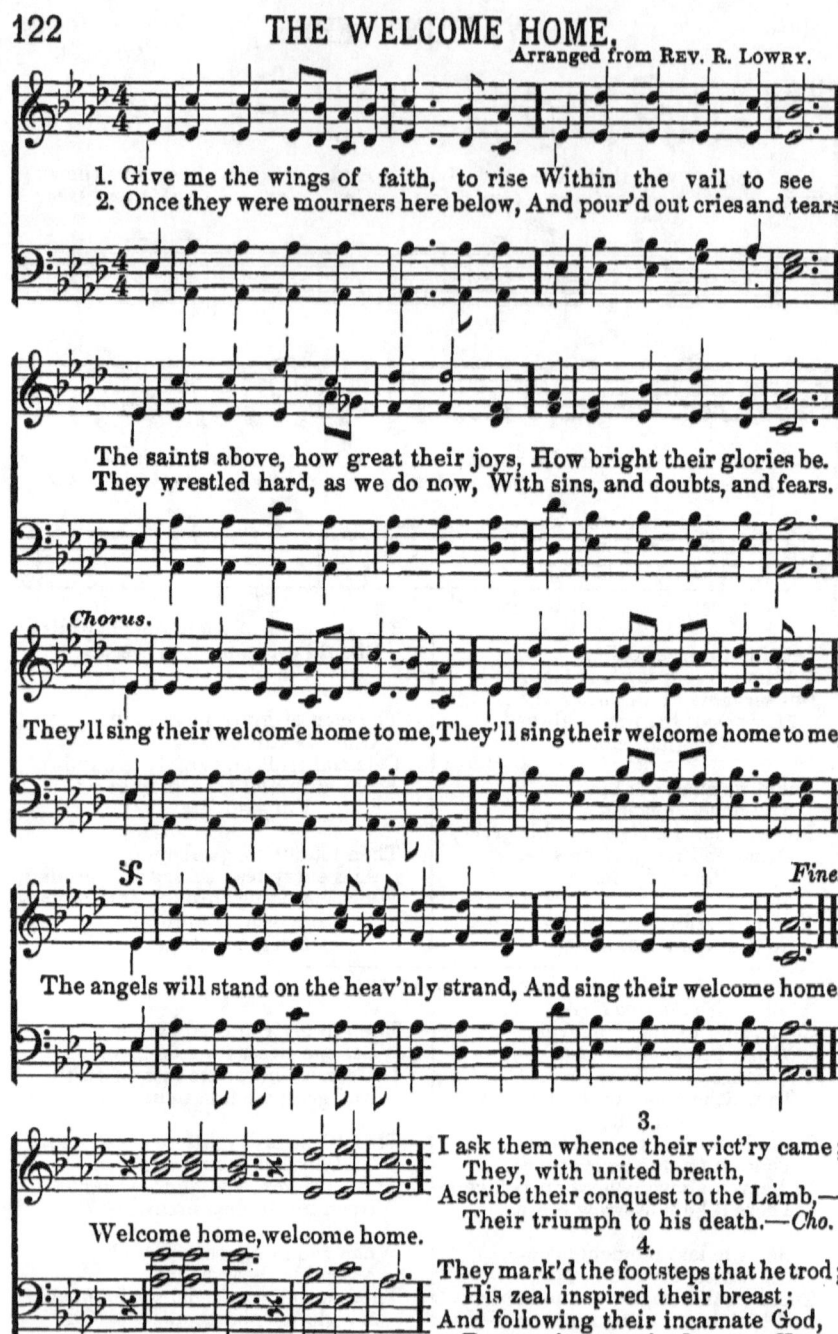

1. Give me the wings of faith, to rise Within the vail to see
The saints above, how great their joys, How bright their glories be.

2. Once they were mourners here below, And pour'd out cries and tears,
They wrestled hard, as we do now, With sins, and doubts, and fears.

Chorus.
They'll sing their welcome home to me, They'll sing their welcome home to me,
The angels will stand on the heav'nly strand, And sing their welcome home.
Welcome home, welcome home.

3.
I ask them whence their vict'ry came;
They, with united breath,
Ascribe their conquest to the Lamb,—
Their triumph to his death.—*Cho.*

4.
They mark'd the footsteps that he trod;
His zeal inspired their breast;
And following their incarnate God,
Possess the promised rest.—*Cho.*

THE SHINING SHORE.
G. F. ROOT.

1. My days are gliding swift-ly by, And I, a pilgrim stranger,
Would not de-tain them as they fly! Those hours of toil and dan-ger.

2. We'll gird our loins, my brethren dear, Our dis-tant home dis-cerning,
Our ab-sent Lord has left us word, Let ev'-ry lamp be burning.
D.S. just be-fore, the shi-ning shore We may al-most dis-cov-er.

Chorus.
For oh! we stand on Jordan's strand, Our friends are passing o-ver; And

3.
Should coming days be cold and dark,
We need not cease our singing;
That perfect rest naught can molest,
Where golden harps are ringing.
For oh! we stand, etc.

4.
Let sorrow's rudest tempests blow,
Each cord on earth to sever; [home,
Our King says, Come, and there's our
Forever, oh, forever!
For oh! we stand, etc.

SECOND HYMN.

The Sweetest Name.

THERE is no name so sweet on earth,
No name so sweet in heaven,
The name before his wondrous birth
To Christ the Saviour given.

CHORUS.

We love to sing around our King,
And hail him blessed Jesus;
For there's no word ear ever heard,
So dear, so sweet as Jesus.

2.
And when he hung upon the tree,
They wrote this name above him,
That all might see the reason we
For evermore must love him.
We love to sing, etc.

3.
So now, upon his Father's throne,
Almighty to release us
From sin and pains, he ever reigns,
The Prince and Saviour, Jesus.
We love to sing, etc.

4.
O Jesus, by that matchless name
Thy grace shall fail us never;
To-day as yesterday the same,
Thou art the same forever.
We love to sing, etc.

HOME, SWEET HOME.

1. 'Mid scenes of con-fu-sion and creature complaints,
   How sweet to my soul is communion with (*Omit.*) saints!
   To find at the ban-quet of mer-cy there's room,
   And feel in the presence of Je-sus at (*Omit.*) home.
   Home, home, sweet, sweet home, Prepare me, dear Saviour, for glory, my home.

2. The pleasures of earth I have seen fade away;
   They bloom for a season, but soon they decay;
   But pleasures more lasting in Jesus are given,
   Salvation on earth, and a mansion in heaven.—Home, etc.

3. Allure me no longer, ye false-glowing charms!
   The Saviour invites me—I'll go to his arms:
   At the banquet of mercy I hear there is room;
   Oh! there may I feast with his children at home.—Home, etc.

SECOND HYMN.

1. Mid pleasures and palaces though we may roam,
   Be it ever so humble, there's no place like home;
   A charm from the skies seems to hallow us there,
   Which, seek thro' the world, is ne'er met with elsewhere.
        Home, home—sweet, sweet home—
   Be it ever so humble, there's no place like home.

2. An exile from home splendor, dazzles in vain;
   Oh! give me my lowly thatched cottage again;
   The birds singing gaily that came at my call,—
   Give me them, with the peace of mind, dearer than all.—Home, etc.

3. I gaze on the moon, as I trace the drear wild,
   And feel that my parents now think of their child;
   They look on that moon from their own cottage door,
   Thro' woodbines whose fragrance shall cheer me no more.—Home, etc.

NEWTON. 125

Arranged.

1. How tedious and tasteless the hours When Jesus no longer I see!
2. His name yields the richest perfume, And sweeter than music his voice;

Sweet prospects, sweet birds, and sweet flow'rs, Have all lost their sweetness to me;
D.S.—But when I am hap-py in him, De-cember's as pleasant as May.

His presence dis-per-ses my gloom, And makes all within me rejoice;
D.S.—No mor-tal so hap-py as I,—My summer would last all the year

The midsummer sun shines but dim, The fields strive in vain to look gay;
I should, were he always thus nigh, Have nothing to wish or to fear;

3.
Content with beholding his face,
  My all to his pleasure resigned,
No changes of season or place
  Would make any change in my mind:
While blest with a sense of his love,
  A palace a toy would appear;
And prisons would palaces prove,
  If Jesus would dwell with me there.

4.
My Lord, if indeed I am thine,
  If thou art my Sun and my Song,
Say, why do I languish and pine?
  And why are my winters so long?
Oh, drive those dark clouds from my sky,
  Thy soul-cheering presence restore;
Or take me to thee up on high,
  Where winter and clouds are no more.

SECOND HYMN.

1.
To Jesus, the Crown of my hope,
  My soul is in haste to be gone;
Oh, bear me, ye cherubim, up,
  And waft me away to his throne:
My Saviour, whom absent I love,
  Whom, not having seen, I adore,
Whose name is exalted above
  All glory, dominion, and power.

2.
Dissolve thou these bands that detain
  My soul from her portion in thee;
Ah! strike off this adamant chain,
  And make me eternally free:
When that happy era begins,
  When array'd in thy glories I shine,
Nor grieve any more, by my sins,
  The bosom on which I recline.

126. I LONG TO BE THERE.

REV. G. D. BROWNE.

1. When I think of that city of light, And of crowns which the glorified wear,
And of garments so pure and so white, Then I long, oh, I long to be there.

2. It is not that I'm weary of pain, Or impatient in trials and cares,
For I know that to die would be gain, And I long, oh, I long to be there.

Chorus.

Oh, I long, with the saints in light, To be cloth'd in the garments of white,
And in songs with the angels unite, Singing, glory, hallelujah to the Lamb.

3.
To that city my Saviour has gone,
A rich mansion and crowns to prepare
For the hosts that are following on;
And I long, oh, I long to be there.
Oh, I long, with the saints, etc.

4.
When I read of the saints gather'd home
To that city of jewels most rare,
I with joy hail the message to "Come,"
For I long, oh, I long to be there.
Oh, I long, with the saints, etc.

3. Peace! O my troubled soul,
   Heav'n is my home;
   I soon shall reach the goal;
   Heav'n is my home;
   Swiftly the race I'll run,
   Yield up my crown to none;
   Forward! the prize is won;
   Heav'n is my home.

4. There, at my Saviour's side,
   Heav'n is my home;
   I shall be glorified;
   Heav'n is my home:
   There are the good and blest,
   Those I loved most and best;
   There, too, I soon shall rest;
   Heav'n is my home.

SECOND HYMN for "Heaven is my Home."

1. More love to thee, O Christ,
     More love to thee!
   Hear thou the prayer I make
     On bended knee;
   This is my earnest plea:
   More love, O Christ, to thee,
   More love, O Christ, to thee,
     More love to thee!

2. Once earthly joy I craved,
     Sought peace and rest,
   Now thee alone I seek,
     Give what is best:
   This all my prayer shall be,
   More love, O Christ, to thee,
   More love, O Christ, to thee,
     More love to thee!

SAVIOUR, LIKE A SHEPHERD. 129

From "Chapel Melodies," by permission.   WM. B. BRADBURY.

1. Saviour, like a shepherd lead us; Much we need thy tend'rest care;
   In thy pleasant pastures feed us; For our use thy folds prepare:
2. We are thine; do thou befriend us; Be the Guardian of our way;
   Keep thy flock; from sin defend us; Seek us when we go a-stray:

Blessed Je-sus, Blessed Je-sus, Thou hast bought us, thine we are,
Blessed Je-sus, Blessed Je-sus, Hear, oh, hear us when we pray,

Blessed Je-sus, Blessed Je-sus, Thou hast bought us, thine we are.
Blessed Je-sus, Blessed Je-sus, Hear, oh, hear us when we pray.

3. Thou hast promised to receive us,
Poor and sinful though we be;
Thou hast mercy to relieve us,
Grace to cleanse, and pow'r to free:
Blessed Jesus, Blessed Jesus,
We will early turn to thee.

4. Early let us seek thy favor;
Early let us do thy will;
Blessed Lord and only Saviour,
With thy love our bosoms fill:
Blessed Jesus, Blessed Jesus,
Thou hast loved us, love us still.

THOUGHTS OF HOME.—Concluded.

3. I've been thinking of the crowns, the robes, the palms,
   Which the glorified shall wear;
   Of those streets of shining gold, and their jasper walls,
   And I long in their glories to share.—I'm watching, etc.

4. I've been thinking of that home, and loved ones there,—
   Those with whom I've walked below;
   They are beck'ning me away to those mansions fair,
   And my spirit's impatient to go.—I'm watching, etc.

A HOME BEYOND THE TIDE.

Arranged from C. DUNBAR.

1. We are out on the ocean sailing; Homeward bound we swiftly glide;
We are out on the ocean sailing To a home beyond the tide.

Chorus.
All the storms will soon be o-ver, Then we'll anchor in the harbor.

2.
Millions now are safely landed
 Over on the golden shore;
Millions more are on their journey,
 Yet there's room for millions more.
  All the storms, etc.

3.
You have kindred over yonder,
 On that bright and happy shore;
By-and-by we'll swell the number,
 When the toils of life are o'er.
  All the storms, etc.

4.
Spread the sails, while heav'nly breezes
 Gently waft our vessel on;
All on board are sweetly singing;
 Free salvation is the song.
  All the storms, etc.

5.
When we all are safely anchored,
 Over on the shining shore,
We will walk about the city,
 And will sing for evermore.
  All the storms, etc.

BETHLEHEM'S STAR.—Concluded.

2.
Once on the raging seas I rode;
 The storm was loud, the night was dark;
The ocean yawned, and rudely blowed
 The wind that toss'd my found'ring bark;
Deep horror then my vitals froze;
 Death-struck, I ceased the tide to stem;
When suddenly a star arose;
 It was the Star of Bethlehem.

3.
It was my guide, my life, my all;
 It bade my dark forebodings cease;
And thro' the storm and danger's thrall,
 It led me, to the port of peace.
Now safely moored, my perils o'er,
 I'll sing, first in night's diadem,
For ever and for evermore,
 It was the Star of Bethlehem.

THE CELESTIAL ARMY.

From "Pilgrim's Harp," by A. Hull.

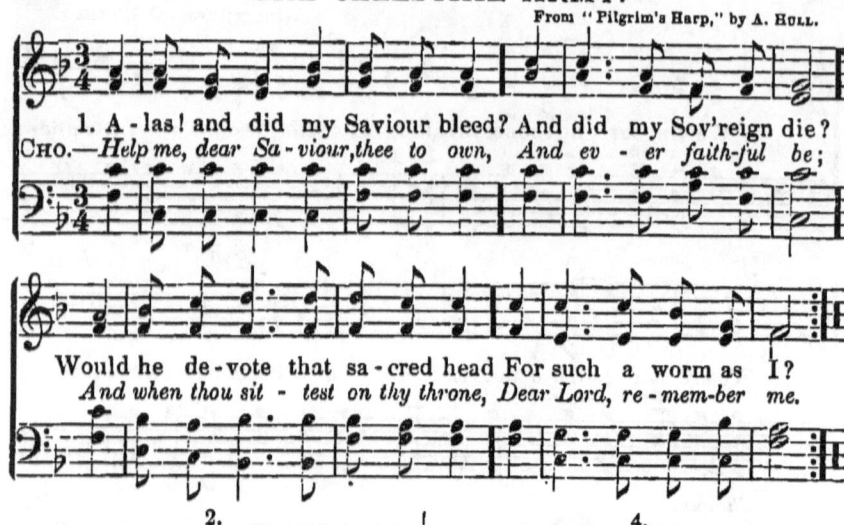

1. A-las! and did my Saviour bleed? And did my Sov'reign die?
Would he de-vote that sa-cred head For such a worm as I?

Cho.—Help me, dear Sa-viour, thee to own, And ev-er faith-ful be;
And when thou sit-test on thy throne, Dear Lord, re-mem-ber me.

2.
Was it for crimes that I have done
 He groaned upon the tree?
Amazing pity! grace unknown!
 And love beyond degree.—*Cho.*

3.
Well might the sun in darkness hide,
 And shut his glory in,
When Christ, the mighty maker, died
 For man, the creature's, sin.—*Cho.*

4.
Thus might I hide my blushing face
 While his dear cross appears;
Dissolve my heart in thankfulness,
 And melt mine eyes to tears.—*Cho.*

5.
But drops of grief can ne'er repay
 The debt of love I owe:
Here, Lord, I give myself away,—
 'Tis all that I can do.—*Cho.*

SECOND HYMN.

1.
Whence came the armies of the sky
 John saw in visions bright?
Whence came their crowns, their robes, their palms,
 Too pure for mortal sight.

CHORUS.
They looked like men in uniform;
 They looked like men of war;
They all were clad in armor bright,
 And conq'ring palms they bore.

2.
Were they tried soldiers of the cross,
 Victorious in the fight?
Were these the trophies they had won
 Reserved in worlds of light?—*Cho.*

3.
Once they were mourners here below,
 And poured out cries and tears:
They wrestled hard, as we do now,
 With sins, and doubts, and fears.—*Cho.*

4.
They saw the star of Bethlehem
 Arise in splendor bright;
They followed long its guiding ray,
 Till beamed a clearer light.—*Cho.*

5.
From desert waste and cities full,
 From dungeons dark they've come,
And now they claim their mansion fair:
 They've found their long-sought home.—*Cho.*

THIRD HYMN.

1.
Am I a soldier of the cross,
 A follower of the Lamb,
And shall I fear to own his cause,
 Or blush to speak his name?—*Cho.*

2.
Must I be carried to the skies
 On flowery beds of ease,
While others fought to win the prize,
 And sailed thro' bloody seas?—*Cho.*

THE GLORIOUS PROSPECT.

Words by MRS. HANNAFORD.
Music by ASA HULL.

1. A-mid the hours that rapid fly, Amid the flow'rs that soon must die,
2. We're going home with saints to dwell, Where angel hosts their chorus swell,

Amid our tears, while here we roam, How sweet the tho't! we're going home.
To join the glorious, ransom'd band Which stand in bliss at God's right hand.

Chorus.   *Rit.*

Going home, going home, How sweet the tho't! we're going, going home.

3.
We'll cling to Jesus in the hour
When sin and Satan use their power,
And murmur not when sorrows come,
For by and by we're going home.
   Going home, etc.

4.
No dying groans shall there be heard,
And we shall speak no parting word;
Oh, sinner, to our Saviour come,
And join the band that's going home.
   Going home, etc.

Concluded from opposite page.

3.
Are there no foes for me to face?
  Must I not stem the flood?
Is this vile world a friend to grace,
  To help me on to God?—*Cho.*

4.
Since I must fight if I would reign,
  Increase my courage, Lord;
I'll bear the toil, endure the pain,
  Supported by thy word.—*Cho.*

5.
Thy saints in all this glorious war
  Shall conquer, though they die:
They see the triumph from afar,—
  By faith they bring it nigh.—*Cho.*

6.
When that illustrious day shall rise,
  And all thy armies shine
In robes of vict'ry through the skies,
  The glory shall be thine.—*Cho.*

HAPPY DAY.   135

1. O happy day, that fix'd my choice On thee, my Saviour and my God!
Well may this glowing heart rejoice, And tell its raptures all abroad.

Hap-py day, hap-py day, When Jesus wash'd my sins away!

He taught me how to watch and pray, And live rejoic-ing every day;

2.
O happy bond, that seals my vows
  To him who merits all my love!
Let cheerful anthems fill his house,
  While to that sacred shrine I move.
    Happy day, etc.

3.
'Tis done! the great transaction's done!
  I am my Lord's, and he is mine:
He drew me, and I follow'd on,
Charm'd to confess the voice divine.
    Happy day, etc.

4.
Now rest, my long-divided heart;
  Fix'd on this blissful centre, rest;
Nor ever from thy Lord depart:
With him, of ev'ry good possess'd.
    Happy day, etc.

5.
High Heav'n that heard the solemn vow,
That vow renew'd shall daily hear,
Till in life's latest hour I bow,
And bless in death a bond so dear.
    Happy day, etc.

SECOND HYMN.

1.
Ho! ev'ry one that thirsts, draw nigh:
'Tis God invites the fallen race;
Mercy and free salvation buy,—
  Buy wine, and milk, and gospel grace.
    Happy day, etc.

2.
Come to the living waters, come!
  Sinners, obey your Maker's call:
Return, ye weary wand'rers home,
  And find his grace is free for all.
    Happy day, etc.

3.
See from the Rock a fountain rise;
For you in healing streams it rolls;
Money ye need not bring, nor price,
Ye lab'ring, burdened, sin-sick souls.
    Happy day, etc.

4.
Nothing ye in exchange shall give;
  Leave all you have, and are, behind;
Frankly the gift of God receive;
  Pardon and peace in Jesus find.
    Happy day, etc.

THE WORLD OF LIGHT.

Arranged from O. Snow.

1. There is a beautiful world, Where saints and angels sing;
   A world where peace and pleasure reigns, And heav'nly praises ring.
2. There is a beautiful world, Where sorrow never comes;
   A world where tears shall never fall In sighing for our home.

Chorus.

We'll be there, we'll be there, Palms of vict'ry, Crowns of glory we shall wear, In that beautiful world on high.

3. There is a beautiful world,
   Unseen to mortal sight,
   And darkness never enters there;
   That home is fair and bright.—*Cho.*

4. There is a beautiful world
   Of harmony and love;
   Oh, may we safely enter there,
   And dwell with God above.—*Cho.*

SECOND HYMN.

1. Come, ye that love the Lord,
   And let your joys be known;
   Join in a song with sweet accord,
   While ye surround his throne.—*Cho.*

2. Let those refuse to sing
   Who never knew our God,
   But servants of the heavenly King
   May speak their joys abroad.—*Cho.*

BETHANY.

Andantino.   DR. L. MASON.

1. Nearer, my God, to thee, Nearer to thee, E'en tho' it be a cross
2. Though like a wanderer, Daylight all gone, Darkness be o-ver me,

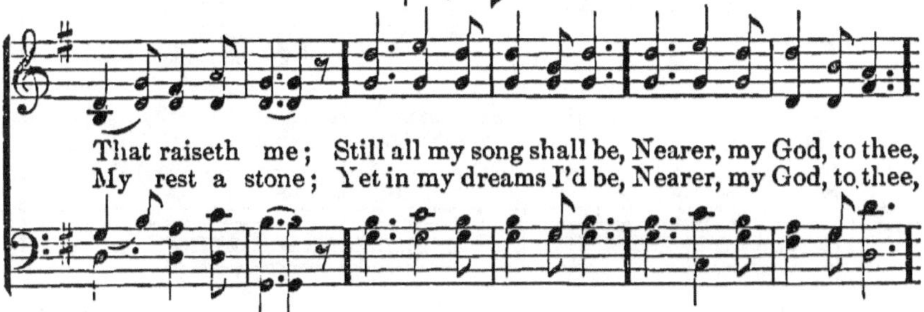

That raiseth me; Still all my song shall be, Nearer, my God, to thee,
My rest a stone; Yet in my dreams I'd be, Nearer, my God, to thee,

Nearer, my God, to thee, Nearer to thee.

3.
There let the way appear
Steps up to heav'n:
All that thou sendest me
In mercy giv'n:
Angels to beckon me
Nearer, my God, to thee,
Nearer, my God, to thee,
Nearer to thee.

4. Then, with my waking thoughts,
Bright with thy praise,
Out of my stony griefs,
Bethel I'll raise;
So by my woes to be
:||: Nearer, my God, to thee, :||:
Nearer to thee.

5. Or, if on joyful wing,
Cleaving the sky,
Sun, moon and stars forgot,
Upward I fly,—
Still all my song shall be,
:||: Nearer, my God, to thee, :||:
Nearer to thee.

THE WORLD OF LIGHT.—Concluded.

3.
There we shall see his face,
And never, never sin;
There, from the rivers of his grace,
Drink endless pleasures in.—*Cho.*

4.
Yea, and before we rise
To that immortal state,
The thoughts of such amazing bliss
Should constant joys create.—*Cho.*

5.
The men of grace have found
Glory begun below:
Celestial fruit on earthly ground
From faith and hope may grow.

6.
Then let our songs abound,
And ev'ry tear be dry: [ground,
We're marching through Immanuel's
To fairer worlds on high.—*Cho.*

138. THE SINNER'S FRIEND.

1. Jesus! the name that charms our fears, That bids our sorrows cease;
'Tis music in the sinner's ears; 'Tis life, and health, and peace.
2. He breaks the pow'r of cancelled sin; He sets the pris'ner free;
His blood can make the foul-est clean; His blood avail'd for me.
D.C.—Jesus alone can do them good; He turns their hell to heav'n.

Chorus.
There is no other name, in earth or sky, No other name to sinners giv'n;

3.
He speaks, and, list'ning to his voice,
New life the dead receive;
The mournful, broken hearts rejoice;
The humble poor believe.—*Cho.*

4.
Hear him, ye deaf! his praise, ye dumb,
Your loosened tongues employ;
Ye blind, behold your Saviour come,
And leap, ye lame, for joy.—*Cho.*

SECOND HYMN.

1.
Jesus, the name high over all
In hell, or earth, or sky;
Angels and men before it fall,
And devils fear and fly.—*Cho.*

2.
Jesus, the name to sinners dear,—
The name to sinners given;
It scatters all their guilty fear;
It turns their hell to heaven.—*Cho.*

3.
Jesus the pris'ner's fetters breaks,
And bruises Satan's head;
Pow'r into strengthless souls he speaks,
And life into the dead.—*Cho.*

4.
Oh, that the world might taste and see
The riches of his grace;
The arms of love that compass me
Would all mankind embrace.—*Cho.*

5.
His only righteousness I show;
His saving truth proclaim;
'Tis all my business, here below,
To cry, Behold the Lamb!—*Cho.*

6.
Happy, if with my latest breath
I may but gasp his name;
Preach him to all, and cry, in death,
Behold, behold the Lamb!—*Cho.*

THE CLEANSING FOUNTAIN. 139
WESTERN MELODY.

1. There is a fountain filled with blood Drawn from Immanuel's veins;
And sinners plunged beneath that flood, Lose all their guil-ty stains,
Lose all their guil-ty stains, Lose all their guil-ty stains.

2.
The dying thief rejoiced to see
  That fountain in his day;
And there may I, though vile as he,
  Wash all my sins away.
3.
Thou dying Lamb! thy precious blood
  Shall never lose its power,
Till all the ransomed Church of God,
  Are saved, to sin no more.

4.
E'er since, by faith, I saw the stream,
  Thy flowing wounds supply,
Redeeming love has been my theme,
  And shall be, till I die.
5.
Then in a nobler, sweeter song,
  I'll sing thy power to save,
When this poor, lisping, stamm'ring
  Lies silent in the grave. [tongue,

SECOND HYMN.

1.
FOREVER here my rest shall be,
  Close to thy bleeding side;
This all my hope, and all my plea,—
  For me the Saviour died.
2.
My dying Saviour and my God,
  Fountain for guilt and sin,
Sprinkle me ever with thy blood,
  And cleanse and keep me clean.

3.
Wash me, and make me thus thine own;
  Wash me, and mine thou art;
Wash me, but not my feet alone,—
  My hands, my head, my heart.
4.
Th' atonement of thy blood apply,
  Till faith to sight improve;
Till hope in full fruition die,
  And all my soul be love.

140 SWEET HOUR OF PRAYER.

From "Chapel Melodies," by permission.
Wm. B. Bradbury.

1. Sweet hour of pray'r, sweet hour of pray'r! That calls me from a world of care,
And bids me at my Father's throne Make all my wants and wishes known.
D.C.—And oft escap'd the tempter's snare By thy return, sweet hour of pray'r.
In sea-sons of distress and grief, My soul has oft-en found relief,

2.
Sweet hour of pray'r!
Sweet hour of pray'r!
Thy wings shall my petition bear
To him, whose truth and faithfulness
Engage the waiting soul to bless;
And since he bids me seek his face,
Believe his word, and trust his grace,
I'll cast on him my every care,
And wait for thee, sweet hour of pray'r.

3.
Sweet hour of pray'r!
Sweet hour of pray'r!
May I thy consolation share,
Till, from Mount Pisgah's lofty height,
I view my home, and take my flight:
This robe of flesh I'll drop, and rise
To seize the everlasting prize,
And shout, while passing thro' the air,
Farewell, farewell, sweet hour of pray'r.

SECOND HYMN.

1.
When pow'r divine, in mortal form,
Hush'd with a word the raging storm,
In soothing accents Jesus said,
Lo, it is I; be not afraid:
So, when in silence nature sleeps,
And lonely watch the mourner keeps,
One thought shall ev'ry pang remove
Trust, feeble man, thy Maker's love.

2.
God calms the tumult and the storm;
He rules the seraph and the worm;
No creature is by him forgot,
Of those who know, or know him not:
And when the last dread hour shall come,
And shudd'ring nature wait her doom,
This voice shall wake the pious dead,
Lo, it is I; be not afraid.

PART SECOND.

OLD HUNDRED. L. M.

1. From all that dwell be-low the skies, Let the Cre-a-tor's praise a-rise;
2. E-ter-nal are thy mercies, Lord, E-ter-nal truth attends thy word;

Let the Redeemer's name be sung, In ev'-ry land, by ev'-ry tongue.
Thy praise shall sound from shore to shore, Till suns shall rise and set no more.

3.
Your lofty themes, ye mortals bring!
In songs of praise divinely sing!
The great salvation loud proclaim,
And shout for joy the Saviour's name.

4.
In every land begin the song—
To every land the strains belong;
In cheerful sounds all voices raise,
And fill the world with loudest praise.

SECOND HYMN.

1.
BEFORE Jehovah's awful throne,
 Ye nations bow with sacred joy;
Know that the Lord is God alone,
 He can create, and he destroy.

2.
His sov'reign power, without our aid,
 Made us of clay, and form'd us men;
And when like wand'ring sheep we stray'd,
 He brought us to his fold again.

3.
We'll crowd thy gates with thankful songs,
 High as the heavens our voices raise;
And earth, with her ten thousand tongues,
 Shall fill thy courts with sounding praise.

4.
Wide as the world is thy command;
 Vast as eternity thy love;
Firm as a rock thy truth shall stand;
 When rolling years shall cease to move.

DOXOLOGY.

Praise God, from whom all blessings flow;
Praise him, all creatures here below;
Praise him above, ye heavenly host;
Praise Father, Son, and Holy Ghost.

HEBRON. L. M.

Dr. L. Mason.

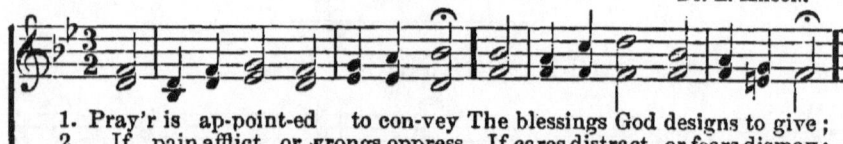
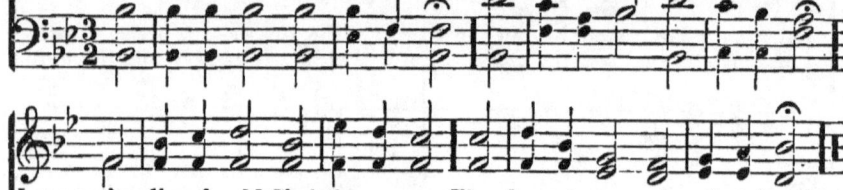
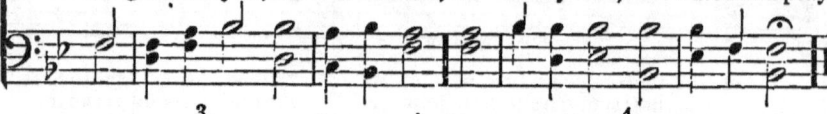

1. Pray'r is ap-point-ed to con-vey The blessings God designs to give;
Long as they live should Christians pray; They learn to pray when first they live.

2. If pain afflict, or wrongs oppress, If cares distract, or fears dismay;
If guilt de-ject, if sin distress, In ev'-ry case, still watch and pray.

3.
'Tis pray'r supports the soul that's weak,
Tho' tho't be broken, language lame;
Pray, if thou canst or canst not speak,
But pray with faith in Jesus' name.

4.
Depend on him—thou can'st not fail;
Make all thy wants and wishes known;
Fear not, his merits must prevail;
Ask but in faith—it shall be done.

SECOND HYMN.

1.
Thus far the Lord hath led me on,
Thus far his pow'r prolongs my days;
And ev'ry evening shall make known
Some fresh memorial of his grace.

2.
Much of my time has run to waste,
And I, perhaps am near my home:
But he forgives my follies past,
And gives me strength for days to come.

3.
I lay my body down to sleep;
Peace is the pillow for my head;
While well-appointed angels keep
Their watchful stations round my bed.

4.
Thus, when the night of death shall come,
My flesh shall rest beneath the ground,
And wait thy voice to rouse my tomb,
With sweet salvation in the sound.

THIRD HYMN.

1.
Author of faith, eternal Word,
Whose Spirit breathes the active flame,
Faith, like its finisher and Lord,
To-day, as yesterday, the same:—

2.
To thee our humble hearts aspire,
And ask the gift unspeakable;
Increase in us the kindled fire,
In us the work of faith fulfil.

3.
By faith we know thee strong to save:
(Save us, a present Saviour thou:)
Whate'er we hope. by faith we have;
Future, and past, subsisting now.

4.
To him that in thy Name believes,
Eternal life with thee is given;
Into himself he all receives,—
Pardon, and holiness, and heaven.

5.
The things unknown to feeble sense,
Unseen by reason's glimm'ring ray,
With strong commanding evidence,
Their heavenly origin display.

6.
Faith lends its realizing light;
The clouds disperse, the shadows fly,
Th' invisible appears in sight,
And God is seen by mortal eye.

SESSIONS. L. M.

L. O. Emerson.

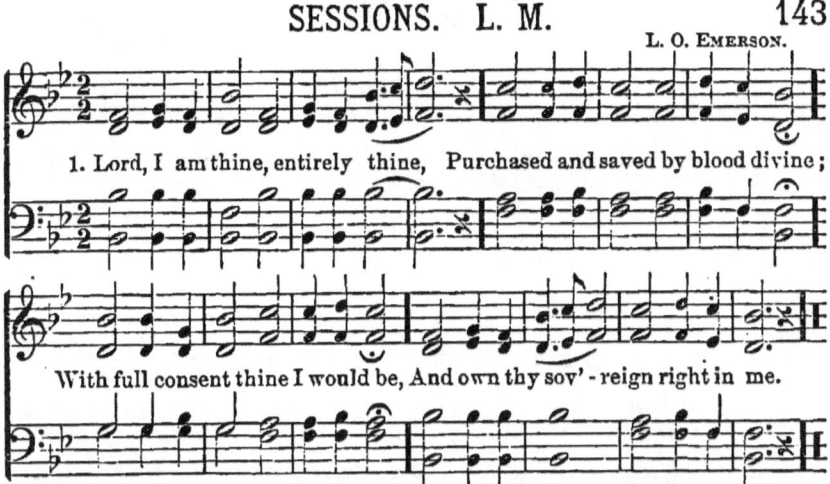

1. Lord, I am thine, entirely thine, Purchased and saved by blood divine;
With full consent thine I would be, And own thy sov'-reign right in me.

2.
Grant one poor sinner more a place
Among the children of thy grace;
A wretched sinner, lost to God,
But ransom'd by Immanuel's blood.

3.
Thine would I live—thine would I die;
Be thine through all eternity;
The vow is past beyond repeal,
And now I set the solemn seal.

4.
Here, at that cross where flows the blood
That bought my guilty soul for God,—
Thee, my new Master, now I call,
And consecrate to thee my all.

5.
Do thou assist a feeble worm,
The great engagement to perform;
Thy grace can full assistance lend,
And on that grace I dare depend.

SECOND HYMN.

1.
O for that flame of living fire,
 Which shone so bright in saints of old;
Which bade their souls to heaven aspire,
 Calm in distress, in danger bold.

2.
Where is that Spirit, Lord, which dwelt
 In Abrah'm's breast, and seal'd him thine?
Which made Paul's heart with sorrow melt,
And glow with energy divine?—

3.
That Spirit, which from age to age
 Proclaim'd thy love, and taught thy ways?

Brighten'd Isaiah's vivid page,
 And breathed in David's hallow'd lays?

4.
Is not thy grace as mighty now
 As when Elijah felt its power;
When glory beam'd from Moses' brow,
 Or Job endured the trying hour?

5.
Remember, Lord, the ancient days;
 Renew thy work; thy grace restore;
And while to thee our hearts we raise,
 On us thy holy Spirit pour.

THIRD HYMN.

1.
Glory to thee, my God, this night,
For all the blessings of the light:
Keep me, O keep me, King of kings,
Beneath the shadow of thy wings.

2.
Forgive me, Lord, for thy dear Son,
The ill which I this day have done:
That with the world, myself, and thee,
I, ere I sleep, at peace may be.

3.
Teach me to live, that I may dread
The grave as little as my bed;
Teach me to die, that so I may
Rise glorious at the judgment-day.

3.
Lord, let my soul forever share
The bliss of thy paternal care:
'Tis heaven on earth, 'tis heaven above,
To see thy face, and sing thy love.

UXBRIDGE. L. M.

Dr. L. Mason.

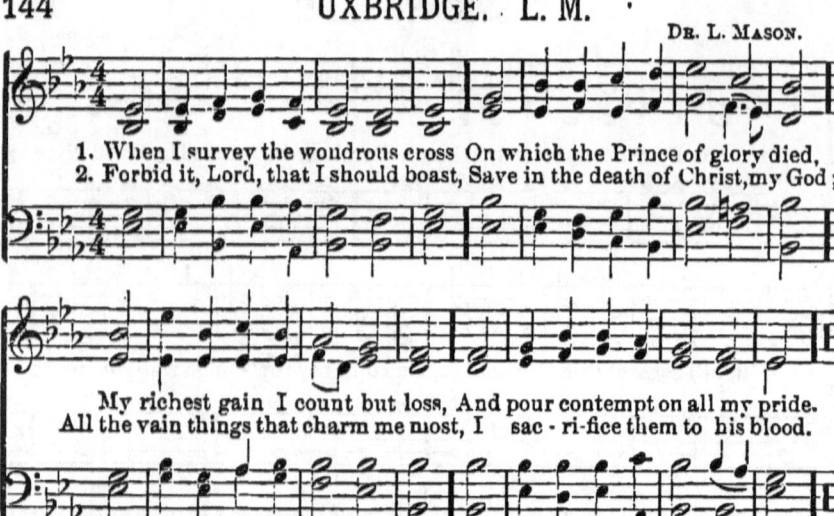

1. When I survey the wondrous cross On which the Prince of glory died,
My richest gain I count but loss, And pour contempt on all my pride.

2. Forbid it, Lord, that I should boast, Save in the death of Christ, my God;
All the vain things that charm me most, I sac-ri-fice them to his blood.

3.
See! from his head, his hands, his feet,
Sorrow and love flow mingled down;
Did e'er such love and sorrow meet,
Or thorns compose so a rich a crown?

4.
Were all the realm of nature mine,
That were a present far too small;
Love so amazing, so divine,
Demands my soul, my life, my all!

SECOND HYMN.

1.
Deep are the wounds which sin has made;
Where shall the sinner find a cure?
In vain, alas! is nature's aid;
The work exceeds her utmost power;

2.
But can no sov'reign balm be found,
And is no kind physician nigh,
To ease the pain, and heal the wound,
Ere life and hope forever fly?

3.
There is a great Physician near;
Look up, O fainting soul, and live:
See, in his heavenly smiles, appear
Such help as nature cannot give.

4.
See, in the Saviour's dying blood,
Life, health, and bliss, abundant flow;
And in that sacrificial flood
A balm for all thy grief and woe.

THIRD HYMN.

1.
Extended on a cursed tree,
Cover'd with dust, and sweat, and [blood,]
See there, the King of glory see!
Sinks and expires the Son of God.

2.
Who, who, my Saviour, this hath done?
Who could thy sacred body wound?
No guilt thy spotless heart hath known,
No guile hath in thy lips been found.

3.
I, I alone have done the deed;
'Tis I thy sacred flesh have torn;
My sins have caused thee, Lord, to bleed,
Pointed the nail, and fix'd the thorn.

4.
For me the burden to sustain
Too great, on thee, my Lord, was laid:
To heal me, thou hast born the pain;
To bless me, thou a curse wast made.

5.
My Saviour, how shall I proclaim,
How pay, the mighty debt I owe?
Let all I have, and all I am,
Ceaseless, to all, thy glory show.

6.
Still let thy tears, thy groans, thy sighs,
O'erflow my eyes, and heave my breast,
Till, loosed from flesh and earth, I rise,
And ever in thy bosom rest.

WARE. L. M.

GEO. KINGSLEY.

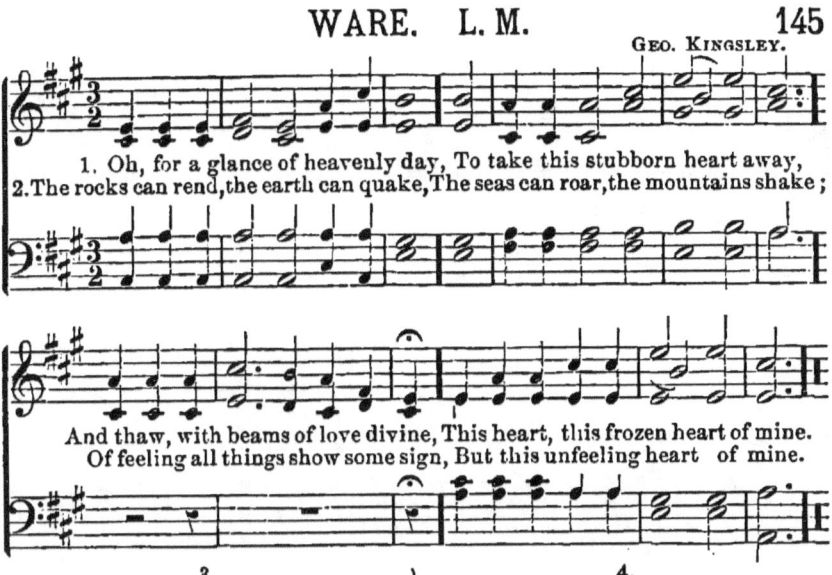

1. Oh, for a glance of heavenly day, To take this stubborn heart away,
And thaw, with beams of love divine, This heart, this frozen heart of mine.

2. The rocks can rend, the earth can quake, The seas can roar, the mountains shake;
Of feeling all things show some sign, But this unfeeling heart of mine.

3.
To hear the sorrows thou hast felt,
O Lord, an adamant would melt;
But I can read each moving line,
And nothing moves this heart of mine.

4.
But power divine can do the deed,
And, Lord, that power I greatly need;
Thy spirit can from dross refine,
And melt and change this heart of mine.

SECOND HYMN.

1.
How vain is all beneath the skies!
How transient ev'ry earthly bliss!
How slender all the fondest ties
 That bind us to a world like this!

2.
The evening cloud, the morning dew,
The with'ring grass, the fading flow'r,
Of earthly hopes are emblems true—
 The glory of a passing hour.

3.
But though earth's fairest blossom die,
And all beneath the skies is vain,
There is a brighter world on high,
 Beyond the reach of care and pain.

4.
Then let the hope of joys to come
 Dispel our cares and chase our fears;
If God be ours, we're trav'ling home,
 Though passing through a vale of tears.

THIRD HYMN.

1.
HE dies! the Friend of sinners dies!
 Lo! Salem's daughters weep around;
A solemn darkness veils the skies,
A sudden trembling shakes the ground:

2.
Come, saints, and drop a tear or two
 For him who groan'd beneath your [load;
He shed a thousand drops for you,
 A thousand drops of richer blood.

3.
Here's love and grief beyond degree:
 The Lord of glory dies for man!
But lo! what sudden joys we see:
 Jesus, the dead, revives again.

4.
The rising God forsakes the tomb;
 (In vain the tomb forbids his rise;)
Cherubic legions guard him home,
 And shout him welcome to the skies.

5.
Break off your tears, ye saints, and tell
 How high your great Deliv'rer reigns;
Sing how he spoil'd the hosts of hell,
 And led the monster death in chains:

6.
Say, Live forever, wondrous King!
 Born to redeem, and strong to save;
Then ask the monster, where's thy sting?
 And where's thy vict'ry, boasting grave?

WARD. L. M.

SCOTCH.

1. How blest the righteous when he dies! When sinks a wea-ry soul to rest, How mildly beam the closing eyes; How gently heaves th'expiring breast.

2.
So fades a summer cloud away;
 So sinks the gale when storms are o'er;
So gently shuts the eye of day;
 So dies a wave along the shore.

3.
A holy quiet reigns around,
 A calm which life nor death destroys;
And naught disturbs the peace profound
 Which his unfettered soul enjoys.

4.
Farewell, conflicting hopes and fears,
 Where light and shade alternate dwell;
How bright th'unchanging happiness!
 Farewell, inconstant world, farewell.

5.
Life's labor done, as sinks the clay,
 Light from the load, the spirit flies,
While heav'n and earth combine to say,
 How blest the righteous when he dies!

SECOND HYMN.

1.
GOD is the refuge of his saints,
 When storms of sharp distress invade;
Ere we can offer our complaints,
 Behold him present with his aid.

2.
Let mountains from their seats be hurled
 Down to the deep, and buried there,
Convulsions shake the solid world;
 Our faith shall never yield to fear.

3.
Loud may the troubled ocean roar;
 In sacred peace our souls abide;
While every nation, every shore,
 Trembles and dreads the swelling tide.

4.
There is a stream, whose gentle flow
 Supplies the city of our God,
Life, love, and joy, still gliding through,
 And watering our divine abode.

5.
That sacred stream, thine holy word,
 Our grief allays, our fear controls;
Sweet peace thy promises afford, [souls.
 And give new strength to fainting

6.
Zion enjoys her Monarch's love,
 Secure against a threatening hour;
Nor can her firm foundations move,
 Built on his truth and armed with power.

THIRD HYMN.

1.
JESUS, I fain would walk in thee,—
 From nature's every path retreat;
Thou art my Way,—my Leader be,
 And set upon the rock my feet.

2.
Uphold me, Saviour, or I fall;
 O reach me out thy gracious hand:
Only on thee for help I call,—
 Only by faith in thee I stand.

HAMBURG. L. M.

Arranged by L. Mason.

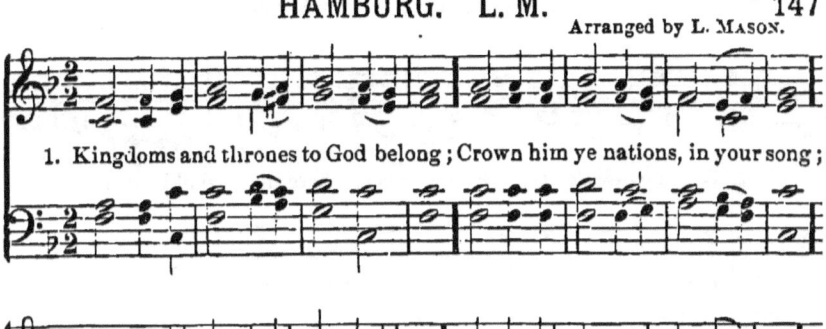

1. Kingdoms and thrones to God belong; Crown him ye nations, in your song;

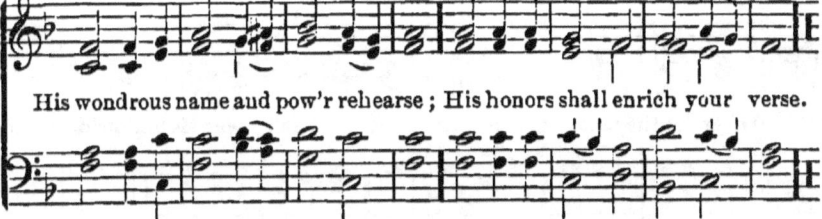

His wondrous name and pow'r rehearse; His honors shall enrich your verse.

2.
He rides and thunders thro' the sky;
His name, Jehovah, sounds on high:
Praise him aloud, ye sons of grace;
Ye saints rejoice before his face.

3.
God is our shield, our joy, our rest;
God is our King, proclaim him blest;
When terrors rise, when nations faint,
He is the strength of every saint.

SECOND HYMN.

1.
WHAT sinners value I resign;
Lord, 'tis enough that thou art mine;
I shall behold thy blissful face,
And stand complete in righteousness.

2.
This life's a dream, an empty show;
But the bright world to which I go
Hath joys substantial and sincere;
When shall I wake and find me there?

3.
Oh, glorious hour! oh, blest abode!
I shall be near and like my God;
And flesh and sin no more control
The sacred pleasures of the soul.

4.
My flesh shall slumber in the ground
Till the last trumpet's joyful sound,
Then burst the chains with sweet sur-
And in my Saviour's image rise! [prise;

THIRD HYMN.

1.
WHILE life prolongs its precious light,
 Mercy is found, and peace is given;
But soon, ah, soon, approaching night
 Shall blot out every hope of heaven.

2.
While God invites, how blest the day!
 How sweet the Gospel's charming
Come,sinner,haste,O haste away,[sound!
 While yet a pard'ning God is found.

3.
Soon, borne on time's most rapid wing,
 Shall death command you to the grave,
Before his bar your spirits bring,
 And none be found to hear or save.

4.
In that lone land of deep despair,
 No Sabbath's heavenly light shall rise,
No God regard your bitter prayer,
 No Saviour call you to the skies.

5.
Now God invites; how blest the day!
 How sweet the gospel's charming
Come,sinner,haste,O haste away,[sound!
 While yet a pard'ning God is found.

DOXOLOGY.
Praise God, from whom all blessings
Praise him, all creatures here below; [flow!
Praise him above, ye heavenly host,
Praise Father, Son, and Holy Ghost.

DUKE STREET. L. M.

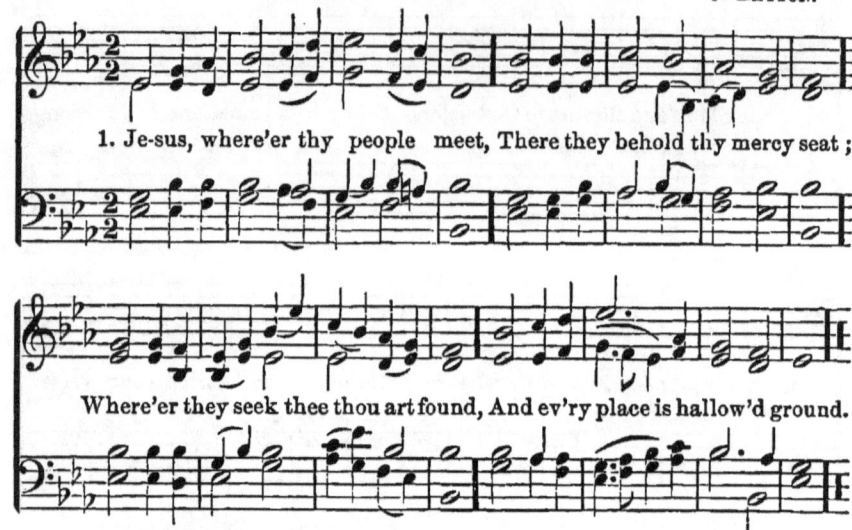

1. Jesus, where'er thy people meet,
There they behold thy mercy seat;
Where'er they seek thee thou art found,
And ev'ry place is hallow'd ground.

2.
For thou, within no walls confined,
Dost dwell with those of humble mind;
Such ever bring thee where they come,
And, going, take thee to their home.

3.
Great Shepherd of thy chosen few,
Thy former mercies here renew;
Here to our waiting hearts proclaim
The sweetness of thy saving name.

SECOND HYMN.

1.
Unto the Lord, unto the Lord,
  Oh, sing a new and joyful song!
Declare his glory, tell abroad
  The wonders that to him belong.

2.
For he is great, for he is great;
  Above all gods his throne is raised;
He reigns in majesty and state,
  In strength and beauty is he praised.

3.
Give to the Lord, give to the Lord
  The glory due unto his name:
Enter his courts with sweet accord;
  In songs of joy his grace proclaim.

4.
For lo! he comes, for lo! he comes
  To judge the earth in truth and love:
His saints in triumph leave their tombs,
  And shout his praise in heaven above.

THIRD HYMN.

1.
How pleasant, how divinely fair,
O Lord of hosts, thy dwellings are;
With long desire my spirit faints,
To meet th' assemblies of thy saints.

2.
My flesh would rest in thine abode;
My panting heart cries out for God:
My God! my King! why should I be
So far from all my joys and thee!

3.
Blest are the saints, who sit on high,
Around thy throne above the sky;
Thy brightest glories shine above,
And all their work is praise and love.

4.
Blest are the souls, who find a place
Within the temple of thy grace;
There they behold thy gentler rays,
And seek thy face, and learn thy praise.

5.
Blest are the men whose hearts are set
To find the way to Zion's gate;
God is their strength; and thro' the road
They lean upon their helper, God.

6. [strength;
Cheerful they walk with growing
Till all shall meet in heaven at length;
Till all before thy face appear,
And join in nobler worship there.

FEDERAL STREET. L. M. 149
H. K. Oliver.

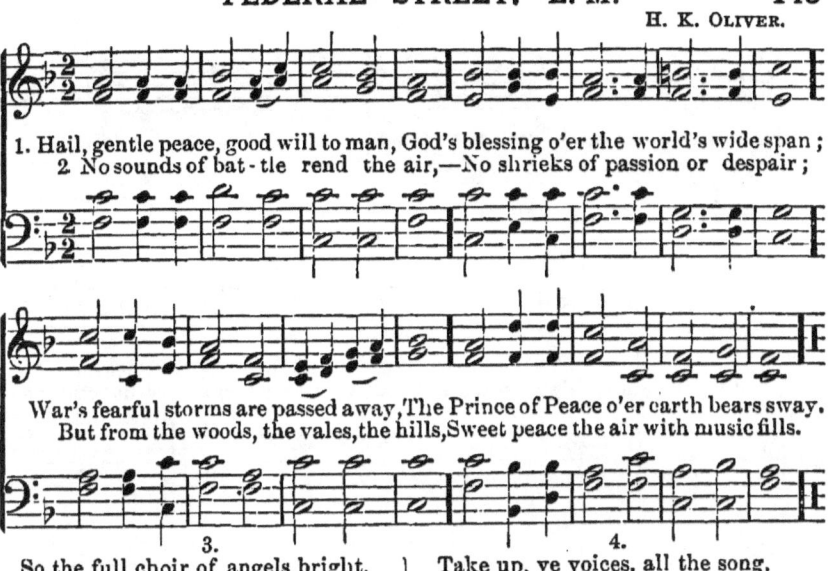

1. Hail, gentle peace, good will to man, God's blessing o'er the world's wide span;
2. No sounds of bat-tle rend the air,—No shrieks of passion or despair;

War's fearful storms are passed away, The Prince of Peace o'er earth bears sway.
But from the woods, the vales, the hills, Sweet peace the air with music fills.

3.
So the full choir of angels bright,
Heralds of Christ, ere early light,
To shepherds sang melodious strains,
On the still air of Bethlehem's plains.

4.
Take up, ye voices, all the song,
With high acclaim the strain prolong,
Earth, join to angel-choir your voice,
And in full harmony rejoice.

SECOND HYMN.

1.
What am I, O thou glorious God!
And what my father's house to thee,
That thou such mercy hast bestowed
On me, the vilest sinner, me?

2.
Me, in my blood, thy love pass'd by,
And stopped my ruin to retrieve;
Wept o'er my soul thy pitying eye;
Thy bowels yearn'd, and sounded, live!

3.
Dying, I heard the welcome sound,
Received the blessing from above,
And pardon in thy mercy found,
Astonish'd at thy boundless love.

4.
Honor, and might, and thanks, and praise,
I render to my pard'ning God;
Extol the riches of thy grace,
And spread thy saving name abroad.

THIRD HYMN.

1.
Show pity, Lord! O Lord, forgive!
Let a repenting rebel live;
Are not thy mercies large and free?
May not a sinner trust in thee?

2.
My crimes are great, but don't surpass
The pow'r and glory of thy grace;
Great God, thy nature hath no bound;
So let thy pard'ning love be found.

3.
Oh, wash my soul from every sin,
And make my guilty conscience clean;
Here, on my heart, the burden lies,
And past offences pain my eyes.

4.
My lips with shame my sins confess,
Against thy law, against thy grace;
Lord, should thy judgments grow severe,
I am condemned, but thou art clear.

5. [breath,
Should sudden vengeance seize my
I must pronounce thee just in death;
And if my soul were sent to hell,
Thy righteous law approves it well.

6.
Yet save a trembling sinner, Lord, [word,
Whose hope still hov'ring round thy
Would light on some sweet promise there,
Some sure support against despair.

BRIDGEWATER. L. M.

EDSON.

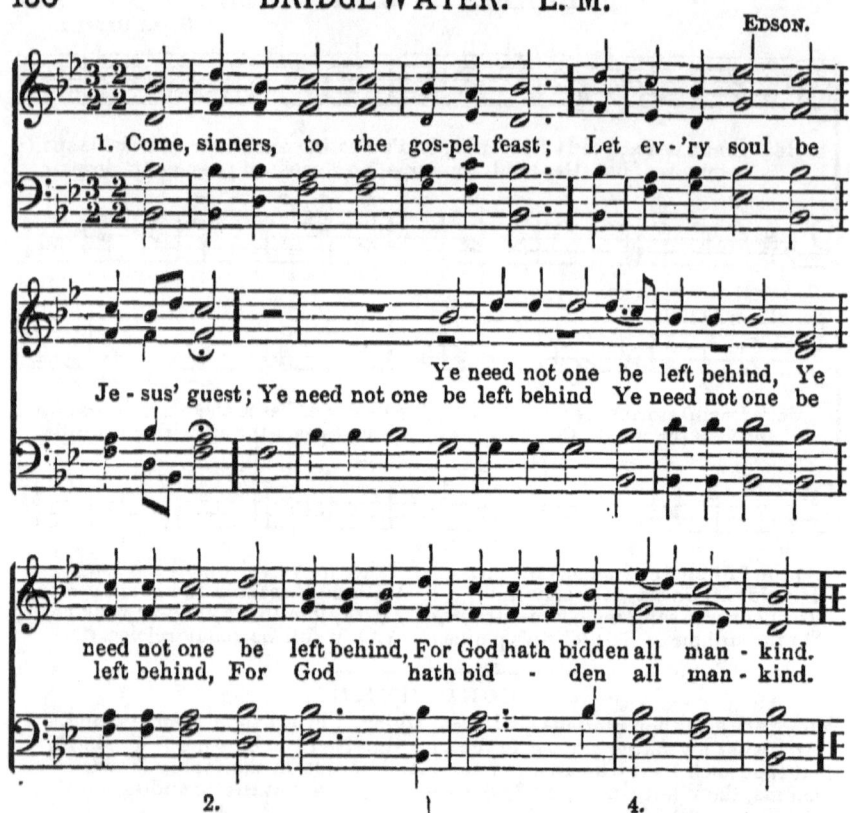

1. Come, sinners, to the gospel feast;
Let ev'ry soul be Jesus' guest;
Ye need not one be left behind,
For God hath bidden all mankind.

2.
Sent by the Lord, on you I call;
The invitation is to all;
Come, all the world! come, sinner, thou!
All things in Christ are ready now.

3.
Come, all ye souls by sin oppressed,
Ye restless wand'rers after rest,
Ye poor, and maim'd, and halt, and blind,
In Christ a hearty welcome find.

4.
My message as from God receive:
Ye all may come to Christ and live;
Oh, let his love your hearts constrain,
Nor suffer him to die in vain.

5.
See him set forth before your eyes,
That precious, bleeding Sacrifice;
His offered benefits embrace,
And freely now be saved by grace.

SECOND HYMN.

1.
GREAT God attend while Zion sings
The joy that from thy presence springs;
To spend one day with thee on earth
Exceeds a thousand days of mirth.

2.
Might I enjoy the meanest place
Within thy house, O God of grace,
Not tents of ease nor thrones of power
Should tempt my feet to leave thy door.

3.
God is our Sun,—he makes our day;
God is our Shield,—he guards our way
From all assaults of hell and sin,
From foes without and foes within.

4.
All needful grace will God bestow,
And crown that grace with glory too;
He gives us all things, and withholds
No real good from upright souls.

DUANE STREET. L. M.

Rev. GEO. COLES.

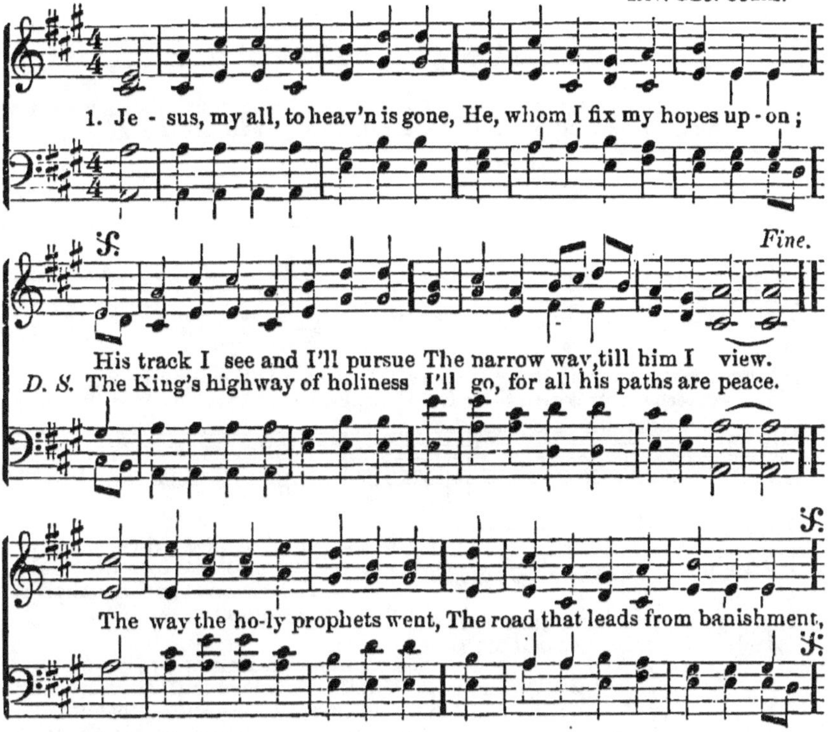

1. Je-sus, my all, to heav'n is gone, He, whom I fix my hopes up-on;
His track I see and I'll pursue The narrow way, till him I view.
D. S. The King's highway of holiness I'll go, for all his paths are peace.
The way the ho-ly prophets went, The road that leads from banishment,

2.
This is the way I long have sought,
And mourn'd because I found it not;
My grief a burden long has been,
Because I was not saved from sin.
The more I strove against its power,
I felt its weight and guilt the more;
Till late I heard my Saviour say,—
"Come hither, soul, I am the way."

3.
Lo! glad I come, and thou, blest Lamb,
Shalt take me to thee, as I am;
Nothing but sin have I to give,
Nothing but love shall I receive.
Then will I tell to sinners round,
What a dear Saviour I have found;
I'll point to thy redeeming blood,
And say, "Behold the way to God!"

SECOND HYMN.

1.
OF Him who did salvation bring,
I could forever think and sing;
Arise, ye needy! he'll relieve;
Arise, ye guilty! he'll forgive.

2.
Ask but his grace, and lo, 'tis given!
Ask, and he turns your hell to heaven;
Though sin and sorrow wound my soul,
Jesus, thy balm will make it whole.

3.
To shame our souls he blushed in blood;
He closed his eyes to show us God;
Let all the world fall down and know
That none but God such love can show.

4.
'Tis thee I love; for thee alone
I shed my tears and make my moan;
Where'er I am, where'er I move
I meet the object of my love.

5.
Insatiate to this spring I fly;
I drink, and yet am ever dry;
Ah! who against thy charms is proof?
Ah! who that loves, can love enough?

ROTHWELL. L. M.

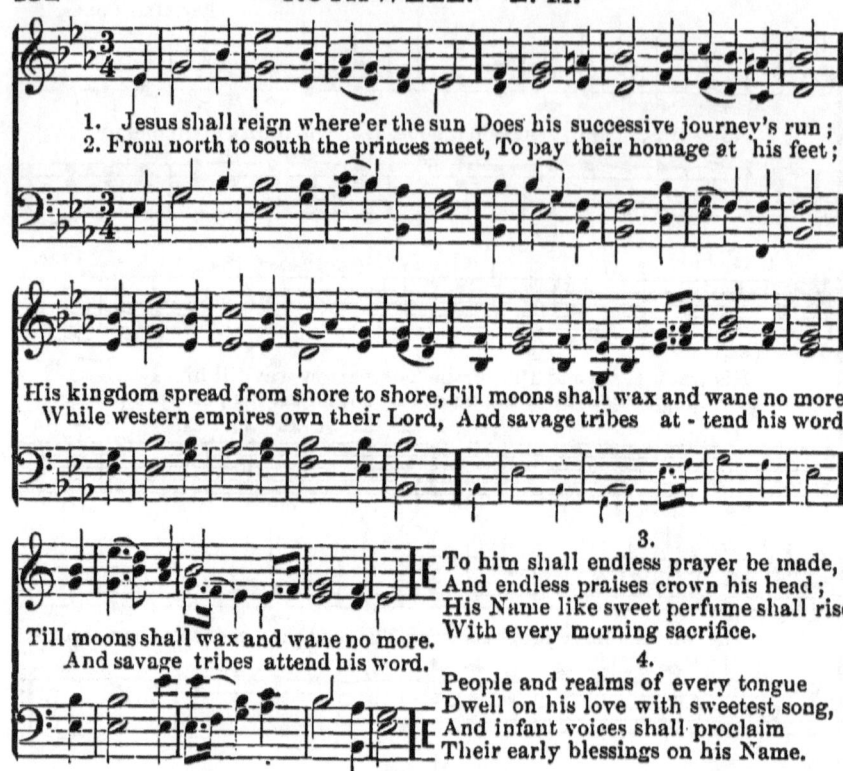

1. Jesus shall reign where'er the sun Does his successive journey's run;
His kingdom spread from shore to shore, Till moons shall wax and wane no more,

2. From north to south the princes meet, To pay their homage at his feet;
While western empires own their Lord, And savage tribes attend his word,

3.
To him shall endless prayer be made,
And endless praises crown his head;
His Name like sweet perfume shall rise
With every morning sacrifice.

4.
People and realms of every tongue
Dwell on his love with sweetest song,
And infant voices shall proclaim
Their early blessings on his Name.

SECOND HYMN.

1.
FAR from my tho'ts, vain world, be gone,
Let my religious hours alone;
Fain would mine eyes my Saviour see;
I wait a visit, Lord, from thee.

2.
O warm my heart with holy fire,
And kindle there a pure desire;
Come, sacred Spirit, from above,
And fill my soul with heav'nly love.

3.
Blest Saviour, what delicious fare!
How sweet thine entertainments are!
Never did angels taste above
Redeeming grace and dying love.

4.
Hail, great Immanuel, all divine!
In thee thy Father's glories shine;
Thy glorious name shall be adored,
And ev'ry tongue confess thee Lord.

THIRD HYMN.

1.
PRAISE waits in Zion, Lord, for thee:
  Thy saints adore thy holy name;
Thy creatures bend th' obedient knee,
  And humbly now thy presence claim.

2.
Eternal Source of truth and light,
  To thee we look, on thee we call;
Lord, we are nothing in thy sight,
  But thou to us art all in all.

3.
Still may thy children in thy word,
  Their common trust and refuge see;
O, bind us to each other, Lord,
  By one great bond,—the love of thee.

4.
So shall our sun of hope arise,
  With brighter still and brighter ray,
Till thou shalt bless our longing eyes,
  With beams of everlasting day.

PARK STREET. L. M.

VENUA.

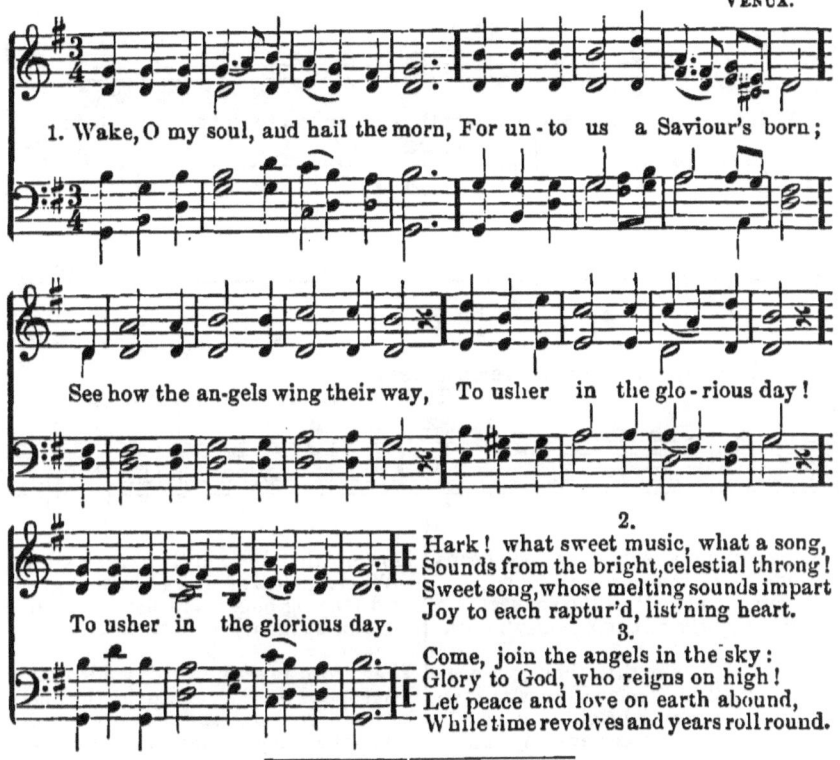

1. Wake, O my soul, and hail the morn, For un-to us a Saviour's born;
See how the an-gels wing their way, To usher in the glo-rious day!
To usher in the glorious day.

2.
Hark! what sweet music, what a song,
Sounds from the bright, celestial throng!
Sweet song, whose melting sounds impart
Joy to each raptur'd, list'ning heart.

3.
Come, join the angels in the sky:
Glory to God, who reigns on high!
Let peace and love on earth abound,
While time revolves and years roll round.

SECOND HYMN.

1.
ASSEMBLED at thy great command,
Before thy face, dread King, we stand:
The voice that marshalled every star,
Has called thy people from afar.

2.
We meet through distant lands to spread
The truth for which the martyrs bled;
Along the line—to either pole—
The anthem of thy praise to roll.

3.
Our prayers assist; accept our praise;
Our hopes revive; our courage raise;
Our counsels aid;—to each impart
The single eye, the faithful heart.

4.
Forth with thy chosen heralds come;
Recall the wand'ring spirits home;
From Zion's mount send forth the sound,
To spread the spacious earth around.

THIRD HYMN.

1.
Lo! round the throne, a glorious band,
The saints in countless myriads stand;
Of every tongue redeemed to God,
Arrayed in garments washed in blood.

2.
Through tribulation great they came;
They bore the cross, despised the shame;
But now from all their labors rest,
In God's eternal glory blest.

3.
They see the Saviour face to face;
They sing the triumphs of his grace;
And day and night, with ceaseless praise,
To him their loud hosannas raise.

4.
O, may we tread the sacred road
That holy saints and martyrs trod;
Wage to the end the glorious strife,
And win, like them, a crown of life.

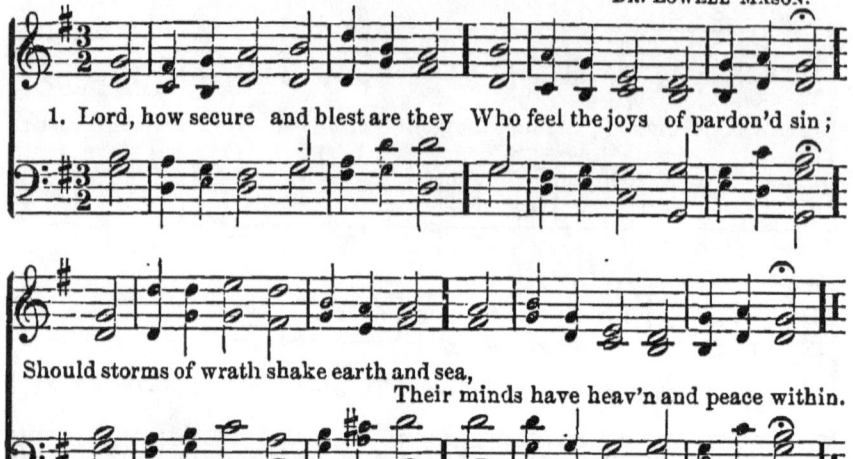

1. Lord, how secure and blest are they Who feel the joys of pardon'd sin;
Should storms of wrath shake earth and sea, Their minds have heav'n and peace within.

2.
The day glides sweetly o'er their heads,
  Made up of innocence and love;
And soft, and silent as the shades,
  Their nightly minutes gently move.

3.
Quick as their thoughts, their joys come on,
  But fly not half so swift away: [
Their souls are ever bright as noon,
  And calm as summer evenings be.

4.
How oft they look to th' heavenly hills,
  Where groves of living pleasure grow;
And longing hopes, and cheerful smiles,
  Sit undisturb'd upon their brow.

5.
They scorn to seek earth's golden toys,
  But spend the day, and share the night,
In numb'ring o'er the richer joys
  That heav'n prepares for their delight.

SECOND HYMN.

1.
I THIRST, thou wounded Lamb of God,
To wash me in thy cleansing blood;
To dwell within thy wounds; then pain
Is sweet, and life or death is gain.

2.
Take my poor heart, and let it be
Forever closed to all but thee:
Seal thou my breast, and let me wear
That pledge of love forever there.

3.
What are our works but sin and death,
Till thou thy quick'ning Spirit breathe,
Thou giv'st the power thy grace to move;
O wondrous grace! O boundless love.

4.
How can it be, thou heavenly King,
That thou shouldst us to glory bring;
Make slaves the partners of thy throne,
Deck'd with a never-fading crown.

THIRD HYMN.

1.
SINNERS, obey the heavenly call;
  Your prison doors stand open wide:
Go forth, for Christ hath ransomed all,
  For every soul of man hath died

2.
'Tis his the drooping soul to raise;
  To rescue all by sin oppressed;
To clothe them with the robes of praise,
  And give their weary spirits rest.

3.
To help their grov'ling unbelief
  Beauty for ashes to confer;
The oil of joy for abject grief;
  Triumphant joy for sad despair.

4.
To make them trees of righteousness,
  The planting of the Lord below;
To spread the honor of his grace,
  And on to full protection go.

RETREAT. L. M.

DR. T. HASTINGS.

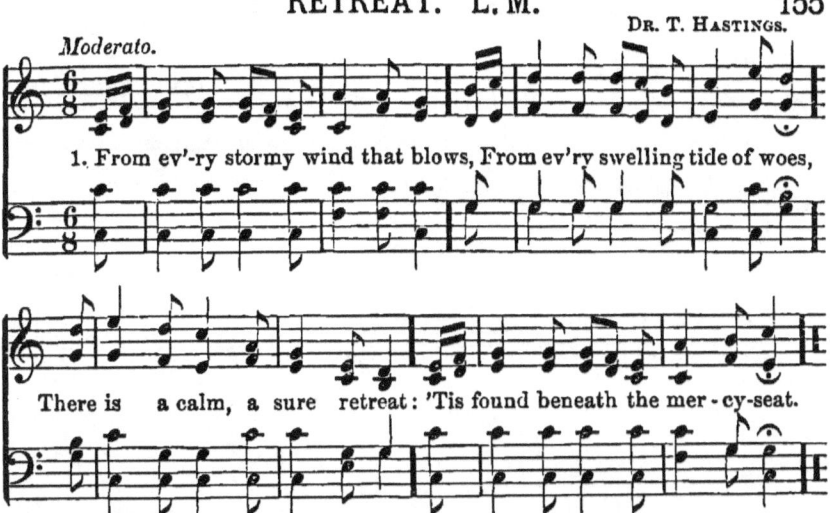

1. From ev'-ry stormy wind that blows, From ev'ry swelling tide of woes, There is a calm, a sure retreat: 'Tis found beneath the mer-cy-seat.

2.
There is a place where Jesus sheds
The oil of gladness on our heads;
A place than all besides more sweet;
It is the blood-bought mercy-seat.

3.
There is a scene where spirits blend,
Where friend holds fellowship with friend:
Though sundered far, by faith they meet,
Around one common mercy-seat.

4.
Ah, whither could we flee for aid,
When tempted, desolate, dismayed?
Or how the hosts of hell defeat,
Had suffering saints no mercy-seat?

5.
There, there on eagle's wings we soar,
And sin and sense molest no more;
And heav'n comes down our souls to greet,
While glory crowns the mercy-seat.

SECOND HYMN.

1.
To Jesus, our exalted Lord,
The name by heaven and earth adored,
Fain would our hearts and voices raise
A cheerful song of sacred praise.

2.
But all the notes which mortals know,
Are weak, and languishing, and low;
Far, far above our humble songs,
The theme demands immortal tongues.

3.
Yet, while around his board we meet,
And humbly worship at his feet,
O let our warm affections move,
In glad returns of grateful love!

4.
Let humble, penitential woe,
In tears of godly sorrow flow;
And thy forgiving smiles impart
Life, hope, and joy to every heart.

THIRD HYMN.

1.
BRETHREN in Christ, and well beloved,
  To Jesus and his servants dear,
Enter, and show yourselves approved;
  Enter, and find that God is here.

2.
Welcome from earth: lo, the right hand
  Of fellowship to you we give:
With open hearts and hands we stand,
  And you in Jesus' name receive.

3.
Jesus, attend: thyself reveal;
  Are we not met in thy great name?
Thee in the midst we wait to feel;
  We wait to catch the spreading flame.

4.
Truly our fellowship below
  With thee, and with the Father is:
In thee eternal life we know,
  And heaven's unutterable bliss.

MISSIONARY CHANT. L. M.

CHAS. ZEUNER.

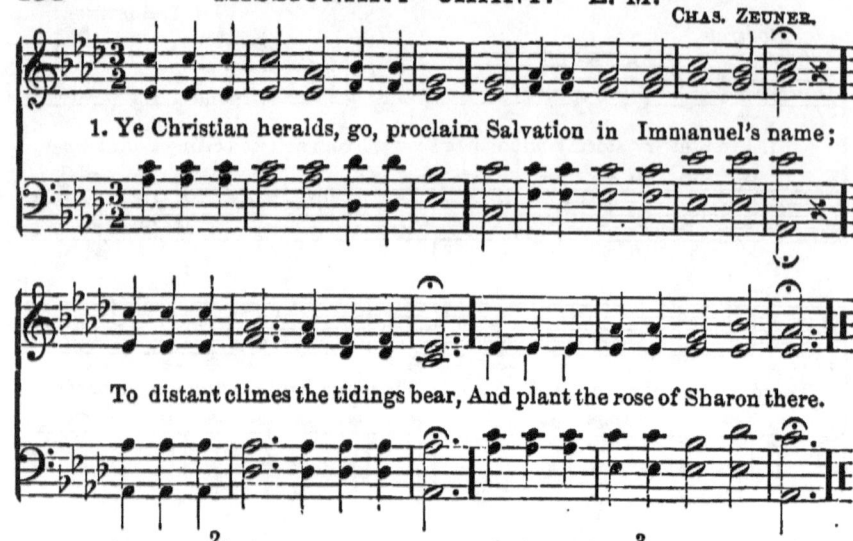

1. Ye Christian heralds, go, proclaim Salvation in Immanuel's name;
To distant climes the tidings bear, And plant the rose of Sharon there.

2.
He'll shield you with a wall of fire,
With holy zeal your hearts inspire,
Bid raging winds their fury cease,
And calm the savage breast to peace.

3.
And when our labors all are o'er,
Then shall we meet to part no more,—
Meet, with the blood-bo't throng to fall,
And crown the Saviour Lord of all.

SECOND HYMN.

1.
Eternal depth of love divine,
In Jesus, God with us, displayed;
How bright thy beaming glories shine;
How wide thy healing streams are
[spread.

2.
With whom dost thou delight to dwell?
Sinners, a vile and thankless race!
O God, what tongue aright can tell
How vast thy love, how great thy grace!

3.
The dictates of thy sov'reign will
With joy our grateful hearts receive;
All thy delight in us fulfil;
Lo, all we are to thee we give.

4.
To thy sure love, thy tender care,
Our flesh, soul, spirit, we resign;
O fix thy sacred presence there,
And seal th' abode forever thine.

THIRD HYMN.

1.
When Israel trod the desert way,
God dwelt within the curtain'd tent;
There gath'ring tribes repair'd to pray,
And found his gracious ear attent.

2.
But when fair Salem's towr's arose,
And massive walls her hosts surround,
When God had scatter'd Zion's foes,
And peace and plenty reign'd around.

3.
Then Lebanon's tall cedars came,
And polished stones majestic rose;
While lofty turrets tipp'd with flame,
Point upward to the saint's repose.

4.
But vain were glitt'ring gems and gold;
And blood, in vain, from altars ran;
Till the unfolding glory told,
Jehovah comes to dwell with man.

5.
Thus here, O God, our off'ring lies,
Cold in its beauty—cold and dead!
O, living fire—burst from the skies—
On us thy hallowing influence shed.

6.
Thy priests shall feel its quick'ning [pow'r,
Thy people catch the rising flame;
While all confess, to time's last hour.
Jehovah here records his name.

ZEPHYR. L. M. 157
WM. B. BRADBURY.

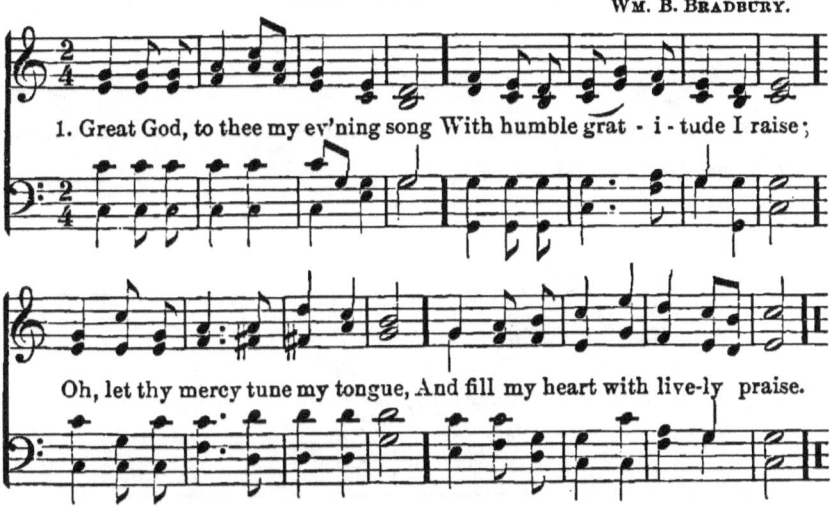

1. Great God, to thee my ev'ning song With humble grat-i-tude I raise;
Oh, let thy mercy tune my tongue, And fill my heart with live-ly praise.

2.
My days, unclouded as they pass,
And ev'ry gently rolling hour,
Are monuments of wondrous grace,
And witness to thy love and pow'r.

3.
And yet this thoughtless, wretched [heart,
Too oft regardless of thy love,
Ungrateful, can from thee depart,
And, fond of trifles, vainly rove.

4.
Seal my forgiveness in the blood
Of Jesus; his dear name alone
I plead for pardon, gracious God,
And kind acceptance at thy throne.

5.
Let this blest hope mine eyelids close;
With sleep refresh my feeble frame;
Safe in thy care may I repose,
And wake with praises to thy name!

SECOND HYMN.

1.
GREAT God, indulge my humble claim;
Be thou my hope, my joy, my rest;
The glories that compose thy name
Stand all engaged to make me blest.

2.
Thou great and good, thou just and wise,
Thou art my Father and my God;
And I am thine by sacred ties,—[blood.
Thy son, thy servant bought with

3.
With heart and eyes, and lifted hands,
For thee I long, to thee I look;
As travellers in thirsty lands
Pant for the cooling water brook.

4.
I'll lift my hands, I'll raise my voice,
While I have breath to pray or praise:
This work shall make my heart rejoice,
And fill the remnant of my days.

THIRD HYMN.

1.
LORD of the Sabbath, hear us pray,
In this thy house, on this thy day;
And own, as grateful sacrifice,
The songs which from thy servants rise.

2.
Thine earthly Sabbaths, Lord, we love,
But there's a nobler rest above;
To that our lab'ring souls aspire,
With ardent hope, and strong desire.

3.
No more fatigue, no more distress,
Nor sin nor hell shall reach the place;
No sighs shall mingle with the songs,
Which warble from immortal tongues.

4.
No rude alarms of raging foes;
No cares to break the long repose;
No midnight shade, no clouded sun;
But sacred, high, eternal noon.

EVENING. L. M.

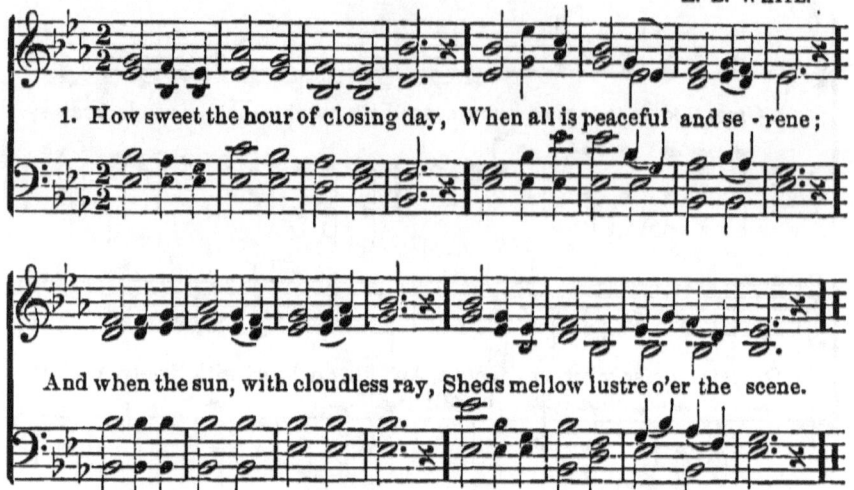

1. How sweet the hour of closing day, When all is peaceful and se-rene; And when the sun, with cloudless ray, Sheds mellow lustre o'er the scene.

2.
Such is the Christian's parting hour;
 So peacefully he sinks to rest; [pow'r,
When faith, endued from heaven with
 Sustains and cheers his languid breast.

3.
Mark but that radiance of his eye,
 That smile upon his wasted cheek;
They tell us of his glory nigh,
 In language that no tongue can speak.

4.
A beam from heaven is sent to cheer
 The pilgrim on his gloomy road;
And angels are attending near,
 To bear him to their bright abode.

5.
Who would not wish to die like those
 Whom God's own Spirit deigns to
To sink into that soft repose, [bless?
 Then wake to perfect happiness?

SECOND HYMN.

1.
How sweetly flow'd the gospel's sound
 From lips of gentleness and grace,
While list'ning thousands gather'd round
 And joy and rev'rence fill'd the place.

2.
From heaven he came, of heaven he
 To heaven he led his foll'wers way; [spoke,
Dark clouds of gloomy night he broke,
 Unveiling an immortal day.

3.
Come, wand'rers, to my Father's home;
 Come, all ye weary ones, and rest.
Yes, sacred Teacher! we will come,
 Obey, and be forever blest.

4.
Decay, then, tenements of dust!
 Pillars of earthly pride, decay!
A nobler mansion waits the just,
 And Jesus has prepared the way.

THIRD HYMN.

1.
UNVAIL thy bosom, faithful tomb;
 Take this new treasure to thy trust:
And give these sacred relics room
 To slumber in the silent dust.

2.
Nor pain, nor grief, nor anxious fear
 Invade thy bounds: no mortal woes
Can reach the peaceful sleeper here,
 While angels watch the soft repose.

3.
So Jesus slept; God's dying Son [bed:
 Pass'd through the grave, and blest the
Rest here, blest saint, till from his throne
 The morning break, and pierce the
 [shade.
4.
Break from his throne, illustrious morn;
 Attend, O earth! his sov'reign word;
Restore thy trust—a glorious form—
 Call'd to ascend and meet the Lord.

LEBANON. L. M.

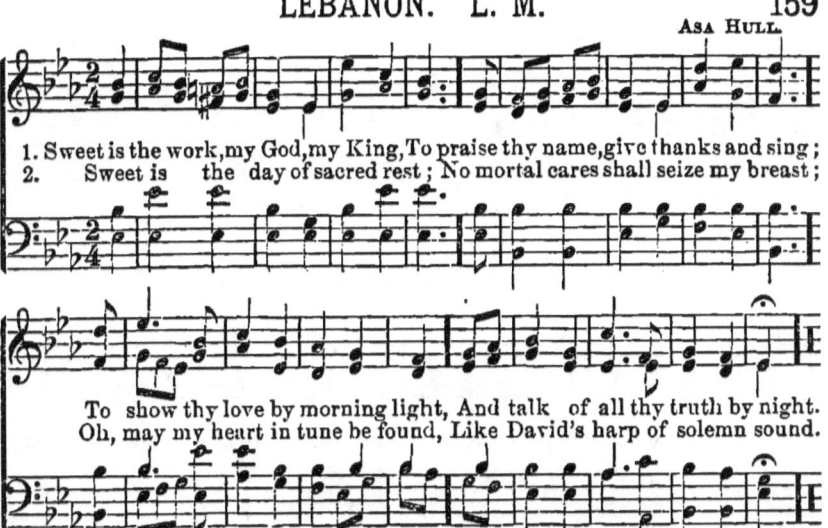

1. Sweet is the work, my God, my King, To praise thy name, give thanks and sing;
To show thy love by morning light, And talk of all thy truth by night.

2. Sweet is the day of sacred rest; No mortal cares shall seize my breast;
Oh, may my heart in tune be found, Like David's harp of solemn sound.

3.
When grace has purified my heart,
Then I shall share a glorious part:
And fresh supplies of joy be shed,
Like holy oil to cheer my head.

4.
Then shall I see, and hear, and know
All I desired or wished below;
And every power find sweet employ
In that eternal world of joy.

SECOND HYMN.

1.
JESUS, and shall it ever be,—
A mortal man ashamed of thee?
Ashamed of thee, whom angels praise,
Whose glories shine thro' endless days?

2.
Ashamed of Jesus, that dear Friend
On whom my hopes of heav'n depend?
No! when I blush, be this my shame—
That I no more revere his name.

3.
Ashamed of Jesus?—yes, I may,
When I've no sins to wash away;
No tears to wipe; no good to crave;
No fears to quell; no soul to save.

4.
Till then—nor is my boasting vain—
Till then I boast a Saviour slain;
And, oh, may this my glory be,—
That Christ is not ashamed of me!

THIRD HYMN.

1.
ETERNAL beam of Light divine,
Fountain of unexhausted love;
In whom the Father's glories shine,
Through earth beneath, and heaven above:—

2.
Jesus, the weary wand'rer's rest,
Give me thy easy yoke to bear;
With steadfast patience arm my breast,
With spotless love and lowly fear.

3.
Thankful I take the cup from thee,
Prepared and mingled by thy skill:
Though bitter to the taste it be,
Powerful the wounded soul to heal.

4.
Be thou, O Rock of Ages, nigh!
So shall each murm'ring thought be gone,
And grief, and fear, and care shall fly,
As clouds before the mid-day sun.

5.
Speak to my warring passions,—Peace;
Say to my trembling heart,—Be still;
Thy power my strength and fortress is,
For all things serve thy sov'reign will.

6.
O death! where is thy sting? Where now
Thy boasted victory, O grave?
Who shall contend with God? or who
Can hurt whom God delights to save.

NAZLAR. L. M.

Words by R. M. MOULTON.
Music Arr'd from SCHUBERT.

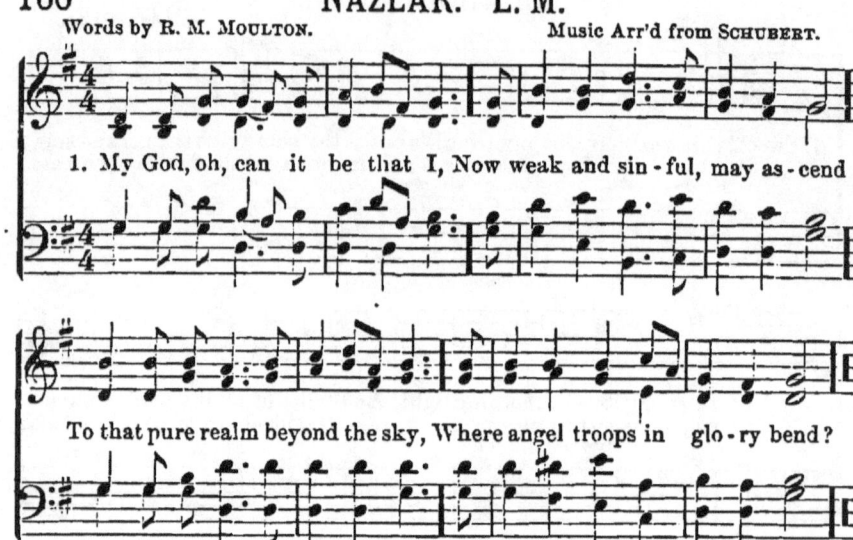

1. My God, oh, can it be that I, Now weak and sinful, may ascend
To that pure realm beyond the sky, Where angel troops in glory bend?

2.
Shall I thy city fair behold;
 And may I pass its pearly gates,
To walk in white its streets of gold,
 And wear the crown the victor waits?

3.
Thy mercy lifts us from our sin;
 What love and praise to thee belong!
The riches of thy grace shall win
 The sweetest notes in heav'nly song.

4.
The angels that excel in strength,
 And shine with glory naught may dim,
Can never, through the blissful length
 Of ceaseless ages, chant that hymn.

5.   [pains
Those ransomed from earth's guilt and
 Alone that grateful song may sing;
And in the most melodious strains,
 Thro' heav'n's high arches shall it ring.

SECOND HYMN.

1.
LET not the wise their wisdom boast,
 The mighty glory in their might;
The rich in flatt'ring riches trust,
 Which take their everlasting flight.

2.
The rush of num'rous years bears down
 The most gigantic strength of man;
And where is all his wisdom gone,
 When, dust, he turns to dust again?

3.
One only gift can justify
 The boasting soul that knows his God;
When Jesus doth his blood apply,
 I glory in his sprinkled blood.

4.
The Lord my righteousness I praise,
 I triumph in the love divine; [grace
The wisdom, wealth, and strength of
 In Christ to endless ages mine.

THIRD HYMN.

1.
HE wills that I should holy be:
 That holiness I long to feel;
That full divine conformity
 To all my Saviour's righteous will.

2.
See, Lord, the travail of thy soul
 Acccomplish'd in the change of mine;
And plunge me, every whit made whole,
 In all the depths of love divine.

3.
On thee, O God, my soul is stay'd,
 And waits to prove thine utmost will;
The promise by thy mercy made,
 Thou canst, thou wilt, in me fulfil.

4.
No more I stagger at thy power,
 Or doubt thy truth, which cannot move:
Hasten the long-expected hour,
 And bless me with thy perfect love.

STONEFIELD. L. M.
Stanley. 161

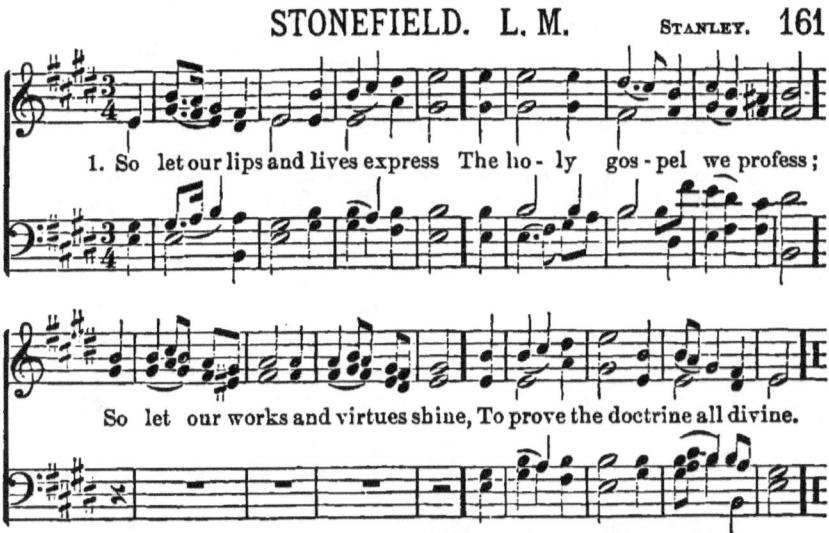

1. So let our lips and lives express The holy gospel we profess;
So let our works and virtues shine, To prove the doctrine all divine.

2.
Thus shall we best proclaim abroad
The honors of our Saviour God,
When his salvation reigns within,
And grace subdues the power of sin.

3.
Religion bears our spirits up,
While we expect that blessed hope,
The bright appearance of the Lord,
And Faith stands leaning on his word.

SECOND HYMN.

1.
How blest the sacred tie that binds,
In union sweet, according minds!
How swift the heavenly course they run,
Whose hearts, and faith, and hopes are one.

2.
To each the soul of each how dear!
What jealous care, what holy fear!
How doth the generous flame within,
Refine from earth and cleanse from sin!

3.
Their streaming tears together flow
For human guilt and human woe;
Their ardent praise united rise,
Like mingling flames in sacrifice.

4.
Together oft they seek the place
Where God reveals his awful face;
How high, how strong their raptures swell
There's none but kindred minds can tell.

5.
Nor shall the glowing flame expire
'Mid nature's drooping sickening fire:
Soon shall they meet in realms above,
A heaven of joy, because of love.

THIRD HYMN.

1.
ABRAHAM, when severely tried,
His faith by his obedience showed;
He with the harsh command complied,
And gave his Isaac back to God.

2.
His son the Father offer'd up,—
Son of his age, his only son;
Object of all his joy and hope,
And less beloved than God alone.

3.
O for a faith like his, that we
The bright example may pursue;
May gladly give up all to thee,
To whom our more than all is due.

4.
Is there a thing than life more dear?
A thing from which we cannot part?
We can; we now rejoice to tear
The idol from our bleeding heart.

5.
Jesus, accept our sacrifice;
All things for thee we count but loss;
Lo! at thy word our idol dies,—
Dies on the altar of thy cross.

6.
For what to thee, O Lord, we give,
A hundred-fold we here obtain;
And soon with thee shall all receive,
And loss shall be eternal gain.

11

CREATION. L. M. 6 L.

Arr'd from HAYDN.

1. The Lord my pasture shall prepare, And feed me with a shepherd's care; His presence shall my wants supply, And guard me with a watchful eye; My noonday walks he shall attend, And all my midnight hours defend.

2. When in the sultry glebe I faint, Or on the thirsty mountain pant, To fertile vales and dewy meads, My weary, wand'ring steps he leads, Where peaceful rivers, soft and slow, Amid the verdant landscape flow.

3.
Though in a bare and rugged way,
Through devious, lonely wilds I stray,
Thy bounty shall my pains beguile;
The barren wilderness shall smile,
With sudden greens and herbage crown'd,
And streams shall murmur all around.

4.
Though in the paths of death I tread,
With gloomy horrors overspread,
My steadfast heart shall fear no ill,
For thou, O Lord, art with me still;
Thy friendly crook shall give me aid,
And guide me through the dreadful shade.

BRIGHTON, L. M. 6 L. 163

1. Pris'ners of hope, be strong, be bold; Cast off your doubts, disdain to fear;
Dare to believe; on Christ lay hold; Wrestle with Christ in mighty pray'r;
Tell him, We will not let thee go, Till we thy name, thy nature know.

2.
Hast thou not died to purge our sin,
  And ris'n, thy death for us to plead?
To write thy law of love within
  Our hearts, and make us free indeed?
That we our Eden might regain,
Thou diedst, and couldst not die in vain.

3.
The promise stands for ever sure,
  And we shall in thine image shine,
Partakers of a nature pure,
  Holy, angelical, divine;
In spirit joined to thee, the Son,
As thou art with the Father one.

SECOND HYMN.

1.
O Love divine, what hast thou done?
  Th' incarnate God has died for me!
The Father's co-eternal Son
  Bore all my sins upon the tree!
The Son of God for me hath died;
My Lord, my Love, is crucified.

2.
Behold him, all ye that pass by,—
  The bleeding Prince of life and peace!
Come, see, ye worms, your Saviour die,
  And say, Was ever grief like his?
Come, feel with me his blood applied:
My Lord, my Love, is crucified:—

3.
Is crucified for me and you,
  To bring us rebels back to God;
Believe, believe the record true,—
  Ye all are bought with Jesus' blood;
Pardon for all flows from his side;
My Lord, my Love, is crucified.

4.
Then let us sit beneath his cross,
  And gladly catch the healing stream;
All things for him account but loss,
  And give up all our hearts to him;
Of nothing think or speak beside,—
My Lord, my Love, is crucified.

Arr'd from H. Bond.

1. O God, of good th'unfathom'd Sea, Who would not give his heart to thee?
2. Thou shin'st with everlasting rays; Before th'insufferable blaze,

Who would not love thee with his might? O Jesus, lover of mankind,
Angels with both wings veil their eyes: Yet free as air thy bounty streams;

Who would not his whole soul, and mind, With all his strength, to thee unite?
On all thy works thy mercy's beams, Diffusive as thy sun's, arise.

3.
Astonished at thy frowning brow, [bow;
Earth, hell, and heaven's strong pillars
 Terrible majesty is thine!
Who then can that vast love express,
Which bows thee down to me,—who less
 Than nothing am, till thou art mine!

4.
High throned on heaven's eternal hill
In number, weight, and measure, still
 Thou sweetly ord'rest all that is;
And yet thou deign'st to come to me,
And guide my steps, that I, with thee
 Enthroned, may reign in endless bliss.

SECOND HYMN.

1.
I'LL praise my Maker while I've breath,
And when my voice is lost in death,
 Praise shall employ my nobler pow'rs;
My days of praise shall ne'er be past,
While life, and thought, and being last,
 Or immortality endures.

2.
Happy the man whose hopes rely
On Israel's God; he made the sky,
 And earth, and seas, with all their
His truth forever stands secure; [train;
He saves th' oppress'd, he feeds the poor,
 And none shall find his promise vain.

3.
The Lord pours eyesight on the blind;
The Lord supports the fainting mind;
 He sends the lab'ring conscience peace;
He helps the stranger in distress,
The widow and the fatherless,
 And grants the pris'ner sweet release.

4.
I'll praise him when he lends me breath,
And when my voice is lost in death,
 Praise shall employ my nobler pow'rs;
My days of praise shall ne'er be past,
While life, and thought, and being last,
 Or immortality endures.

PALESTINE. L.P.M. — Mazzinghi. 165

1. Peace, troubled soul, whose plaintive moan Hath taught.. these rocks the notes of woe; Cease thy complaint, suppress thy groan, And let... thy tears for-get to flow; Be-hold the pre-cious balm is found, To lull... thy pain, to heal thy wound.

2. Come, free-ly come, by sin op-pressed, Un-bur--den here thy weight-y load; Here find thy ref-uge and thy rest, And trust.. the mer-cy of thy God; Thy God's thy Sa-viour— glo-rious word! For ev--er love and praise the Lord.

SECOND HYMN.

1.
Would Jesus have the sinner die?
  Why hangs he, then, on yonder tree?
What means that strange, expiring cry?
  (Sinners, he prays for you and me;)
Forgive them, Father, oh, forgive!
They know not that by me they live.

2.
Jesus descended from above,
  Our loss of Eden to retrieve;
Great God of universal love,
  If all the world through thee may live,
In us a quick'ning spirit be,
And witness thou hast died for me.

3.
Thou loving, all-atoning Lamb,
  Thee, by thy painful agony,
Thy bloody sweat, thy grief and shame,
  Thy cross and passion on the tree,
Thy precious death and life,—I pray,
Take all, take all my sins away.

4.
Oh, let thy love my heart constrain,
  Thy love, for every sinner free,
That every fallen son of man
  May taste the grace that found out me;
That all mankind with me may prove
Thy sov'reign, everlasting love.

CORONATION. C. M.

O. HOLDEN.

1. All hail the pow'r of Je-sus name! Let an-gels prostrate fall;
Bring forth the roy-al di-a-dem, And crown him Lord of all,
Bring forth the roy-al di-a-dem, And crown him Lord of all!

2.
Ye chosen seed of Israel's race,
 Ye ransom'd from the fall,
Hail him who saves you by his grace,
 And crown him Lord of all!

3.
Sinners, whose love can ne'er forget
 The wormwood and the gall,
Go, spread your trophies at his feet,
 And crown him Lord of all!

4.
Let every kindred, every tribe,
 On this terrestrial ball,
To him all majesty ascribe,
 And crown him Lord of all!

5.
Oh, that with yonder sacred throng,
 We at his feet may fall!
We'll join the everlasting song,
 And crown him Lord of all.

SECOND HYMN.

1.
How happy every child of grace
 Who knows his sins forgiven;
This earth, he cries, is not my place;
 I seek my place in heav'n,—

2.
A country far from mortal sight,
 Yet, Oh, by faith I see;
The land of rest, the saints' delight,
 The heaven prepared for me.

3.
Oh, what a blessed hope is ours!
 While here on earth we stay,
We more than taste the heav'nly pow'rs,
 And ante-date that day.

4.
We feel the resurrection near,
 Our life in Christ concealed,
And with his glorious presence here
 Our earthen vessels filled.

5.
Oh, would he more of heaven bestow,
 And, when the vessels break,
Let our triumphant spirits go
 To grasp the God we seek;

6.
In rapt'rous awe on Him to gaze,
 Who bought the sight for me,
And shout and wonder at his grace
 To all eternity.

NORTHFIELD. C. M.

1. Oh, for a thousand tongues, to sing My great Redeemer's praise, The glories of my God and King, The triumphs of his grace.

2. My gracious Master and my God,
 Assist me to proclaim,
To spread through all the earth abroad,
 The honors of thy name.

3. Jesus!—the name that charms our fears,
 That bids our sorrows cease;
'Tis music in the sinners ears;
 'Tis life, and health, and peace.

4. He breaks the power of cancelled sin;
 He sets the pris'ner free;
His blood can make the foulest clean;
 His blood availed for me.

5. He speaks—and list'ning to his voice,
 New life the dead receive;
The mournful, broken hearts rejoice;
 The humble poor believe.

6. Hear him, ye deaf; his praise, ye dumb,
 Your loosened tongues employ;
Ye blind, behold your Saviour come;
 And leap, ye lame, for joy!

SECOND HYMN.

1. How sweet the name of Jesus sounds
 In a believer's ear;
It soothes his sorrows, heals his wounds,
 And drives away his fear.

2. It makes the wounded spirit whole,
 And calms the troubled breast;
'Tis manna to the hungry soul,
 And to the weary, rest.

3. Dear Name, the rock on which I build,
 My shield and hiding place,
My never-failing treasure, filled
 With boundless stores of grace:

4. I would thy boundless love proclaim
 With every fleeting breath;
So shall the music of thy name
 Refresh my soul in death.

VARINA. C. M.

2.
Sweet fields, beyond the swelling flood,
  Stand dressed in living green;
So, to the Jews, old Canaan stood,
  While Jordan rolled between:
But tim'rous mortals start, and shrink
  To cross this narrow sea,
And linger, shiv'ring, on the brink,
  And fear to launch away.

3.
Oh, could we make our doubts remove,
  Those gloomy doubts that rise,
And see the Canaan that we love
  With unbeclouded eyes,—
Could we but climb where Moses stood,
  And view the landscape o'er, [flood,
Not Jordan's stream, nor death's cold
  Should fright us from the shore.

SECOND HYMN.

1.
Let worldly minds the world pursue;
  It has no charms for me;
Once I admired its trifles too,
  But grace hath set me free;
Its pleasures can no longer please,
  Nor happiness afford;
Far from my heart be joys like these,
  Now I have seen the Lord.

2.
As by the light of opening day
  The stars are all concealed,
So earthly pleasures fade away,
  When Jesus is revealed.
Creatures no more divide my choice;
  I bid them all depart:
His name, his love, his gracious voice,
  Have fixed my roving heart.

JERUSALEM. C. M.

E. L. WHITE.

1. Je-ru-sa-lem, my glorious home, Name ev-er dear to me! When shall my la-bors have an end, In joy, and peace, and thee? D. S. Thy bulwarks, with salvation strong, And streets of shining gold. When shall these eyes thy heav'n-built walls, And pear-ly gates behold?

2.
There happier bow'rs than Eden's bloom,
  Nor sin, nor sorrow know;
Blest seats, thro' rude and stormy scenes,
  I onward press to you.
Why should I shrink at pain or woe,
  Or feel at death dismay?
I've Canaan's goodly land in view,
  And realms of endless day.

3.
Apostles, martyrs, prophets there,
  Around my Saviour stand;
And soon, my friends in Christ below,
  Will join the glorious band.
Jerusalem my glorious home,
  My soul still pants for thee!
Then shall my labors have an end,
  When I thy joys shall see.

SECOND HYMN.

1.
To our Redeemer's glorious name
  Awake the sacred song;
Oh, may his love—immortal flame!
  Tune every heart and tongue;
His love, what mortal thought can reach
  What mortal tongue display!
Imagination's utmost stretch
  In wonder dies away.

2.
Dear Lord, while we adoring, pay
  Our humble thanks to thee,
May every heart with rapture say,
  "The Saviour died for me!"
Oh, may the sweet, the blissful theme,
  Fill every heart and tongue!
Till strangers love thy charming name,
  And join the sacred song.

170   ANTIOCH. C. M.   Arr'd by Dr. L. Mason.

1. Hark, the glad sound! the Saviour comes, The Saviour promised long; Let ev'ry heart prepare a throne, And ev'ry voice a song, And ev'ry voice a song, And ev'ry, ev' ry voice a song. And ev' ry voice a song.

2.
He comes, the pris'ner to release,
 In Satan's bondage held:
The gates of brass before him burst;
 The iron fetters yield.

3.
He comes, from thickest films of vice
 To clear the mental ray,
And on the eyes oppressed with night
 To pour celestial day.

4.
He comes, the broken heart to bind,
 The wounded soul to cure,
And, with the treasures of his grace,
 T' enrich the humble poor.

5.
Our glad hosannas, Prince of peace,
 The welcome shall proclaim,
And heav'n's eternal arches ring
 With thy beloved name.

SECOND HYMN.

1.
Give me the wings of faith, to rise
 Within the vail, and see
The saints above, how great their joys,
 How bright their glories be.

2.
Once they were mourners here below,
 And poured out cries and tears;
They wrestled hard, as we do now,
 With sins, and doubts and fears.

3.
I ask them, whence their vict'ry came:
 They, with united breath,

Ascribe their conquest to the Lamb,—
 Their triumph to his death.

4.
They mark'd the footsteps that he trod;
 His zeal inspired their breast;
And, following their incarnate God,
 Possess the promised rest.

5.
Our glorious Leader claims our praise
 For his own pattern given,
While the long cloud of witnesses
 Show the same path to hea'vn.

HEBER. C. M.

Geo. Kingsley.

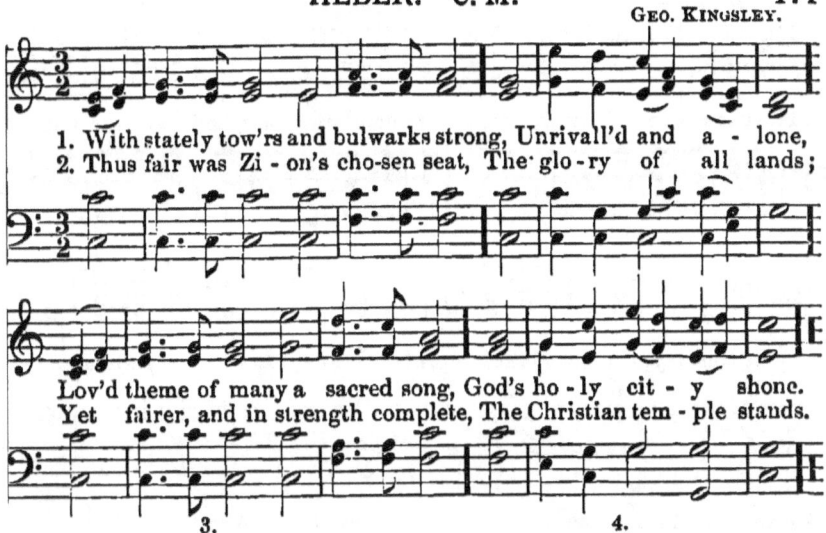

1. With stately tow'rs and bulwarks strong, Unrivall'd and alone,
Lov'd theme of many a sacred song, God's ho-ly cit-y shone.
2. Thus fair was Zi-on's cho-sen seat, The glo-ry of all lands;
Yet fairer, and in strength complete, The Christian tem-ple stands.

3.
The faithful of each clime and age
 This glorious Church compose;
Built on a Rock, with idle rage
 The threat'ning tempest blows.

4.
Fear not; though hostile bands alarm,
 Thy God is thy defence;
And weak and powerless every arm
 Against Omnipotence.

SECOND HYMN.

1.
Awake, my soul! stretch ev'ry nerve,
 And press with vigor on;
A heavenly race demands thy zeal,
 And an immortal crown.

2.
'Tis God's all-animating voice
 That calls thee from on high;
'Tis he whose hand presents the prize
 To thine aspiring eye.

3.
A cloud of witnesses around,
 Hold thee in full survey;
Forget the steps already trod,
 And onward urge thy way.

4.
Blest Saviour! introduced by thee,
 Our race have we begun;
And, crown'd with vict'ry, at thy feet
 We'll lay our trophies down.

THIRD HYMN.

1.
Far from the world, O Lord! I flee,
 From strife and tumult far;
From scenes, where Satan wages still
 His most successful war.

2.
The calm retreat, the silent shade,
 With prayer and praise agree;
And seem, by thy sweet bounty, made
 For those who follow thee.

3.
There, if thy Spirit touch the soul,
 And grace her mean abode,
O! with what peace, and joy, and love,
 Does she commune with God.

4.
There, like the nightingale, she pours
 Her solitary lays;
Nor asks a witness of her song,
 Nor thirsts for human praise.

5.
Author and Guardian of my life,—
 Sweet Source of light divine,—
And,—all harmonious names in one—
 Blest Saviour! thou art mine.

6.
The thanks I owe thee, and the love
 And praise, an endless store,
Shall echo through the realms above
 When time shall be no more.

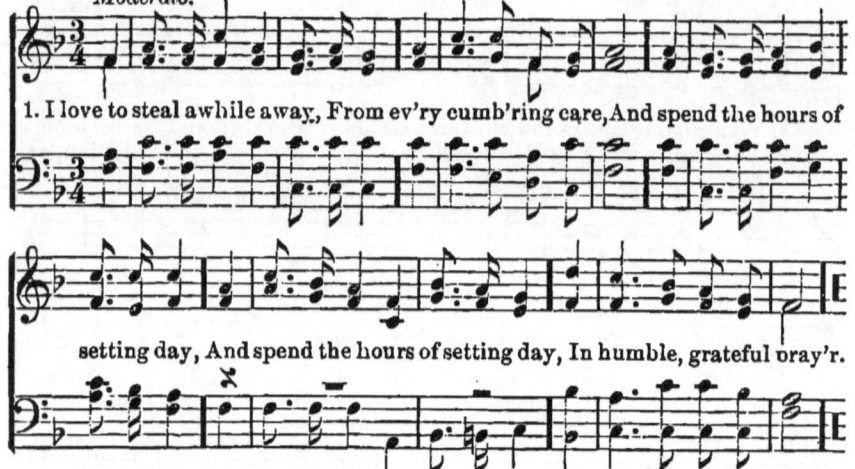

1. I love to steal awhile away, From ev'ry cumb'ring care, And spend the hours of setting day, And spend the hours of setting day, In humble, grateful pray'r.

2.
I love in solitude to shed
 The penitential tear,
And all his promises to plead,
 Where none but God can hear.
3.
I love to think on mercies past,
 And future good implore;
And all my cares and sorrows cast
 On him whom I adore.

4.
I love by faith to take a view
 Of brighter scenes in heaven:
The prospect doth my strength renew,
 While here by tempest driven.
5.
Thus, when life's toilsome day is o'er,
 May its departing ray
Be calm as this impressive hour,
 And lead to endless day.

SECOND HYMN.

1.
There is an hour of peaceful rest,
 To mourning wand'rers given;
There is a joy for souls distress'd,
A balm for every wounded breast,
 'Tis found above in heaven.
2.
There is a home for weary souls
 By sin and sorrow driven,
When toss'd on life's tempestuous shoals,
Where storms arise and ocean rolls,
 And all is drear but heaven.

3.
There faith lifts up the tearless eye,
 To brighter prospects given;
And views the tempest passing by,
The evening shadows quickly fly,
 And all serene in heaven.
4.
There fragrant flowers immortal bloom,
 And joys supreme are given;
There rays divine disperse the gloom;
Beyond the confines of the tomb
 Appears the dawn of heaven.

THIRD HYMN.

1.
GREAT God, to thee my evening song
 With gratitude I raise;
O let thy mercy tune my tongue,
 And fill my heart with praise.
2.
My days, unclouded as they pass,
 And every fleeting hour,
Are monuments of wondrous grace,—
 Of mercy, love, and power.

3.
Thy love and power, celestial guard,
 Preserve me from all harm:
Can danger reach me while the Lord
 Extends his mighty arm?
4.
Let this blest hope mine eyelids close;
 With sleep refresh my frame;
Safe in thy care may I repose,
 And wake to praise thy name.

ARLINGTON. C. M. 173

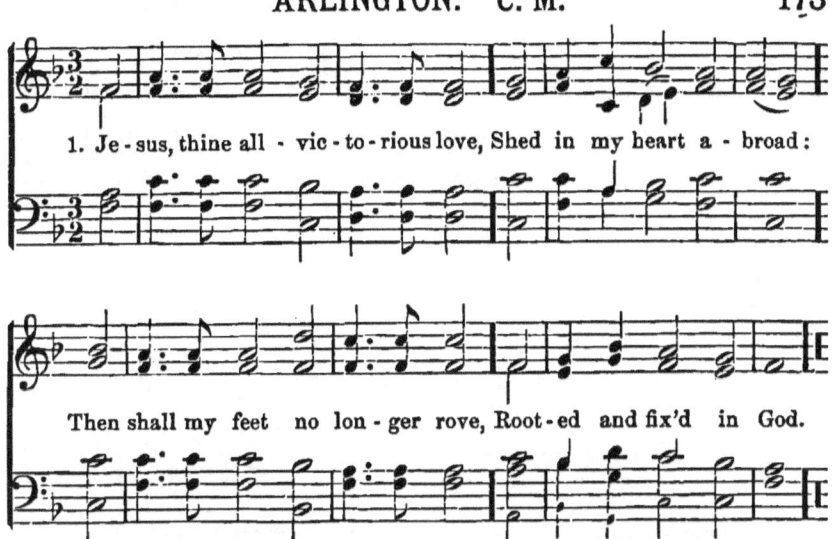

1. Jesus, thine all-victorious love, Shed in my heart abroad: Then shall my feet no longer rove, Rooted and fix'd in God.

2. O that in me the sacred fire
   Might now begin to glow;
   Burn up the dross of base desire,
   And make the mountains flow.

3. O that it now from heaven might fall,
   And all my sins consume:
   Come, Holy Ghost, for thee I call;
   Spirit of burning, come.

4. Refining fire, go through my heart;
   Illuminate my soul;
   Scatter thy life through every part,
   And sanctify the whole.

5. My steadfast soul, from falling free,
   Shall then no longer move;
   While Christ is all the world to me,
   And all my heart is love.

SECOND HYMN.

1.
Thou art the Way; to thee alone
From sin and death we flee;
And he who would the Father seek,
Must seek him, Lord, by thee.

2.
Thou art the Truth; thy word alone
True wisdom can impart;
Thou only canst inform the mind,
And purify the heart.

3.
Thou art the Life; the rending tomb
Proclaims thy conq'ring arm;
And those who put their trust in thee,
Nor death nor hell shall harm.

4.
Thou art the Way, the Truth, the Life;
Grant us that way to know,
That truth to keep, that life to win,
Whose joys eternal flow.

THIRD HYMN.

1.
Once more, my soul, the rising day
Salutes thy waking eyes;
Once more, my voice, thy tribute pay
To Him that rules the skies.

2.
Night unto night his Name repeats,
The day renews the sound:
Wide as the heavens on which he sits,
To turn the seasons round.

3.
'Tis he supports my mortal frame;
My tongue shall speak his praise;
My sins might rouse his wrath to flame,
But yet his wrath delays.

4.
O God, let all my hours be thine,
Whilst I enjoy the light!
Then shall my sun in smiles decline,
And bring a peaceful night.

AZMON. C. M.
Arranged from GLASER.

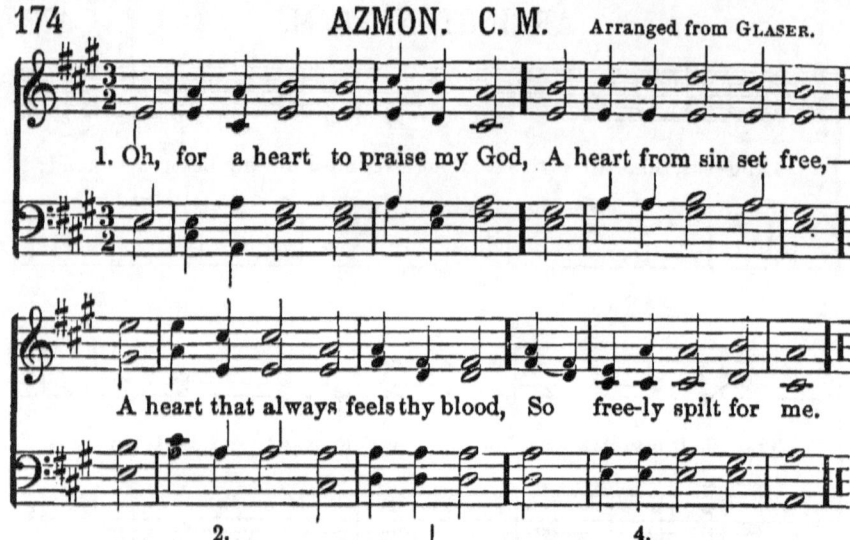

1. Oh, for a heart to praise my God, A heart from sin set free,—
A heart that always feels thy blood, So freely spilt for me.

2.
A heart resigned, submissive, meek,
My great Redeemer's throne,
Where only Christ is heard to speak:
Where Jesus reigns alone.

3.
Oh, for a lowly, contrite heart,
Believing, true, and clean,
Which neither life nor death can part
From him that dwells within:—

4.
A heart in every thought renewed,
And full of love divine;
Perfect, and right, and pure, and good,
A copy, Lord, of thine.

5.
Thy nature, gracious Lord, impart:
Come quickly from above;
Write thy new name upon my heart—
Thy new, best name of love.

SECOND HYMN.

1.
Yes, I will bless thee, O my God,
Through all my fleeting days;
And to eternity prolong
Thy vast, thy boundless praise.

2.
Nor shall my tongue alone proclaim
The honors of my God;
My life, with all its active powers,
Shall spread thy praise abroad.

3.
Nor will I cease thy praise to sing,
When death shall close mine eyes;
My thoughts shall then to nobler heights,
And sweeter raptures rise.

4.
Then shall my lips in endless praise,
Their grateful tribute pay;
The theme demands an angel's tongue,
And an eternal day.

THIRD HYMN.

1.
O God, unseen, yet ever near,
Thy presence may we feel;
And thus, inspired with holy fear,
Before thy table kneel.

2.
Here may thy faithful people know
The blessings of thy love;
The streams that thro' the desert flow,
The manna from above.

3.
We come, obedient to thy word,
To feast on heavenly food;
Our meat, the body of the Lord,
Our drink, his precious blood.

4.
Thus may we all thy words obey;
For we, O Lord, are thine;
And go rejoicing on our way,
Renewed with strength divine.

DUNDEE. C. M.   175

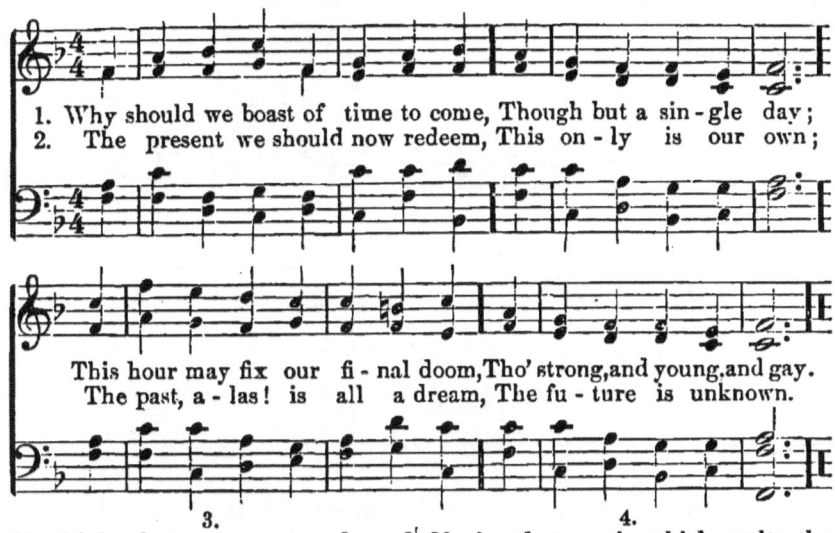

1. Why should we boast of time to come, Though but a single day;
This hour may fix our final doom, Tho' strong, and young, and gay.

2. The present we should now redeem, This only is our own;
The past, alas! is all a dream, The future is unknown.

3.
Oh, think what vast concerns depend
 Upon a moment's space;
When life and all its cares shall end
 In vengeance or in grace.

4.
Oh, for that pow'r which melts the heart,
 And lifts the soul on high,
Where sin, and grief, and death depart,
 And pleasures never die.

SECOND HYMN.

1.
HIGH on a throne of light, O Lord,
 Dost thou exalted shine:
What can our poverty bestow,
 Since all the world is thine?

2.
But thou hast brethren here below,
 Partakers of thy grace,
Whose humble names thou wilt confess
 Before thy Father's face.

3.
In them may'st thou be clothed and fed,
 And visited and cheer'd;
And, in their accents of distress,
 The Saviour's voice be heard.

4.
Whate'er our willing hands can give,
 Lord, at thy feet we lay;
Grace will the humble gift receive,
 And grace at length repay.

THIRD HYMN.

1.
JESUS, to thy dear wounds we flee;
 We shelter in thy side;
Assured that all who trust in thee
 Shall evermore abide.

2.
Then let the thund'ring trumpet sound;
 The latest lightnings glare;
The mountains melt; the solid ground
 Dissolve as liquid air;

3.
The huge celestial bodies roll
 Amidst the gen'ral fire;
And shrivel as a parchment scroll,
 And all in smoke expire:—

4.
Sublime on his eternal throne,
 He speaks th' almighty word;
His fiat is obeyed: 'tis done;
 And paradise restored.

5.
So be it; let this system end;
 This ruinous earth and skies;
The new Jerusalem descend,—
 The new creation rise.

6.
Thy power omnipotent assume,
 Thy brightest majesty;
And when thou dost in glory come,
 My Lord, remember me.

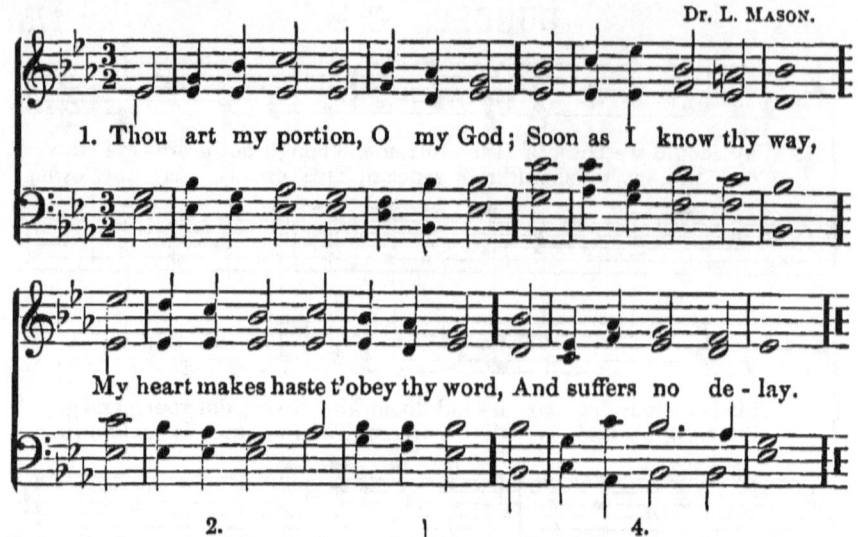

Dr. L. Mason.

1. Thou art my portion, O my God; Soon as I know thy way, My heart makes haste t'obey thy word, And suffers no de-lay.

2.
I choose the path of heavenly truth,
 And glory in my choice;
Not all the riches of the earth
 Could make me so rejoice.

3.
The testimonies of thy grace
 I set before mine eyes;
Thence I derive my daily strength,
 And there my comfort lies.

4.
If once I wander from thy path,
 I think upon my ways;
Then turn my feet to thy commands,
 And trust thy pardoning grace.

5.
Now I am thine—forever thine—
 Oh, save thy servant, Lord!
Thou art my shield, my hiding place;
 My hope is in thy word.

SECOND HYMN.

1.
GREAT God! the nations of the earth,
 Are by creation thine;
Are in thy works, by all beheld,
 Thy power and glory shine.

2.
But, Lord, thy greater love hath sent
 Thy gospel to mankind,
Unvailing what rich stores of grace
 Are treasured in thy mind.

3.
Oh, when shall these glad tidings spread
 The spacious earth around,
Till every tribe and every soul
 Shall hear the joyful sound?

4.
Smile, Lord, on each divine attempt
 To spread the gospel's rays,
And build on sin's demolished throne
 The temples of thy praise.

THIRD HYMN.

1.
ONCE more we come before our God;
 Once more his blessing ask;
O may not duty seem a load,
 Nor worship prove a task.

2.
Father, thy quick'ning Spirit send
 From heaven, in Jesus' name,
And bid our waiting minds attend,
 And put our souls in frame.

3.
May we receive the word we hear,
 Each in an honest heart;
And keep the precious treasure there,
 And never with it part.

4.
To seek thee, all our hearts dispose;
 To each thy blessing suit;
And let the seed thy servant sows,
 Produce abundant fruit.

GENEVA. C. M. 177
JOHN COLE.

2.
Oh, how can words with equal warmth
  The gratitude declare,
That glows within my ravish'd heart?
  But thou canst read it there.

3.
To all my weak complaints and cries
  Thy mercy lent an ear,
Ere yet my feeble thoughts had learn'd
  To form themselves in prayer.

4.
When in the slippery paths of youth,
  With heedless steps, I ran;
Thine arm, unseen, conveyed me safe,
  And led me up to man.

5.
Thro' hidden dangers, toils and deaths,
  It gently clear'd my way;
And thro' the pleasing snares of vice,
  More to be feared than they.

SECOND HYMN.

1.
WHAT glory gilds the sacred page!
  Majestic, like the sun,
It gives a light to every age;
  It gives, but borrows none.

2.
The power that gave it still supplies
  The gracious light and heat;
Its truths upon the nations rise:
  They rise, but never set.

3.
Lord! everlasting thanks be thine
  For such a bright display,
As makes a world of darkness shine
  With beams of heavenly day.

4.
Our souls rejoicingly pursue
  The steps of him we love,
Till glory break upon our view
  In brighter worlds above.

THIRD HYMN.

1.
COME, ye that love the Saviour's name,
  And joy to make it known,
The Sov'reign of your hearts proclaim,
  And bow before his throne.

2.
Behold your Lord, your Master, crown'd
  With glories all divine:
And tell the wond'ring nations round,
  How bright those glories shine.

12

NAOMI. C. M. — Dr. L. Mason.

1. Father, whate'er of earthly bliss Thy sov'reign will de-nies;
Ac'-cep-ted at thy throne of grace, Let this pe-ti-tion rise.

2.
Give me a calm, a thankful heart,
From every murmur free;
The blessings of thy grace impart,
And let me live to thee.

3.
Oh, let me hope that thou art mine,
My life and death attend;
Thy presence thro' my journey shine,
And crown my journey's end.

SECOND HYMN.

1.
WITH joy we hail the sacred day,
Which God has called his own;
With joy the summons we obey,
To worship at his throne.

2.
Thy chosen temple, Lord, how fair!
As here thy servants throng
To breathe the humble, fervent prayer,
And pour the grateful song.

3.
Spirit of grace! O deign to dwell
Within thy Church below;
Make her in holiness excel,
With pure devotion glow.

4.
Let peace within her walls be found,
Let all her sons unite,
To spread with holy zeal around,
Her clear and shining light.

THIRD HYMN.

1.
FATHER of mercies, in thy word
What endless glory shines;
Forever be thy Name adored
For these celestial lines.

2.
Here may the wretched sons of want
Exhaustless riches find;
Riches above what earth can grant,
And lasting as the mind.

3.
Here the fair tree of knowledge grows,
And yields a free repast;
Sublimer sweets than nature knows
Invite the longing taste.

4.
Here the Redeemer's welcome voice
Spreads heavenly peace around;
And life, and everlasting joys,
Attend the blissful sound.

5.
O may these heavenly pages be
Our ever dear delight;
And still new beauties may we see,
And still increasing light.

6.
Divine Instructor, gracious Lord,
Be thou forever near;
Teach us to love the sacred word,
And view the Saviour there.

WARWICK. C. M.

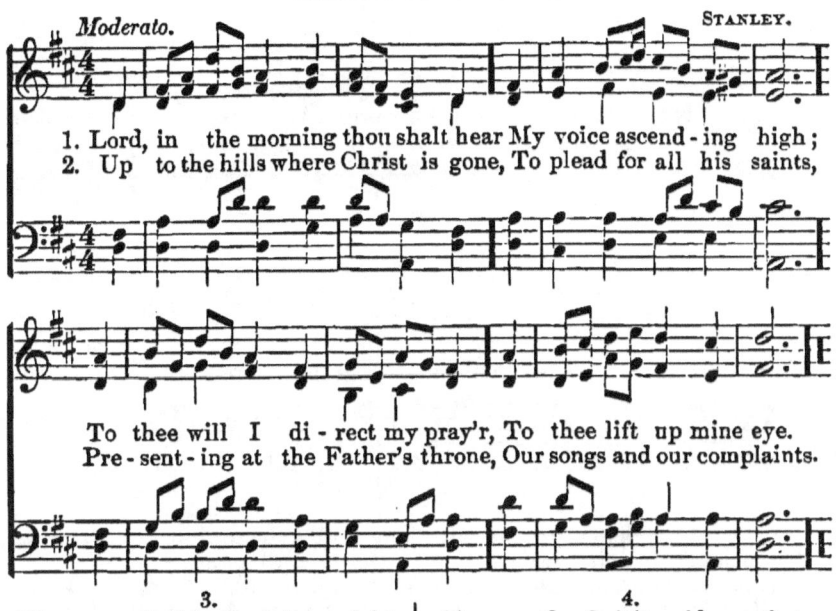

1. Lord, in the morning thou shalt hear My voice ascending high;
   To thee will I direct my pray'r, To thee lift up mine eye.
2. Up to the hills where Christ is gone, To plead for all his saints,
   Presenting at the Father's throne, Our songs and our complaints.

3.
Thou art a God before whose sight
 The wicked shall not stand;
Sinners shall ne'er be thy delight,
 Nor dwell at thy right hand.

4.
Oh, may thy Spirit guide my feet
 In ways of righteousness;
Make every path of duty straight
 And plain before my face.

SECOND HYMN.

1.
Now from the altar of our hearts,
 Let warmest thanks arise;
Assist us, Lord, to offer up
 Our evening sacrifice.

2.
This day God was our sun and shield,
 Our keeper and our guide;
His care was on our weakness shown,
 His mercies multiplied.

3.
Minutes and mercies multiplied,
 Have made up all this day;
Minutes came quick, but mercies were
 More swift and free than they.

4.
New time, new favors, and new joys,
 Do a new song require;
Till we shall praise thee as we would,
 Accept our hearts' desire.

THIRD HYMN.

1.
Let him to whom we now belong,
 His sov'reign right assert;
And take up every thankful song,
 And every loving heart.

2.
He justly claims us for his own,
 Who bought us with a price:
The Christian lives to Christ alone;
 To Christ alone he dies.

3.
Jesus, thine own at last receive;
 Fulfil our heart's desire;
And let us to thy glory live,
 And in thy cause expire.

4.
Our souls and bodies we resign;
 With joy we render thee
Our all,—no longer ours, but thine
 To all eternity.

HOWARD. C. M.

1. I love the Lord—he heard my cries, And pit-ied ev'-ry groan: Long as I live, when troubles rise, I'll has-ten to his throne.

2.
I love the Lord,—he bowed his ear,
   And chased my grief away;
Oh, let my heart no more despair,
   While I have breath to pray.

3.
The Lord beheld me sore distressed,
   He bade my pains remove;
Return, my soul, to God, thy Rest,
   For thou hast known his love.

SECOND HYMN.

1.
O WHY should gloomy thoughts arise,
   And darkness fill the mind? [sighs,
Why should the bosom heave with
   And yet no refuge find?

2.
Hast thou not heard of Gilead's balm,
   The great Physician there,
Who can thine every fear disarm,
   And save thee from despair?

3.
Still art thou overwhelm'd with grief,
   And filled with sore dismay?
Still looking downward for relief,
   Without one cheering ray?

4.
Lift up thy streaming eyes to heaven;
   The great atonement see;
And all thy sins shall be forgiven:—
   Believe, and thou art free.

THIRD HYMN.

1.
ACCORDING to thy gracious word,
   In meek humility,
This will I do, my dying Lord,—
   I will remember thee.

2.
Thy body, broken for my sake,
   My bread from heaven shall be:
Thy testamental cup I take,
   And thus remember thee.

3.
Gethsemane can I forget?
   Or there thy conflict see,
Thine agony and bloody sweat,
   And not remember thee?

4.
When to the cross I turn mine eyes,
   And rest on Calvary,
O Lamb of God, my Sacrifice,
   I must remember thee!

5.
Remember thee and all thy pains,
   And all thy love to me;
Yea, while a breath, a pulse remains,
   Will I remember thee.

6.
And when these failing lips grow dumb,
   And mind and mem'ry flee,
When thou shalt in thy kingdom come,
   Jesus, remember me.

CHRISTMAS. C. M.

Arranged from HANDEL.

1. Come, let us lift our joyful eyes Up to the courts a-bove, And smile to see our Fa-ther there, Up-on a throne of love.
2. Come, let us bow before his feet, And venture near the Lord: No fi-ery cherubs guard his seat, Nor double-flaming sword,

3. The peaceful gates of heavenly bliss
Are opened by the Son;
High let us raise our notes of praise,
And reach th' almighty throne.

4. To thee ten thousand thanks we bring,
Great Advocate on high;
And glory to th' eternal King,
Who lays his anger by.

SECOND HYMN.

1.
WHILE shepherds watch'd their flocks
All seated on the ground, [by night,
The angel of the Lord came down,
And glory shone around.

2.
Fear not, said he, (for mighty dread
Had seized their troubled mind,)
Glad tidings of great joy I bring,
To you and all mankind.

3.
To you, in David's town, this day
Is born, of David's line,
The Saviour, who is Christ the Lord;
And this shall be the sign:

4.
The heavenly babe you there shall find
To human view display'd, [bands,
All meanly wrapp'd in swathing-
And in a manger laid.

5.
Thus spake the seraph; and forthwith
Appear'd a shining throng
Of angels, praising God on high,
Who thus address'd their song:

6.
All glory be to God on high,
And to the earth be peace: [men,
Good-will henceforth, from heaven to
Begin and never cease.

ORTONVILLE. C. M.

T. HASTINGS.

1. Come, humble sinner, in whose breast A thousand tho'ts revolve,
Come, with your guilt and fear oppress'd, And make this last re-solve,

And make this last re-solve.

2. I'll go to Jesus, though my sin
Like mountains round me close;
I know his courts, I'll enter in,
Whatever may oppose.

3. Prostrate I'll lie before his throne,
And there my guilt confess:
I'll tell him I'm a wretch undone,
Without his sovereign grace.

4.
Perhaps he will admit my plea,
Perhaps will hear my prayer;
But, if I perish, I will pray,
And perish only there.

5.
I can but perish, if I go;
I am resolved to try;
For if I stay away, I know
I must forever die.

SECOND HYMN.

1.
I want a principle within,
Of jealous, godly fear;
A sensibility of sin,—
A pain to feel it near:

2.
I want the first approach to feel,
Of pride, or fond desire;
To catch the wand'ring of my will,
And quench the kindling fire.

3.
From thee that I no more may part,
No more thy goodness grieve,
The filial awe, the fleshly heart,
The tender conscience, give.

4.
Quick as the apple of an eye,
O God, my conscience make;
Awake, my soul, when sin is nigh,
And keep it still awake.

5.
If to the right or left I stray,
That moment, Lord, reprove;
And let me weep my life away,
For having grieved thy love.

6.
O may the least omission pain
My well-instructed soul,
And drive me to the blood again,
Which makes the wounded whole.

ST. MARTIN'S. C. M.

TANSUR.   183

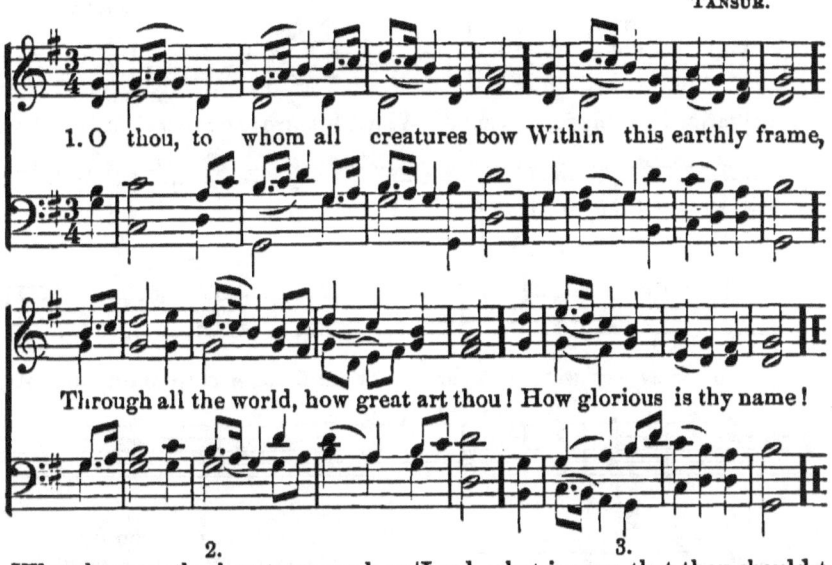

1. O thou, to whom all creatures bow Within this earthly frame, Through all the world, how great art thou! How glorious is thy name!

2.
When heaven, thy beauteous work on high,
Employs my wondering sight;
The moon that nightly rules the sky,
With stars of feebler light;—

3.
Lord, what is man, that thou shouldst deign
To bear him in thy mind! [prove
Or what his race, that thou shouldst
To them so wondrous kind!

SECOND HYMN.

1.
BEHOLD the sure foundation-stone
Which God in Zion lays,
To build our heavenly hopes upon,
And his eternal praise.

2.
Chosen of God, to sinners dear,
We now adore thy name;
We trust our whole salvation here,
Nor can we suffer shame.

3.
The foolish builders, scribe and priest,
Reject it with disdain;
Yet on this Rock the church shall rest,
And envy rage in vain.

4.
What though the gates of hell withstood,
Yet must this building rise; [stood,
'Tis thine own work, almighty God,
And wondrous in our eyes.

THIRD HYMN.

1.
TRY us, O God, and search the ground
Of every sinful heart:
Whate'er of sin in us is found,
O bid it all depart.

2.
If to the right or left we stray,
Leave us not comfortless;
But guide our feet into the way
Of everlasting peace.

3.
Help us to help each other, Lord,
Each other's cross to bear:
Let each his friendly aid afford,
And feel his brother's care.

4.
Help us to build each other up;
Our little stock improve;
Increase our faith, confirm our hope,
And perfect us in love.

5.
Up into thee, our living Head,
Let us in all things grow,
Till thou hast made us free indeed,
And spotless here below.

CAMBRIDGE. C. M.

Dr. Randall.

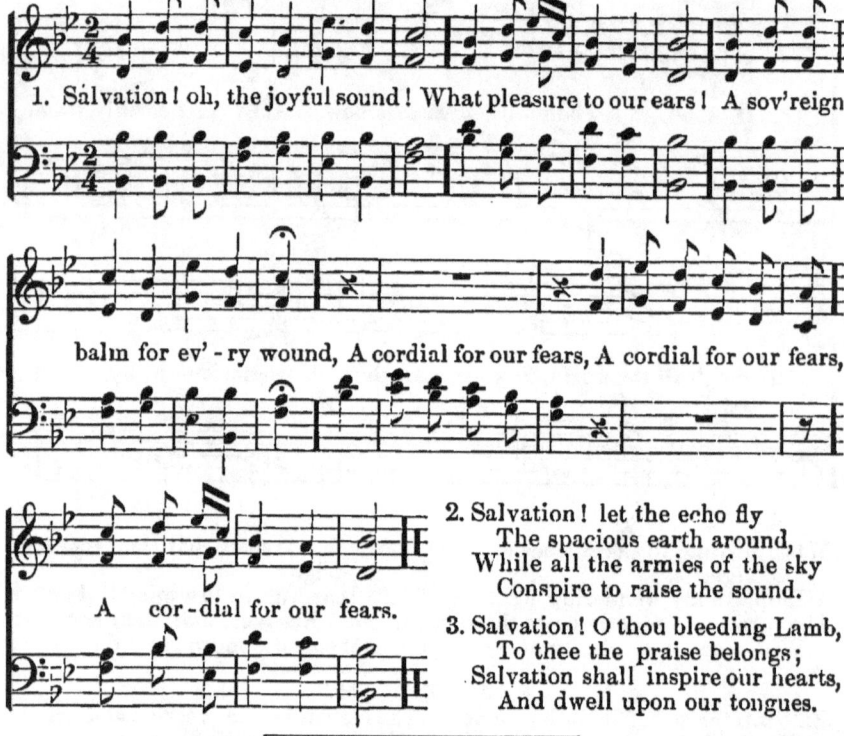

1. Salvation! oh, the joyful sound! What pleasure to our ears! A sov'reign balm for ev'-ry wound, A cordial for our fears, A cordial for our fears, A cor-dial for our fears.

2. Salvation! let the echo fly
The spacious earth around,
While all the armies of the sky
Conspire to raise the sound.

3. Salvation! O thou bleeding Lamb,
To thee the praise belongs;
Salvation shall inspire our hearts,
And dwell upon our tongues.

SECOND HYMN.

1.
Let Zion's watchmen all awake,
And take th' alarm they give;
Now let them from the mouth of God
Their awful charge receive.

2.
'Tis not a cause of small import,
The pastor's care demands;
But what might fill an angel's heart,
And fill'd a Saviour's hands.

3.
They watch for souls for which the Lord
Did heavenly bliss forego;
For souls, which must forever live
In raptures, or in wo.

4.
May they in Jesus, whom they preach,
Their own Redeemer see;
And watch thou daily o'er their souls,
That they may watch for thee.

THIRD HYMN

1.
My Saviour, my almighty Friend,
When I begin thy praise,
Where will the growing numbers end,
The numbers of thy grace?

2.
I trust in thy eternal word;
Thy goodness I adore:
Send down thy grace, O blessed Lord,
That I may love thee more.

3.
My feet shall travel all the length
Of the celestial road;
And march, with courage in thy strength,
To see the Lord my God.

4.
Awake! awake! my tuneful powers,
With this delightful song;
And entertain the darkest hours,
Nor think the season long.

MERTON. C. M.

H. K. OLIVER.

1. Ye gold-en lamps of heav'n! farewell, With all your fee-ble light;
2. And thou re-ful-gent orb of day, In brighter flames array'd,

Farewell, thou ever-changing moon, Pale em-press of the night!
My soul, that springs beyond thy sphere, No more demands thine aid.

3.
Ye stars are but the shining dust
  Of my divine abode;
The pavement of those heavenly [courts,
  Where I shall reign with God.

4.
The Father of eternal light
  Shall there his beams display;
Nor shall one moment's darkness mix
  With that unvaried day.

5.
No more the drops of piercing grief,
  Shall swell into my eyes;
Nor the meridian sun decline
  Amid those brighter skies.

6.
There all the millions of his saints
  Shall in one song unite,
And each the bliss of all shall view,
  With infinite delight.

SECOND HYMN.

1.
ALL glory to the dying Lamb,
  And never-ceasing praise,
While angels live to know thy name,
  Or men to feel thy grace.

2.
With this cold stony heart of mine,
  Jesus, to thee I flee;
And to thy grace my soul resign,
  To be renew'd by thee.

3.
O may the uncorrupted seed
  Abide and reign within;
And thy life-giving word forbid
  My new-born soul to sin.

THIRD HYMN.

1.
DELIGHTFUL work! young souls to [win,
  And turn the rising race
From the deceitful paths of sin,
  To seek redeeming grace.

2.
Children our kind protection claim;
  And God will well approve
When infants learn to lisp his name,
  And their Redeemer love.

3.
Be ours the bliss, in wisdom's way
  To guide untutored youth,
And show the mind which went astray,
  The Way, the Life, the Truth.

4.
Almighty God, thine influence shed,
  To aid this blest design:
The honors of thy Name be spread,
  And all the glory thine.

EMMONS. C. M.

Arranged from BURGMULLER.

1. Thou dear Redeemer, dying Lamb, I love to hear of thee;
   No music like thy charming name, Nor half so sweet can be,
   Nor half so sweet can be.
2. Oh, may I ever hear thy voice In mercy to me speak!
   In thee, my Priest, will I rejoice, And thy salvation seek,
   And thy salvation seek.
3. My Jesus shall be still my theme,
   While on this earth I stay,
   I'll sing my Jesus' lovely name,
   When all things else decay.
4. When I appear in yonder cloud,
   With all his favored throng,
   Then will I sing more sweet, more loud,
   And Christ shall be my song.

SECOND HYMN.

1. JESUS, the Life, the Truth, the Way,
   In whom I now believe,
   As taught by thee, in faith I pray,
   Expecting to receive.
2. Thy will by me on earth be done,
   As by the powers above,
   Who always see thee on thy throne,
   And glory in thy love.
3. I ask in confidence the grace,
   That I may do thy will,
   As angels, who behold thy face,
   And all thy words fulfil.
4. Surely I shall, the sinner I,
   Shall serve thee without fear,
   If thou my nature sanctify
   In answer to my prayer.

THIRD HYMN.

1. I WOULD be thine; O take my heart,
   And fill it with thy love;
   Thy sacred image, Lord, impart,
   And seal it from above.
2. I would be thine; but while I strive
   To give myself away,
   I feel rebellion still alive,
   And wander while I pray.

ELIM. C. M.

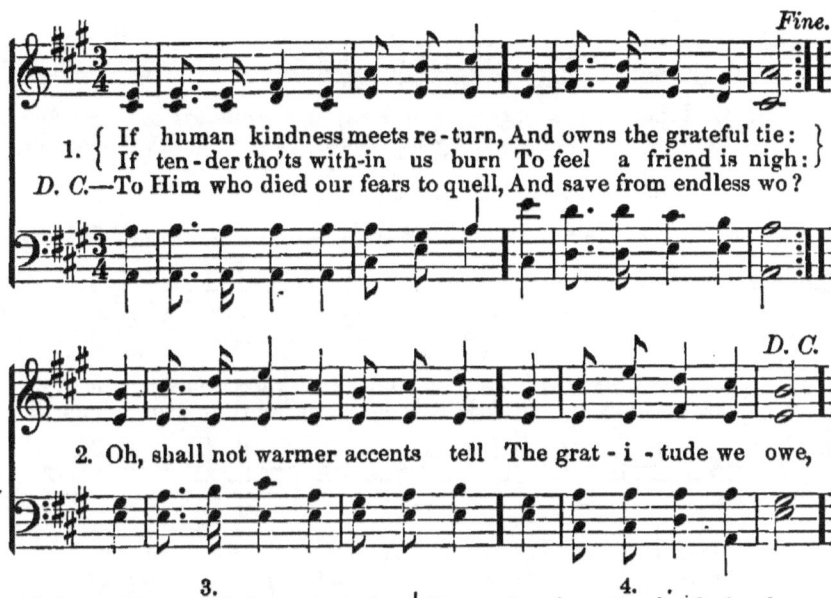

1. { If human kindness meets re-turn, And owns the grateful tie:
   { If ten-der tho'ts with-in us burn To feel a friend is nigh:
   D. C.—To Him who died our fears to quell, And save from endless wo?

2. Oh, shall not warmer accents tell The grat-i-tude we owe,

3.
While yet in anguish he surveyed
  Those pangs he would not flee,
What love his latest words display'd!
  Meet and remember me.

4.
Remember thee! thy death, thy shame,
  The griefs which thou didst bear!
O mem'ry, leave no other name
  So deeply graven there.

SECOND HYMN.

1.
PRAISE ye the Lord, ye heav'nly choirs
  That fill the worlds above;
Praise him who formed you of his fires,
  And feeds you with his love.

2.
Shine to his praise, ye crystal skies,
  The floor of his abode;
Or veil in shades your thousand eyes,
  Before your brighter God.

3.
Thou restless globe of golden light,
  Whose beams create our days,
Join with the silver queen of night,
  To own your borrowed rays.

4.
Thunder and hail, and fire and storms,
  The troops of his command,
Appear in all your dreadful forms,
  And speak his awful hand.

5.
Shout to the Lord, ye surging seas,
  In your eternal roar;
Let wave to wave resound his praise,
  And shore reply to shore.

6.
Thus while the meaner creatures sing,
  Ye mortals, catch the sound;
Echo the glories of your King
  Through all the nations round.

Concluded from opposite page.

3.
I WOULD be thine; but Lord, I feel
  Evil still lurks within:—
Do thou thy majesty reveal,
  And overcome my sin.

4.
I would be thine; I would embrace
  The Saviour, and adore;
Inspire with faith, infuse thy grace,
  And now my soul restore.

BALERMA. C. M.
Scottish Melody.

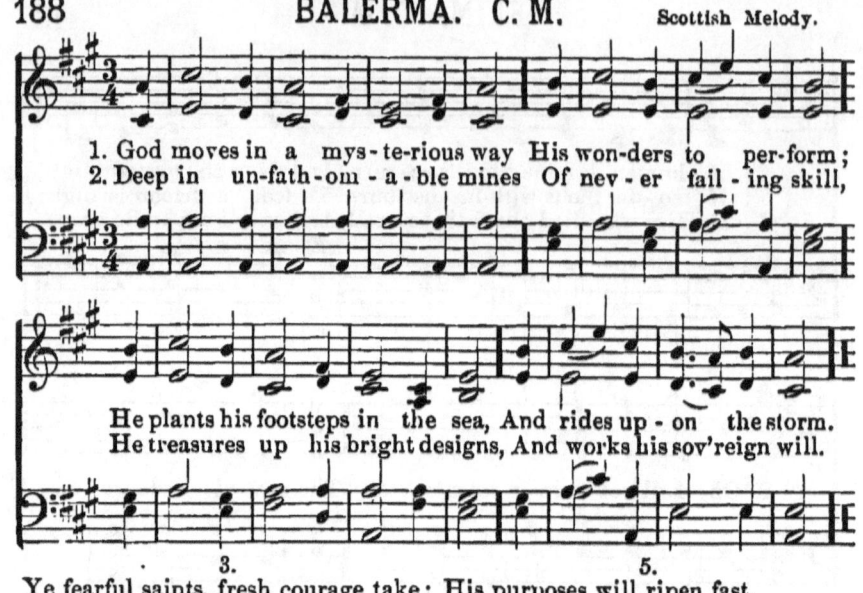

1. God moves in a mys-te-rious way His won-ders to per-form;
He plants his footsteps in the sea, And rides up-on the storm.

2. Deep in un-fath-om-a-ble mines Of nev-er fail-ing skill,
He treasures up his bright designs, And works his sov'reign will.

3.
Ye fearful saints, fresh courage take;
The clouds ye so much dread
Are big with mercy, and shall break
In blessings on your head.

4.
Judge not the Lord by feeble sense,
But trust him for his grace;
Behind a frowning providence
He hides a smiling face.

5.
His purposes will ripen fast,
Unfolding every hour;
The bud may have a bitter taste,
But sweet will be the flow'r.

6.
Blind unbelief is sure to err,
And scan his work in vain;
God is his own interpreter,
And he will make it plain.

SECOND HYMN.

1.
Come, Holy Ghost, our hearts inspire;
Let us thine influence prove;—
Source of the old prophetic fire;
Fountain of life and love.

2.
Come Holy Ghost, for moved by thee
The prophets wrote and spoke:
Unlock the truth, thyself the key;
Unseal the sacred book.

3.
Expand thy wings, Celestial Dove;
Brood o'er our nature's night;
On our disorder'd spirits move,
And let there now be light.

4.
God, thro' himself, we then shall know,
If thou within us shine;
And sound, with all thy saints below,
The depth of love divine.

THIRD HYMN.

1.
Lord, while for all mankind we pray,
Of every clime and coast,
O hear us for our native land,—
The land we love the most.

2.
O guard our shores from every foe;
With peace our borders bless—
Our cities with prosperity,
Our fields with plenteousness.

3.
Unite us in the sacred love
Of knowledge, truth, and thee;
And let our hills and valleys chant
The songs of liberty.

4.
Lord of the nations, thus to thee
Our country we commend;
Be thou her refuge and her trust—
Her everlasting friend.

CROSS AND CROWN. C. M. 189

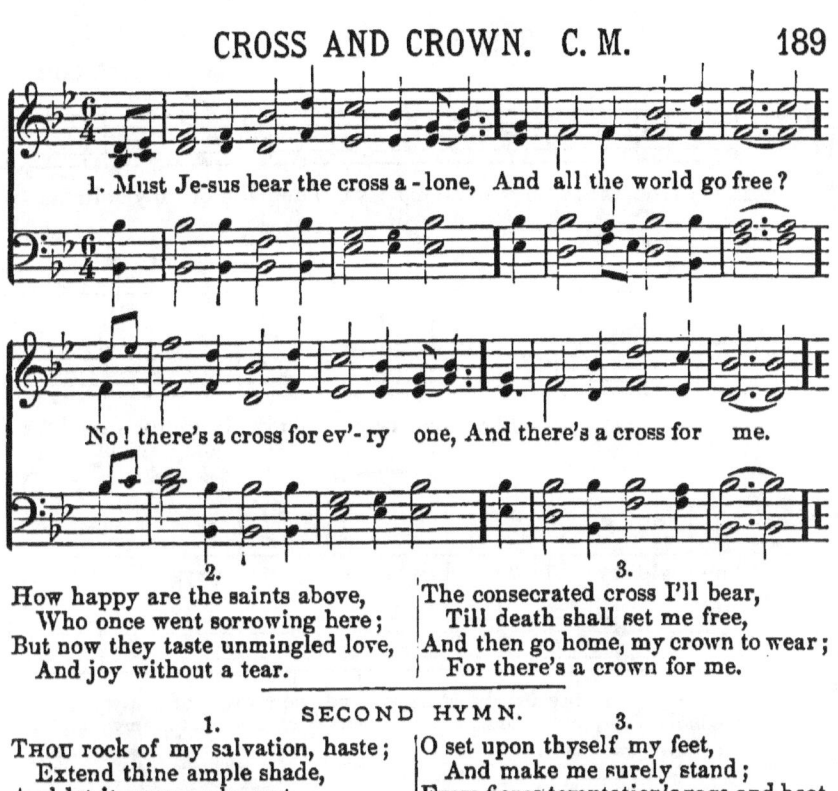

1. Must Jesus bear the cross alone, And all the world go free?
No! there's a cross for ev'ry one, And there's a cross for me.

2.
How happy are the saints above,
 Who once went sorrowing here;
But now they taste unmingled love,
 And joy without a tear.

3.
The consecrated cross I'll bear,
 Till death shall set me free,
And then go home, my crown to wear;
 For there's a crown for me.

SECOND HYMN.

1.
THOU rock of my salvation, haste;
 Extend thine ample shade,
And let it over me be cast,
 To screen my naked head.

2.
Defend me in this trying hour;
 My sure protection be;
My shelter from the tempest's pow'r,
 Till I am fixed on thee.

3.
O set upon thyself my feet,
 And make me surely stand;
From fierce temptation's rage and heat
 Protect me with thy hand.

4.
Now let me in the cleft be placed:
 Nor my defence remove;
Within thine arms of love embraced,
 Thine arms of endless love.

THIRD HYMN.

1.
JESUS, immortal King, arise;
 Assert thy rightful sway;
Till earth, subdued, its tribute brings,
 And distant lands obey.

2.
Ride forth, victorious conq'ror, ride,
 Till all thy foes submit,
And all the powers of hell resign
 Their trophies at thy feet.

3.
Send forth thy word, and let it fly
 The spacious earth around,
Till every soul beneath the sun
 Shall hear the joyful sound.

4.
O may the great Redeemer's name
 Through every clime be known,
And heathen gods, forsaken, fall,
 And Jesus reign alone.

5.
From sea to sea, from shore to shore,
 Be thou, O Christ, adored,
And earth, with all her millions shout
 Hosannas to the Lord.

Doxology.
To Father, Son, and Holy Ghost,
 Who sweetly all agree,
To save a world of sinners lost,
 Eternal glory be.

TURNER. C. M.

MAXIM.

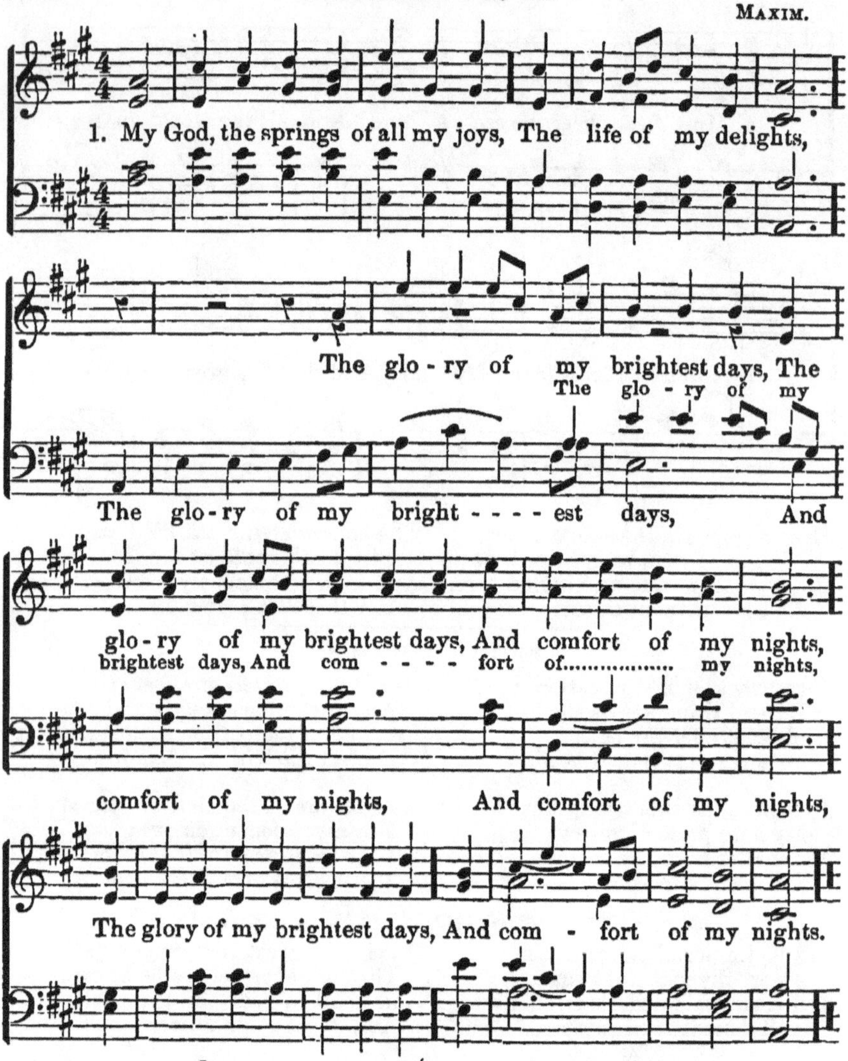
1. My God, the springs of all my joys, The life of my delights,
The glo - ry of my brightest days, The
The glo - ry of my
The glo-ry of my bright - - - - est days, And
glo-ry of my brightest days, And comfort of my nights,
brightest days, And com - - - - fort of.................. my nights,
comfort of my nights, And comfort of my nights,
The glory of my brightest days, And com - fort of my nights.

2.
In darkest shades, if thou appear,
My dawning is begun; [star,
Thou art my soul's bright morning
And thou my rising sun.

3.
The op'ning heavens around me shine
With beams of sacred bliss,
If Jesus shows his mercy mine,
And whispers I am his.

4.
My soul would leave this heavy clay
At that transporting word,
Run up with joy the shining way,
To see and praise my Lord.

5.
Fearless of hell and ghastly death,
I'd break through ev'ry foe;
The wings of love, and arms of faith,
Would bear me conqu'ror through.

EXHORTATION. C. M. 191

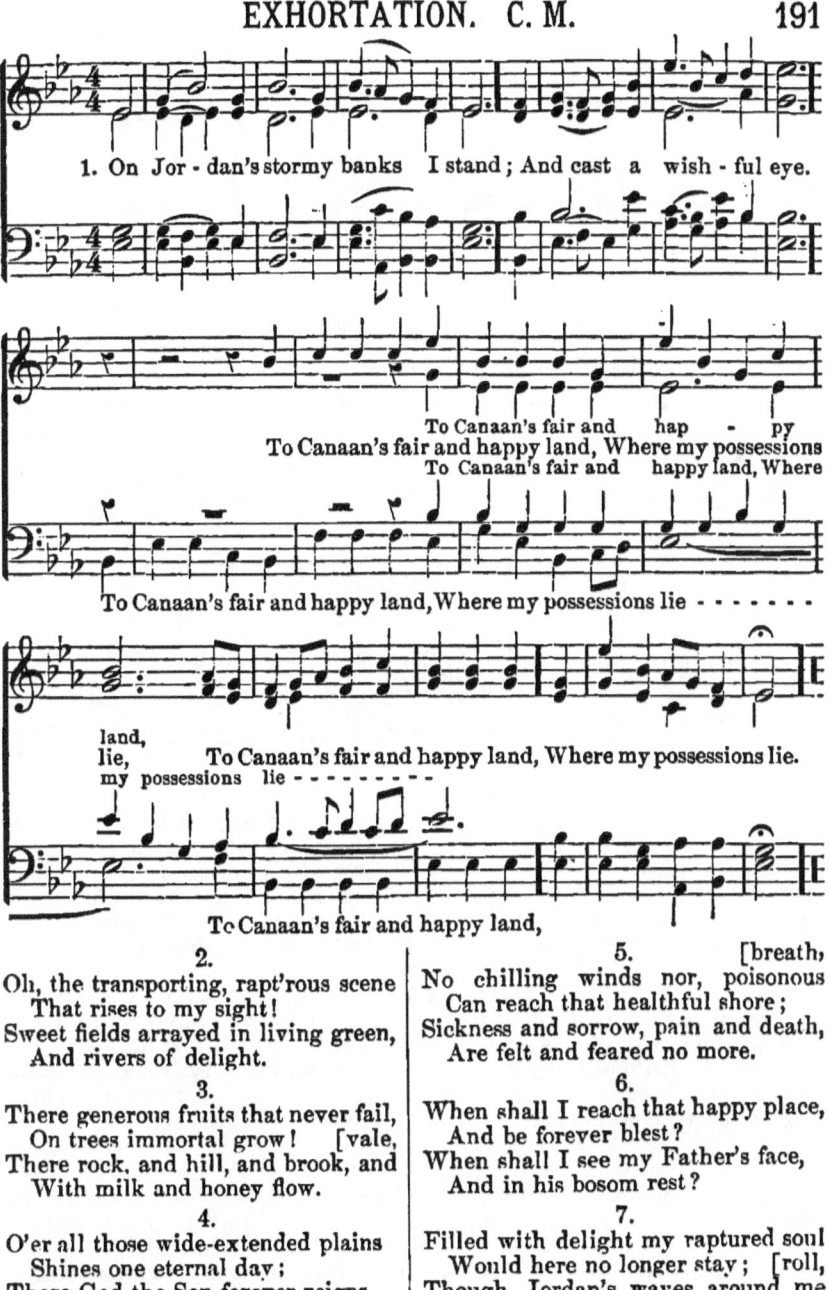

1. On Jordan's stormy banks I stand; And cast a wishful eye. To Canaan's fair and happy land, Where my possessions lie.

2.
Oh, the transporting, rapt'rous scene
  That rises to my sight!
Sweet fields arrayed in living green,
  And rivers of delight.

3.
There generous fruits that never fail,
  On trees immortal grow! [vale,
There rock, and hill, and brook, and
  With milk and honey flow.

4.
O'er all those wide-extended plains
  Shines one eternal day;
There God the Son forever reigns,
  And scatters night away.

5. [breath,
No chilling winds nor, poisonous
  Can reach that healthful shore;
Sickness and sorrow, pain and death,
  Are felt and feared no more.

6.
When shall I reach that happy place,
  And be forever blest?
When shall I see my Father's face,
  And in his bosom rest?

7.
Filled with delight my raptured soul
  Would here no longer stay; [roll,
Though Jordan's waves around me
  Fearless I'd launch away.

192 — MERIBAH. C. P. M.
L. Mason.

1. Lo! on a narrow neck of land, 'Twixt two unbounded seas, I stand, Secure, insensible: A point of time, a moment's space, Removes me to that heav'nly place, Or shuts me up in hell.

2.
O God, mine inmost soul convert,
And deeply on my thoughtful heart
  Eternal things impress:
Give me to feel their solemn weight,
And tremble on the brink of fate,
  And wake to righteousness.

3.
Before me place, in dread array,
The pomp of that tremendous day,
  When thou with clouds shalt come
To judge the nations at thy bar;
And tell me, Lord, shall I be there,
  To meet a joyful doom?

4.
Be this my one great business here—
With serious industry and fear
  Eternal bliss t' ensure;
Thine utmost counsel to fulfil,
And suffer all thy righteous will,
  And to the end endure.

5.
Then, Saviour, then my soul receive,
Transported from this vale, to live
  And reign with thee above,
Where faith is sweetly lost in sight,
And hope in full, supreme delight,
  And everlasting love.

SECOND HYMN.

1.
Come on, my partners in distress,
My comrades thro' the wilderness,
  Who still your bodies feel:
Awhile forget your griefs and fears,
And look beyond this vale of tears,
  To that celestial hill.

2.
Beyond the bounds of time and space,
Look forward to that heav'nly place,
  The saints secure abode;
On faith's strong eagle-pinions rise,
And force your passage to the skies,
  And scale the mount of God.

ARIEL. C. P. M.

Dr. L. Mason.

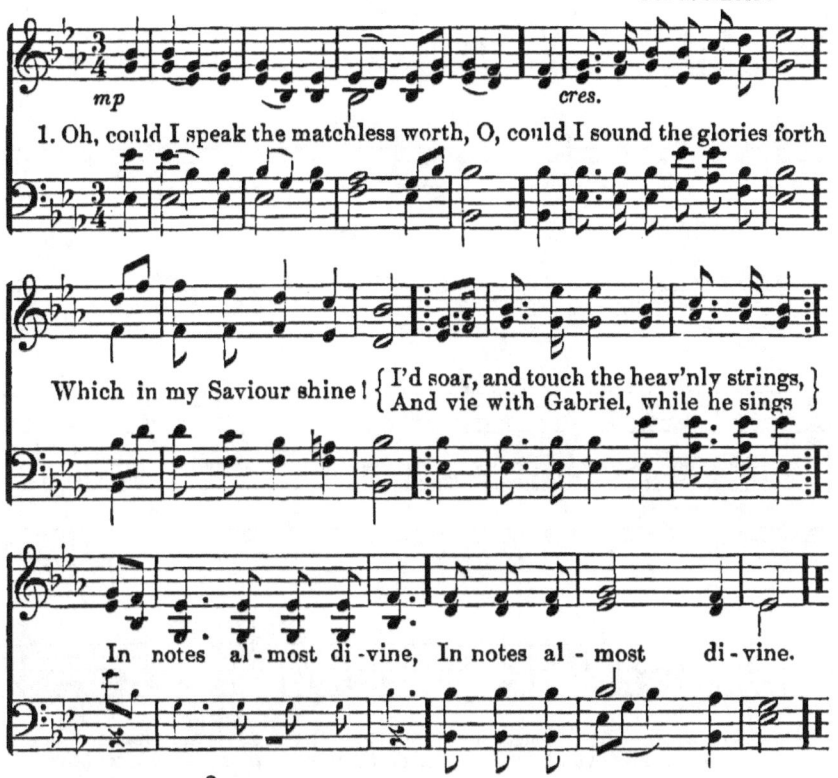

2.
I'd sing the precious blood he spilt,
My ransom from the dreadful guilt
  Of sin and wrath divine;
I'd sing his glorious righteousness,
In which all-perfect, heav'nly dress,
  My soul shall ever shine.
3.
I'd sing the characters he bears,
And all the forms of love he wears,
  Exalted on his throne;

In loftiest songs of sweetest praise,
I would to everlasting days
  Make all his glories known.
4.
Well, the delightful day will come
When my dear Lord will bring me home,
  And I shall see his face;
Then with my Saviour, Brother, Friend,
A blest eternity I'll spend,
  Triumphant in his grace.

Concluded from opposite page.

3.
Who suffer with our master here,
We shall before his face appear,
  And by his side sit down;
To patient faith the prize is sure;
And all that to the end endure
  The cross, shall wear the crown.

4.
Thrice blessed, bliss-inspiring hope!
It lifts the fainting spirits up;
  It brings to life the dead:
Our conflict here shall soon be past,
And you and I ascend at last,
  Triumphant with our Head.

3.
Yet doubts still intervene,
  And all my comfort flies;
Like Noah's dove, I flit between
  Rough seas and stormy skies;
Anon the clouds depart,
  The winds and waters cease, [heart
While sweetly o'er my gladden'd
  Expands the bow of peace.
Bow of peace, bow of peace, etc.

4.
So, when my latest breath
  Shall rend the vail in twain,
By death, I shall escape from death,
  And life-eternal gain;
Knowing "as I am known,"
  How shall I love that word,
And oft repeat before the throne,
  "Forever with the Lord."
With the Lord, with the Lord, etc.

MORNINGTON. S. M. 195

1. Welcome, sweet day of rest, That saw the Lord arise;
Welcome to this reviving breast, And these rejoicing eyes!

2. The King himself comes near, And feasts his saints to-day;
Here we may sit, and see him here, And love, and praise and pray.

3.
One day in such a place,
 Where thou, my God, art seen,
Is sweeter than ten thousand days,
 Of pleasurable sin.

4.
My willing soul would stay
 In such a frame as this,
And sit and sing herself away
 To everlasting bliss.

SECOND HYMN.

1.
WE know, by faith we know,
 If this vile house of clay,
This tabernacle, sink below,
 In ruinous decay—

2.
We have a house above,
 Not made with mortal hands;
And firm as our Redeemer's love
 That heavenly fabric stands.

3.
It stands securely high,
 Indissolubly sure:
Our glorious mansion in the sky
 Shall evermore endure.

4.
Full of immortal hope,
 We urge the restless strife,
And hasten to be swallow'd up
 Of everlasting life.

5.
Lord, let us put on thee
 In perfect holiness,
And rise prepared thy face to see,
 Thy bright, unclouded face.

6.
Thy grace with glory crown,
 Who hast the earnest given;
And then triumphantly come down,
 And take us up to heaven.

THIRD HYMN.

1.
Come, sound his praise abroad,
 And hymns of glory sing;
Jehovah is the sovereign God,
 The universal King.

2.
He formed the deeps unknown;
 He gave the seas their bound;
The wat'ry worlds are all his own,
 And all the solid ground.

3.
Come, worship at his throne;
 Come, bow before the Lord;
We are his works and not our own;
 He formed us by his word.

4.
To-day attend his voice,
 Nor dare provoke his rod;
Come, like the people of his choice,
 And own your gracious God.

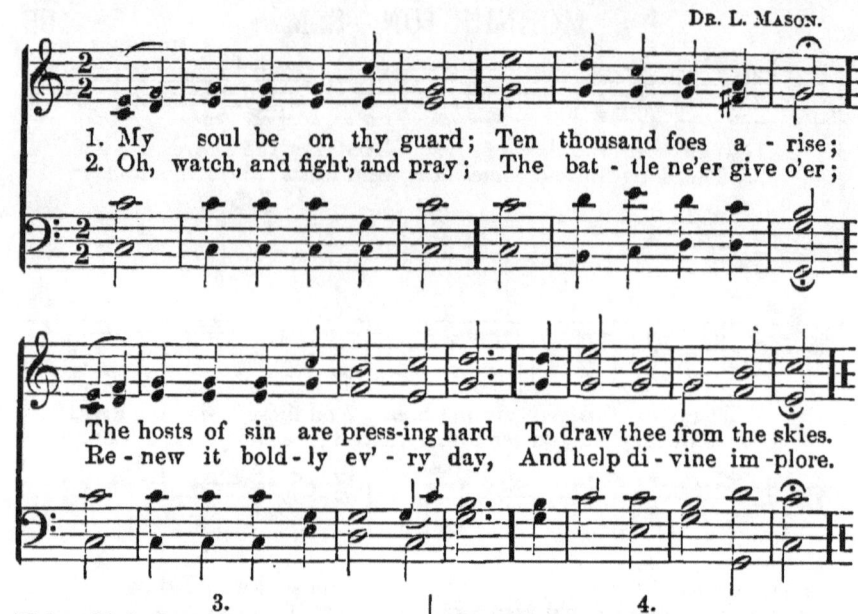

DR. L. MASON.

1. My soul be on thy guard; Ten thousand foes a-rise;
   The hosts of sin are press-ing hard To draw thee from the skies.
2. Oh, watch, and fight, and pray; The bat-tle ne'er give o'er;
   Re-new it bold-ly ev'-ry day, And help di-vine im-plore.

3.
Ne'er think the vict'ry won,
  Nor lay thine armor down;
The work of faith will not be done,
  Till thou obtain a crown.

4.
Then persevere till death
  Shall bring thee to thy God;
He'll take thee, at thy parting breath,
  To his divine abode.

SECOND HYMN.

1.
EQUIP me for the war,
  And teach my hands to fight;
My simple, upright heart prepare,
  And guide my words aright.

2.
Control my every thought;
  My whole of sin remove;
Let all my works in thee be wrought;
  Let all be wrought in love.

3.
O arm me with the mind,
  Meek Lamb, that was in thee;
And let my knowing zeal be joined
  With perfect charity.

4.
With calm and temper'd zeal
  Let me enforce thy call;
And vindicate thy gracious will,
  Which offers life to all.

THIRD HYMN.

1.
Sow in the morn thy seed;
  At eve hold not thy hand;
To doubt and fear give thou no heed,
  Broad-cast it o'er the land.

2.
Thou know'st not which shall thrive,
  The late or early sown;
Grace keeps the precious germ alive,
  When and wherever strown:

3.
And duly shall appear,
  In verdure, beauty, strength,
The tender blade, the stalk, the ear,
  And the full corn at length.

4.
Thou canst not toil in vain:
  Cold, heat, and moist, and dry,
Shall foster and mature the grain
  For garners in the sky.

ST. THOMAS. S. M.
A. WILLIAMS.

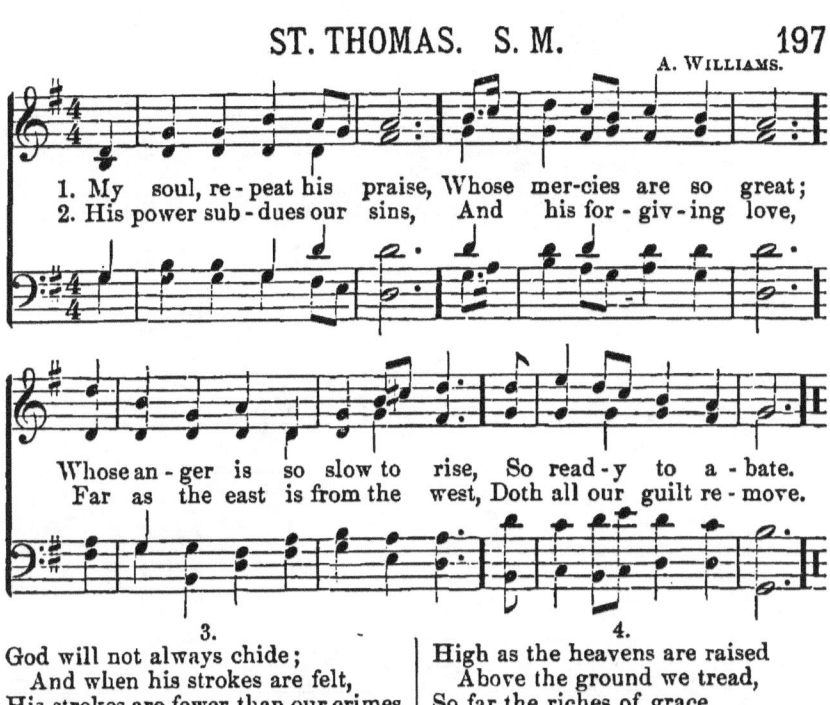

1. My soul, repeat his praise, Whose mercies are so great;
Whose anger is so slow to rise, So ready to abate.

2. His power subdues our sins, And his forgiving love,
Far as the east is from the west, Doth all our guilt remove.

3.
God will not always chide;
  And when his strokes are felt,
His strokes are fewer than our crimes,
  And lighter than our guilt.

4.
High as the heavens are raised
  Above the ground we tread,
So far the riches of grace
  Our highest thoughts exceed.

SECOND HYMN.

1.
BEHOLD the throne of grace;
  The promise calls us near;
There Jesus shows a smiling face,
  And waits to answer prayer.

2.
Thine image, Lord, bestow,—
  Thy presence and thy love,—
That we may serve thee here below,
  And reign with thee above.

3.
Teach us to live by faith,—
  Conform our wills to thine;
Let us victorious be in death,
  And then in glory shine.

4.
If thou these blessings give,
  And thou our portion be,
All worldly joys we'll gladly leave,
  To find our heaven in thee.

THIRD HYMN.

1.
AWAKE, and sing the song
  Of Moses and the Lamb;
Wake, every heart and every tongue,
  To praise the Saviour's name.

2.
Sing of his dying love;
  Sing of his rising power;
Sing how he intercedes above
  For those whose sins he bore.

3.
Ye pilgrims, on the road
  To Zion's city, sing;
Rejoice ye in the Lamb of God,—
  In Christ th' eternal King.

4.
Soon shall we hear him say,—
  Ye blessed children, come;
Soon will he call us hence away,
  To our eternal home.

5.
There shall each raptured tongue
  His endless praise proclaim;
And sweeter voices tune the song
  Of Moses and the Lamb.

198. THE WANDERER. S. M.

1. I was a wand'ring sheep,
    I did not love the fold;
  I did not love my Shepherd's voice,
    I would not be controlled:
  I was a way-ward child,
    I did not love my home,
  I did not love my Fa-ther's voice,
    I lov'd a-far to roam.

2.
The Shepherd sought his sheep,
  The Father sought his child;
They followed me o'er vale and hill,
  O'er desert waste and wild:
They found me nigh to death,
  Famish'd, and faint, and lone;
They bound me with the bands of love,
  They saved the wand'ring one.

3.
They spoke in tender love,
  They raised my drooping head,
They gently closed my bleeding wounds,
  My fainting soul they fed;
They washed my filth away,
  They made me clean and fair,
They brought me to my home in peace,
  The long-sought wanderer.

4.
Jesus my Shepherd is;
  'Twas he that loved my soul,
'Twas he that washed me in his blood,
  'Twas he that made me whole,
'Twas he that sought the lost,
  That found the wand'ring sheep:
'Twas he that brought me to the fold,
  'Tis he that still doth keep.

SECOND HYMN.

1. And are we yet alive,
    And see each other's face?
  Glory and praise to Jesus give,
    For his redeeming grace.

  Preserved by pow'r divine
    To full salvation here,
  Again in Jesus' praise we join,
    And in his sight appear.

WILLIAMSVILLE. S. M.
ASA HULL.

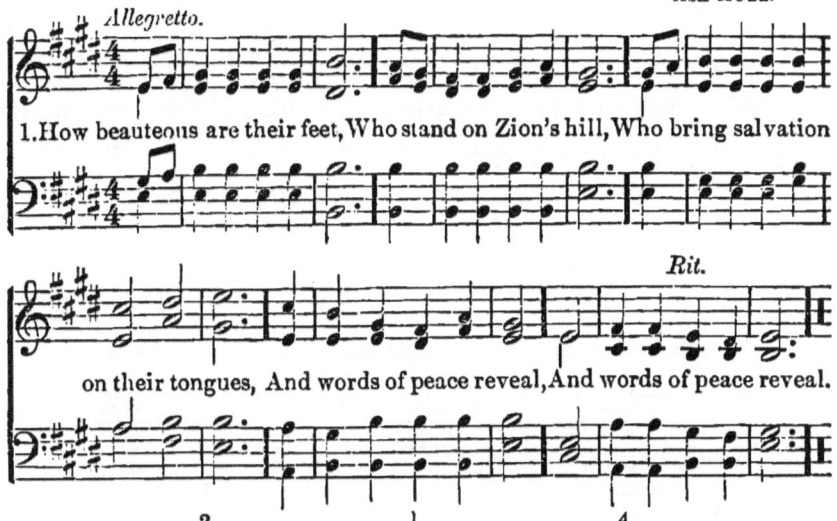

1. How beauteous are their feet, Who stand on Zion's hill, Who bring salvation on their tongues, And words of peace reveal, And words of peace reveal.

2.
How charming is their voice!
 How sweet the tidings are!
"Zion, behold thy Saviour King,
 He reigns and triumphs here."

3.
So happy are our ears,
 That hear the joyful sound,
Which kings and prophets waited for,
 And sought, but never found.

4.
How blessed are our eyes,
 That see the heavenly light;
Prophets and kings desired it long,
 But died without the sight.

5.
The watchmen join their voice,
 And tuneful notes employ;
Jerusalem breaks forth in songs,
 And deserts learn the joy.

SECOND HYMN.

1.
JESUS, the word bestow,—
 The true immortal seed;
Thy gospel then shall greatly grow,
 And all our land o'erspread;

2.
Through earth extended wide
 Shall mightily prevail,—
Destroy the works of self and pride,
 And shake the gates of hell.

3.
Its energy exert
 In the believing soul;
Diffuse thy grace through every part,
 And sanctify the whole.

4.
Its utmost virtue show
 In pure consummate love,
And fill with all thy life below,
 And give us thrones above.

Concluded from opposite page.

2.
What troubles have we seen,—
 What conflicts have we past;
Fightings without and fears within,
 Since we assembled last!
But out of all, the Lord
 Hath brought us by his love;
And still he doth his help afford,
 And hides our life above.

3.
Then let us make our boast
 Of his redeeming power,
Which saves us to the uttermost,
 Till we can sin no more:
Let us take up the cross,
 Till we the crown obtain;
And gladly reckon all things loss,
 So we may Jesus gain.

200 OLMUTZ. S. M.

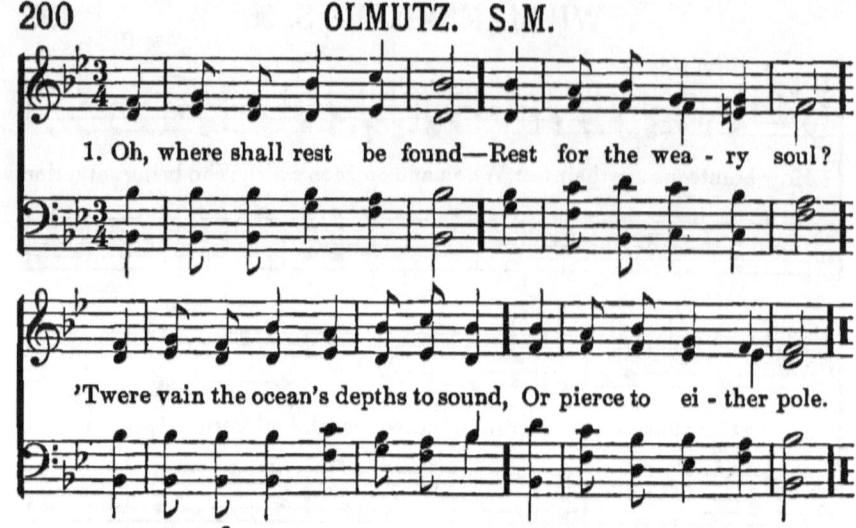

1. Oh, where shall rest be found—Rest for the wea-ry soul? 'Twere vain the ocean's depths to sound, Or pierce to ei-ther pole.

2.
The world can never give
  The bliss for which we sigh;
'Tis not the whole of life to live,
  Nor all of death to die.

3.
Beyond this vale of tears
  There is a life above,
Unmeasured by the flight of years;
  And all that life is love.

4.
There is a death whose pang
  Outlasts the fleeting breath;
Oh, what eternal horrors hang
  Around the second death!

5.
Thou God of truth and grace,
  Teach us that death to shun,
Lest we be banished from thy face,
  For evermore undone.

SECOND HYMN.

1.
Come, weary sinners, come,
  Groaning beneath your load,
The Saviour calls his wand'rers home;
  Haste to your pard'ning God.

2.
Come, all by guilt oppressed,
  Answer the Saviour's call—
O come, and I will give you rest,
  And I will save you all.

3.
Redeemer, full of love,
  We would thy word obey,
And all thy faithful mercies prove:
  O take our guilt away.

4.
We would on thee rely;
  On thee would cast our care;
Now to thine arms of mercy fly,
  And find salvation there.

THIRD HYMN.

1.
Lord of the harvest, hear
  Thy needy servants' cry;
Answer our faith's effectual prayer,
  And all our wants supply.

2.
On thee we humbly wait,—
  Our wants are in thy view;
The harvest, truly, Lord, is great,
  The laborers are few.

3.
Convert and send forth more
  Into thy Church abroad,
And let them speak thy word of pow'r,
  As workers with their God.

4.
O let them spread thy name,—
  Their mission fully prove;
The universal grace proclaim,—
  Thine all-redeeming love.

SEIR. S. M.

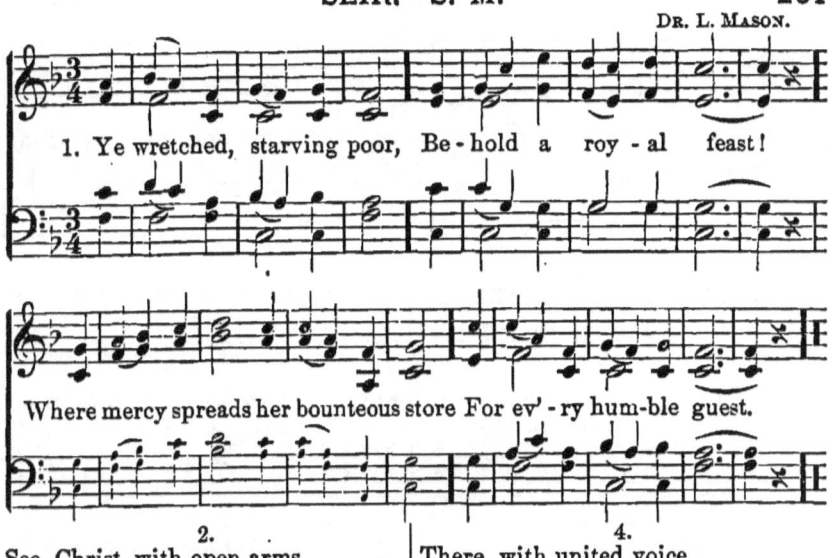

1. Ye wretched, starving poor, Behold a royal feast! Where mercy spreads her bounteous store For ev'ry humble guest.

2.
See, Christ, with open arms,
  Invites, and bids you come;
O stay not back, though fear alarms;
  For yet there still is room.
3.
O come, and with us taste
  The blessings of his love:
While hope expects the sweet repast
  Of nobler joys above.

4.
There, with united voice,
  Before th' eternal throne,
Ten thousand thousand souls rejoice,
  In ecstasies unknown.
5.
Ten thousand thousand more
  Are welcome still to come:
Ye longing souls, the grace adore;
  Approach,—there yet is room.

SECOND HYMN.

1.
O MY offended God!
  If now at last I see
That I have trampled on thy blood,
  And done despite to thee;
2.
If I begin to wake
  Out of my deadly sleep;
Into thine arms of mercy take,
  And there forever keep.

3.
No other right have I,
  Than what the world may claim;
And all may to their God draw nigh,
  Through faith in Jesus' name;
4.
Thy death hath wrought the power
  For every sinful soul:
That all may know the gracious hour,
  And be by faith made whole.

THIRD HYMN.

1.
WITH joy we lift our eyes
  To those bright realms above,
That glorious temple in the skies,
  Where dwells eternal Love.
2.
Before thy throne we bow,
  O thou almighty King;
Here we present the solemn vow,
  And hymns of praise we sing.

3.
While in thy house we kneel,
  With trust and holy fear,
Thy mercy and thy truth reveal,
  And lend a gracious ear.
4.
Lord, teach our hearts to pray,
  And tune our lips to sing;
Nor from thy presence cast away
  The sacrifice we bring.

202 TIME. S. M.
Moderato. ASA HULL.

1. An-oth-er day is past, The hours for-ev-er fled,
And time is bear-ing us a-way, To min-gle with the dead.

2.
Our minds in perfect peace
Our Father's care shall keep;
We yield to gentle slumber now,
For thou canst never sleep.

3.
How blessed, Lord, are they
On thee securely stayed!
Nor shall they be in life alarmed,
Nor be in death dismayed.

SECOND HYMN.

1.
FAR from these scenes of night,
Unbounded glories rise,
And realms of joy and pure delight,
Unknown to mortal eyes.

2.
Fair land!—could mortal eyes
But half its charms explore,
How would our spirits long to rise,
And dwell on earth no more!

3.
No cloud those regions know,—
Realms ever bright and fair;
For sin, the source of mortal woe,
Can never enter there.

4.
O may the prospect fire
Our hearts with ardent love,
Till wings of faith, and strong desire,
Bear every thought above.

THIRD HYMN.

1.
THE day is past and gone,
The evening shades appear;
O, may we all remember well
The night of death draws near.

2.
We lay our garments by,
Upon our beds to rest;
So death will soon disrobe us all
Of what we here possess.

3.
Lord, keep us safe this night,
Secure from all our fears;
May angels guard us while we sleep,
Till morning light appears.

4.
And if we early rise,
And view th' unwearied sun,
May we set out to win the prize,
And after glory run.

5.
And when our days are past,
And we from time remove,
O, may we in thy bosom rest—
The bosom of thy love!

DOXOLOGY.
To God, the Father, Son,
And Spirit, One in Three,
Be glory, as it was, is now,
And shall forever be.

OLNEY. S. M.

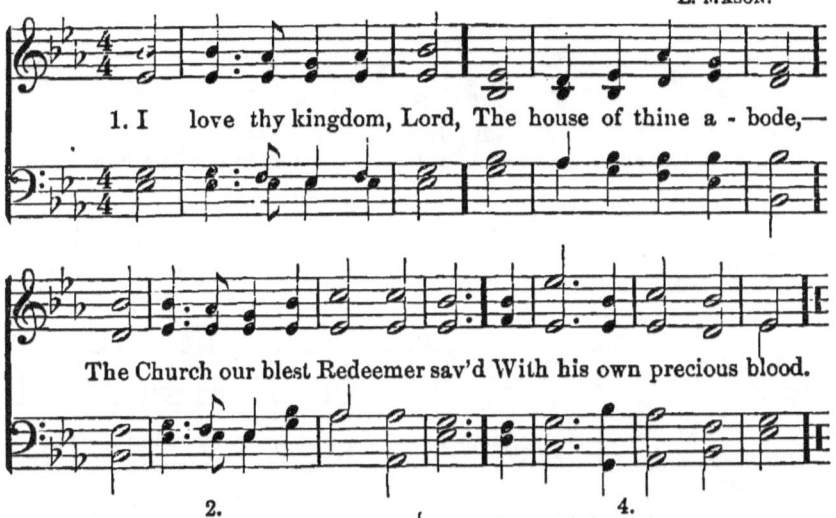

1. I love thy kingdom, Lord, The house of thine abode,—
The Church our blest Redeemer sav'd With his own precious blood.

2.
I love thy Church, O God!
 Her walls before thee stand,
Dear as the apple of thine eye,
 And graven on thy hand.

3.
For her my tears shall fall;
 For her my prayers ascend;
To her my cares and toils be given,
 Till toils and cares shall end.

4.
Beyond my highest joy
 I prize her heavenly ways;
Her sweet communion, solemn vows,
 Her hymns of love and praise.

5.
Sure as thy truth shall last,
 To Zion shall be given
The brightest glories earth can yield,
 And brighter bliss of heaven.

SECOND HYMN.

1.
AND can I yet delay
 My little all to give?
To tear my soul from earth away,
 For Jesus to receive.

2.
Nay, but I yield, I yield;
 I can hold out no more;
I sink, by dying love compelled,
 And own thee conqueror.

3.
Though late, I all forsake,
 My friends, my all, resign;
Gracious Redeemer, take, oh, take,
 And seal me ever thine.

4.
Come, and possess me whole,
 Nor hence again remove;
Settle and fix my wav'ring soul,
 With all thy weight of love.

THIRD HYMN.

1.
O THOU that wouldst not have
 One wretched sinner die;
Who diedst thyself, my soul to save
 From endless misery;—

2.
Show me the way to shun
 Thy dreadful wrath severe,
That when thou comest on thy throne,
 I may with joy appear.

3.
Thou art thyself the way;
 Thyself in me reveal;
So shall I spend my life's short day
 Obedient to thy will.

4.
So shall I love my God,
 Because he first loved me;
And praise thee in thy bright abode,
 To all eternity.

204 SHIRLAND. S. M.

STANLEY.

1. My son, know thou the Lord; Thy Father's God obey;
Seek his protecting care by night, His guardian hand by day.

2. Call while he may be found; Oh, seek him while he's near;
Serve him with all thy heart and mind, And worship him with fear.

3.
If thou wilt seek his face,
 His ear will hear thy cry;
Then shalt thou find his mercy sure,
 His grace forever nigh.

4.
But if thou leave thy God,
 Nor choose the path to heaven,
Then shalt thou perish in thy sins,
 And never be forgiven.

SECOND HYMN.

1.
YE praying souls, rejoice,
 And bless your Father's name;
With joy to him lift up your voice,
 And all his love proclaim.

2.
Your mournful cry he hears;
 He marks your feeblest groan,
Supplies your wants, dispels your fears,
 And makes his mercy known.

3.
To all his praying saints
 He ever will attend,
And to their sorrows and complaints,
 His ear in mercy bend.

4.
Then let us still go on
 In his appointed ways,
Rejoicing in his name alone,
 In prayer and humble praise.

THIRD HYMN.

1.
BLEST are the sons of peace
 Whose hearts and hopes are one;
Whose kind designs to serve and please
 Through all their actions run.

2.
Blest is the pious house
 Where zeal and friendship meet;
Their songs of praise, their mingled [vows,
 Make their communion sweet.

3.
From those celestial springs
 Such streams of pleasure flow,
As no increase of riches brings,
 Nor honors can bestow.

4.
Thus on the heavenly hills
 The saints are blest above;
There joy, like morning dew distils,
 And all the air is love.

GERAR. S. M. 205

DR. L. MASON.

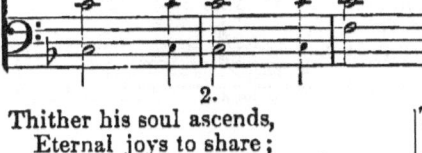

1. While thro' this world we roam, From infancy to age, Heav'n is the Chris-tian pil-grim's home, His rest at ev' - ry stage.

2.
Thither his soul ascends,
  Eternal joys to share;
There his adoring spirit bends,
  While here he kneels in prayer.
3.
His freed affections rise,
  To fix on things above,
Where all his hope of glory lies,—
  Where all is perfect love.

4.
There we our treasure place,
  There let our hearts be found;
That still, where sin abounded, grace
  May more and more abound.
5.
Henceforth our converse be
  With Christ before the throne;
Ere long we eye to eye shall see,
  And know as we are known.

SECOND HYMN.

1.
SOLDIERS of Christ, arise,
  And put your armor on, [supplies
Strong in the strength which God
  Through his eternal Son;
2.
Strong in the Lord of Hosts,
  And in his mighty power,
Who in the strength of Jesus trusts,
  Is more than conqueror.

3.
Stand, then, in his great might,
  With all his strength endued;
But take, to arm you for the fight,
  The panoply of God:
4.
That having all things done,
  And all your conflicts past,
Ye may o'ercome, thro' Christ alone,
  And stand entire at last.

THIRD HYMN.

1.
GRACE! 'tis a charming sound,
  Harmonious to the ear;
Heaven with the echo shall resound,
  And all the earth shall hear.
2.
Grace first contrived a way
  To save rebellious man;
And all the steps that grace display,
  Which drew the wondrous plan.

3.
Grace taught my roving feet
  To tread the heavenly road;
And new supplies each hour I meet,
  While pressing on to God.
4.
Grace all the work shall crown,
  Through everlasting days;
It lays in heaven the topmost stone,
  And well deserves our praise.

BOYLSTON. S. M.

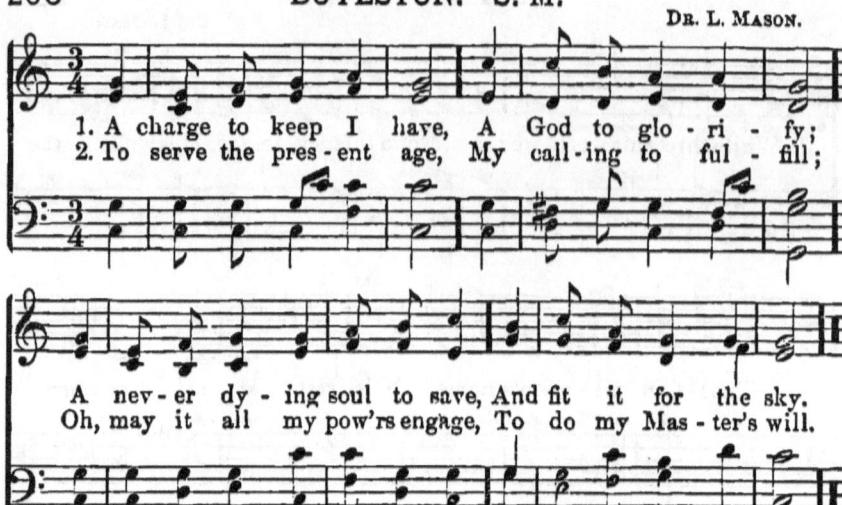

Dr. L. Mason.

1. A charge to keep I have, A God to glo-ri-fy;
A nev-er dy-ing soul to save, And fit it for the sky.

2. To serve the pres-ent age, My call-ing to ful-fill;
Oh, may it all my pow'rs engage, To do my Mas-ter's will.

3.
Arm me with jealous care,
  As in thy sight to live;
And oh, thy servant, Lord, prepare,
  A strict account to give.

4.
Help me to watch and pray,
  And on thyself rely;
Assured, if I thy trust betray,
  I shall forever die.

SECOND HYMN.

1.
How helpless nature lies,
  Unconscious of her load!
The heart unchanged can never rise
  To happiness and God.

2.
Can aught but power divine
  The stubborn will subdue?
'Tis thine, eternal Spirit, thine
  To form the heart anew:—

3.
The passions to recall,
  And upward bid them rise;
To make the scales of error fall
  From reason's darken'd eyes.

4.
O change these hearts of ours,
  And give them life divine;
Then shall our passions and our pow'rs,
  Almighty Lord, be thine.

THIRD HYMN.

1.
And am I born to die?
  To lay this body down?
And must my trembling spirit fly
  Into a world unknown?—

2.
A land of deepest shade,
  Unpierced by human thought;
The dreary regions of the dead,
  Where all things are forgot!

3.
Soon as from earth I go,
  What will become of me?
Eternal happiness or woe
  Must then my portion be:

4.
Waked by the trumpet's sound,
  I from my grave shall rise,
And see the Judge, with glory crown'd,
  And see the flaming skies!

5.
How shall I leave my tomb—
  With triumph or regret?
A fearful or a joyful doom,
  A curse or blessing meet.

6.
Will angel bands convey
  Their brother to the bar?
Or devils drag my soul away,
  To meet its sentence there?

DENNIS. S. M. From NAGELI. 207

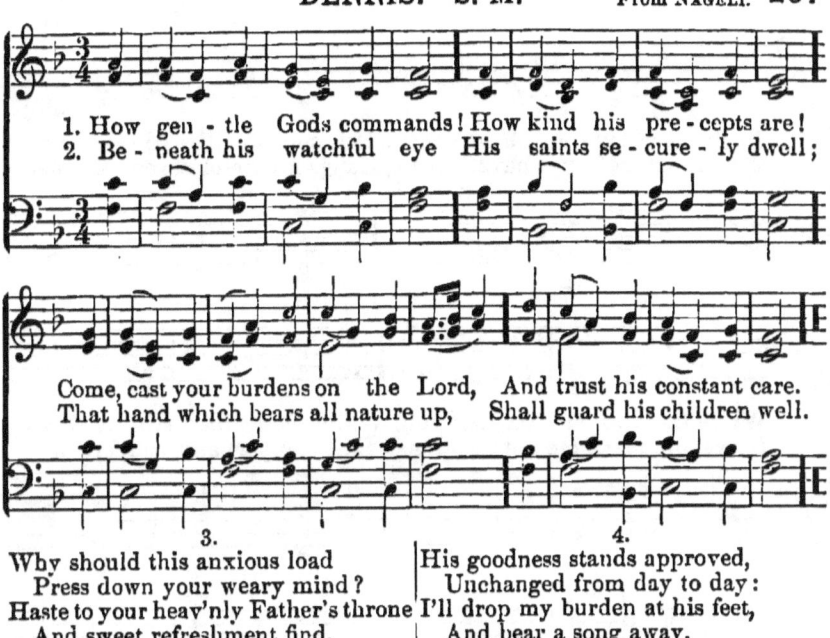

1. How gentle Gods commands! How kind his precepts are!
Come, cast your burdens on the Lord, And trust his constant care.

2. Beneath his watchful eye His saints securely dwell;
That hand which bears all nature up, Shall guard his children well.

3.
Why should this anxious load
 Press down your weary mind?
Haste to your heav'nly Father's throne
 And sweet refreshment find.

4.
His goodness stands approved,
 Unchanged from day to day:
I'll drop my burden at his feet,
 And bear a song away.

SECOND HYMN.

1.
THE pity of the Lord
 To those that fear his name,
Is such as tender parents feel;
 He knows our feeble frame.

2.
He knows we are but dust,
 Shatter'd with ev'ry breath;
His anger, like a rising wind,
 Can send us swift to death.

3.
Our days are as the grass,
 Or like the morning flower; [field,
When blasting winds sweet o'er the
 It withers in an hour.

4.
But thy compassions, Lord,
 To endless years endure;
And children's children ever find
 Thy words of promise sure.

THIRD HYMN.

1.
BLEST be the tie that binds
 Our hearts in Christian love;
The fellowship of kindred minds
 Is like to that above.

2.
Before our Father's throne,
 We pour our ardent prayers;
Our fears, our hopes, our aims are one,
 Our comforts and our cares.

3.
We share our mutual woes;
 Our mutual burdens bear;
And often for each other flows
 The sympathizing tear.

4.
When we asunder part,
 It gives us inward pain;
But we shall still be join'd in heart,
 And hope to meet again.

5.
This glorious hope revives
 Our courage by the way;
While each in expectation lives,
 And longs to see the day.

6.
From sorrow, toil, and pain,
 And sin we shall be free;
And perfect love and friendship reign
 Through all eternity.

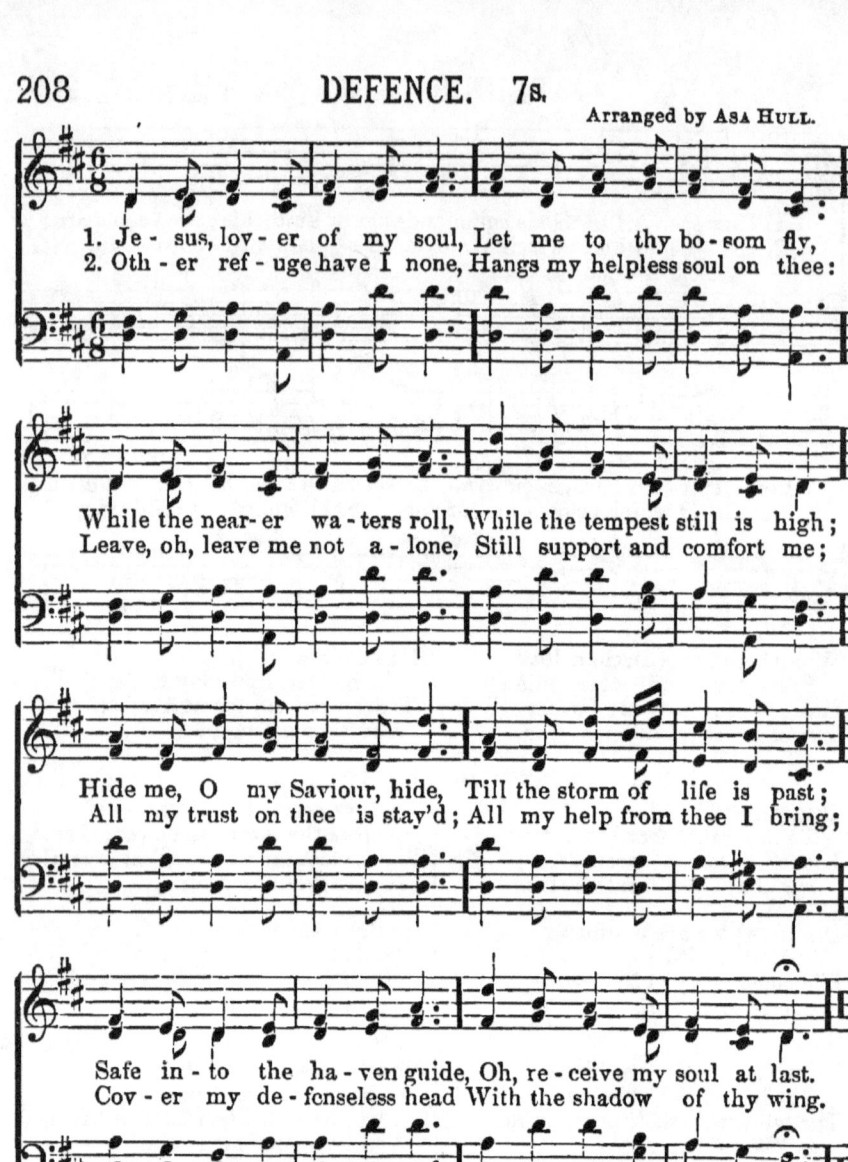

3. Thou, O Christ, art all I want
   More than all in thee I find;
   Raise the fallen, cheer the faint,
   Heal the sick, and lead the blind.
   Just and holy is thy name,—
   I am all unrighteousness;
   False and full of sin I am—
   Thou art full of truth and grace.

4. Plenteous grace with thee is found,
   Grace to cover all my sin;
   Let the healing streams abound;
   Make and keep me pure within.
   Thou of life the Fountain art—
   Freely let me take of thee;
   Spring thou up within my heart;
   Rise to all eternity.

MARTYN. 7s.

MARSH.

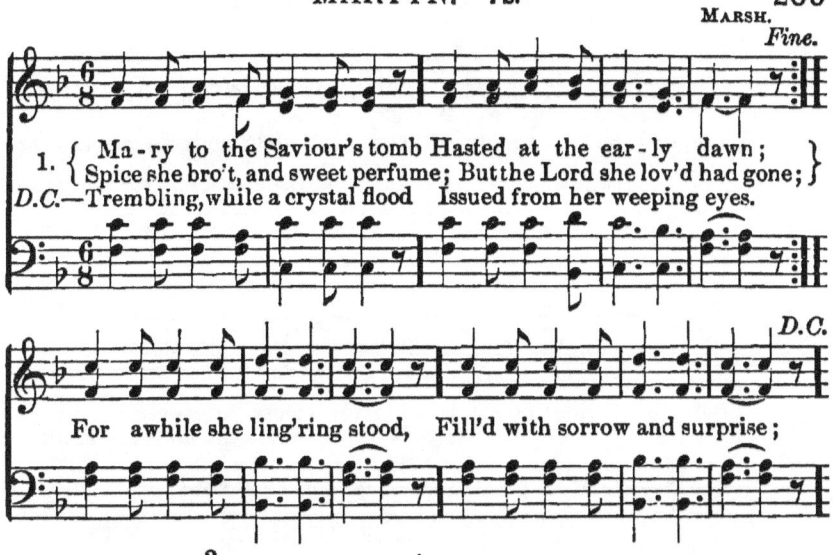

1. Mary to the Saviour's tomb Hasted at the early dawn;
Spice she bro't, and sweet perfume; But the Lord she lov'd had gone;
D.C.—Trembling, while a crystal flood Issued from her weeping eyes.
For awhile she ling'ring stood, Fill'd with sorrow and surprise;

2.
But her sorrows quickly fled
When she heard his welcome voice:
Christ had risen from the dead;
Now he bids her heart rejoice.

What a change his word can make,
Turning darkness into day!
Ye who weep for Jesus' sake,
He will wipe your tears away.

SECOND HYMN.

1.
LIGHT of life,—seraphic fire,—
Love divine,—thyself impart:
Every fainting soul inspire;
Shine in every drooping heart:
Every mournful sinner cheer;
Scatter all our guilty gloom;
Son of God, appear! appear!—
To thy human temples come.

2.
Come in this accepted hour;
Bring thy heavenly kingdom in;
Fill us with thy glorious power,
Rooting out the seeds of sin:
Nothing more can we require,—
We will covet nothing less;
Be thou all our heart's desire,—
All our joy, and all our peace.

SECOND HYMN for "Defence."

1.
WATCHMAN, tell us of the night,
What its signs of promise are.
Trav'ler, o'er yon mountain's height
See the glory-beaming star.
Watchman, does its beauteous ray
Aught of hope or joy foretell?
Trav'ler, yes, it brings the day—
Promised day of Israel.

2.
Watchman, tell us of the night;
Higher yet that star ascends.
Trav'ler, blessedness and light,
Peace and truth, its course portends.

Watchman, will its beams, alone,
Gild the spot that gave them birth?
Trav'ler, ages are its own;
See, it bursts o'er all the earth.

3.
Watchman, tell us of the night,
For the morning seems to dawn.
Trav'ler, darkness takes its flight;
Doubt and terror are withdrawn.
Watchman, let thy wand'ring cease;
Hie thee to thy quiet home.
Trav'ler, lo! the Prince of Peace,
Lo! the Son of God is come.

BENEVENTO. 7s.

S. WEBBE.

1. While, with ceaseless course, the sun Hasted through the former year,

Man-y souls their race have run, Nevermore to meet us here:
D.S.—We a lit-tle lon-ger wait, But how lit-tle, none can know.

Fix'd in an e-ter-nal state, They have done with all be-low;

2.
As the winged arrow flies,
  Speedily the mark to find;
As the lightning from the skies
  Darts and leaves no trace behind,—
Swiftly thus our fleeting days
  Bear us down life's rapid stream;
Upward, Lord, our spirits raise;
  All below is but a dream.

3.
Thanks for mercies past receive;
  Pardon of our sins renew;
Teach us henceforth how to live,
  With eternity in view:
Bless thy word to young and old;
  Fill us with a Saviour's love;
And when life's short tale is told,
  May we reign with thee above.

SECOND HYMN.

1.
For a season called to part,
  Let us now ourselves commend
To the gracious eye and heart
  Of our ever-present friend.
Jesus! hear our humble prayer;
  Tender Shepherd of thy sheep!
Let thy mercy and thy care
  All our souls in safety keep.

2.
In thy strength may we be strong;
  Sweeten every cross and pain;
Grant, that if we live, ere long
  We may meet in peace again.
Then, if thou thy help afford,
  Joyful songs to thee shall rise,
And our souls shall praise the Lord,
  Who regards our humble cries.

LEAVENWORTH. 7s.

Spanish Melody.

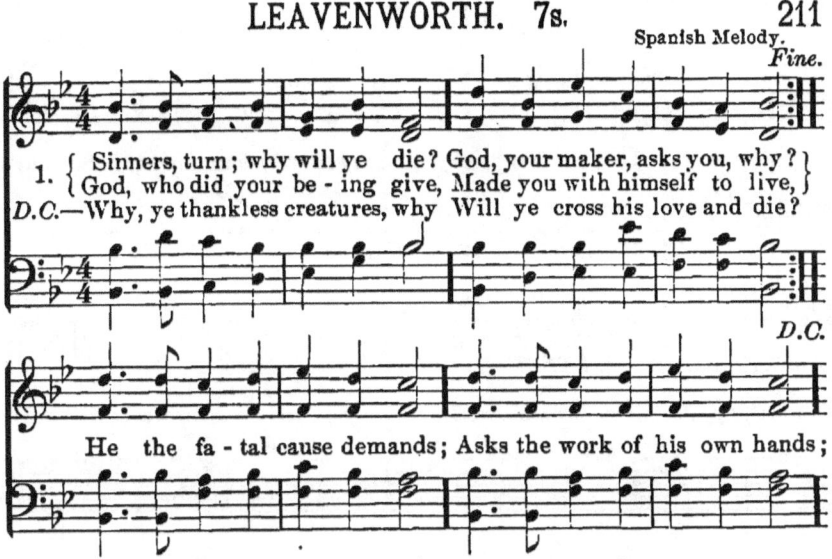

1. { Sinners, turn; why will ye die? God, your maker, asks you, why? }
   { God, who did your be-ing give, Made you with himself to live, }
D.C.—Why, ye thankless creatures, why Will ye cross his love and die?

He the fa-tal cause demands; Asks the work of his own hands;

2.
Sinners, turn; why will ye die?
God, your Saviour, asks you, why?
He, who did your souls retrieve,
Died himself, that ye might live.
Will ye let him die in vain?
Crucify your Lord again?
Why, ye ransom'd sinners, why
Will ye slight his grace and die?

3.
Sinners, turn; why will ye die?
God, the Spirit, asks you, why?
He, who all your lives hath strove,
Urged you to embrace his love.
Will ye not his grace receive?
Will ye still refuse to live?
Oh, ye dying sinners, why,
Why will ye forever die?

SECOND HYMN.

1.
Lift your eyes of faith, and see
  Saints and angels joined in one:
What a countless company
  Stand before yon dazzling throne!
Each before his Saviour stands,
  All in whitest robes arrayed;
Palms they carry in their hands,
  Crowns of glory on their head.

2.
Saints, begin the endless song;
  Cry aloud, in heavenly lays,—
Glory doth to God belong;
  God the glorious Saviour praise.
All salvation from him came,
  Him who reigns enthroned on high:
Glory to the bleeding Lamb,—
  Let the morning stars reply.

THIRD HYMN.

1.
Go, ye messengers of God;
  Like the beams of morning, fly;
Take the wonder-working rod;
  Wave the banner cross on high.
Go to many a tropic isle
  In the bosom of the deep,
Where the skies forever smile,
  And th' oppress'd forever weep.

2.
O'er the pagan's night of care
  Pour the living light of heaven;
Chase away his wild despair;
  Bid him hope to be forgiven.
Where the golden gates of day
  Open on the palmy east,
High the bleeding cross display;
  Spread the gospel's richest feast.

HENDON. 7s.
Dr. Malan.

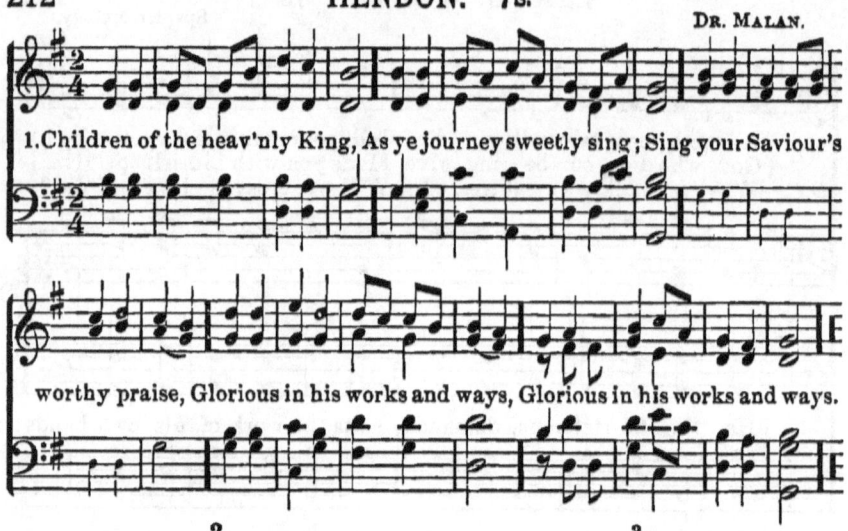

1. Children of the heav'nly King,
As ye journey sweetly sing;
Sing your Saviour's worthy praise,
Glorious in his works and ways,
Glorious in his works and ways.

2.
We are trav'ling home to God,
In the way our fathers trod;
They are happy now, and we
Soon their happiness shall see.

3.
Oh, ye banish'd seed, be glad;
Christ our Advocate is made:
Us to save, our flesh assumes,—
Brother to our souls becomes.

SECOND HYMN.

1.
Prince of peace, control my will;
Bid this struggling heart be still;
Bid my fears and doubtings cease,—
Hush my spirit into peace.

2.
Thou hast bought me with thy blood,
Opened wide the gate to God:
Peace I ask—but peace must be,
Lord, in being one with thee.

3.
May thy will, not mine, be done;
May thy will and mine be one:
Chase these doubtings from my heart;
Now thy perfect peace impart.

4.
Saviour! at thy feet I fall;
Thou my life, my God, my all!
Let thy happy servant be
One for evermore with thee!

THIRD HYMN.

1.
In thy presence we appear;
Lord! we love to worship here,
When, within the vail, we meet
Thee upon thy mercy-seat.

2.
While thy glorious name is sung,
Touch our lips, and loose our tongue;
Then our joyful souls shall bless
Thee, the Lord our righteousness.

3.
While to thee our prayers ascend,
Let thine ear in love attend;
Hear, for Jesus intercedes;
Hear us, for thy Spirit pleads.

4.
While thy word is heard with awe,
And we tremble at thy law,
Let thy gospel's wondrous love
Every doubt and fear remove.

5.
While thy ministers proclaim
Peace and pardon through thy name,
In their voices let us own
Jesus, speaking from the throne.

6.
From thy house when we return,
Let our hearts within us burn;
That at evening we may say,—
We have walk'd with God to-day.

PLEYEL'S HYMN. 7s.

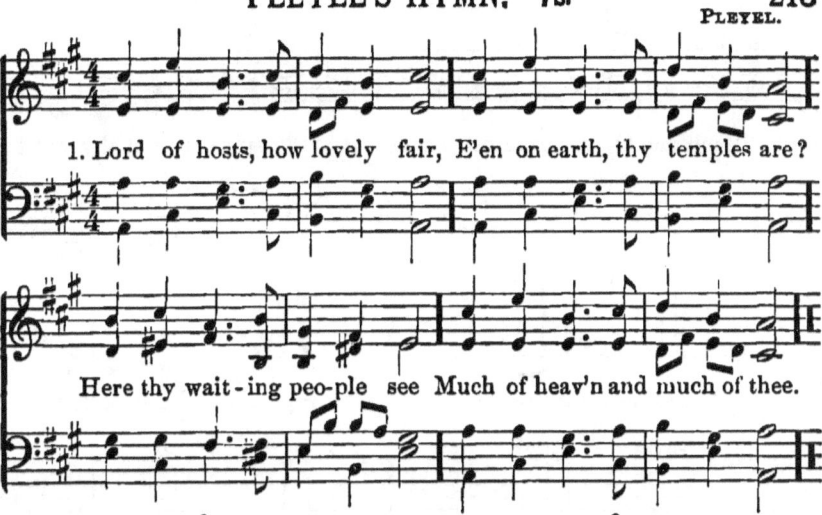

1. Lord of hosts, how lovely fair, E'en on earth, thy temples are? Here thy wait-ing peo-ple see Much of heav'n and much of thee.

2.
From thy gracious presence flows
Bliss that softens all our woes;
While thy Spirit's holy fire
Warms our hearts with pure desire.

3.
Here we supplicate thy throne;
Here thy pard'ning grace is known;
Here we learn thy righteous ways,
Taste thy love, and sing thy praise.

SECOND HYMN.

1.
LORD of hosts! to thee we raise
Here a house of prayer and praise:
Thou thy people's hearts prepare,
Here to meet for praise and prayer.

2.
Let the living here be fed
With thy word, the heavenly bread:
Here, in hope of glory blest,
May the dead be laid to rest.

3.
Here to thee a temple stand,
While the sea shall gird the land
Here reveal thy mercy sure,
While the sun and moon endure.

4.
Hallelujah! earth and sky
To the joyful sound reply:
Hallelujah! hence ascend
Prayer and praise till time shall end.

THIRD HYMN.

1.
LORD! we come before thee now;
At thy feet we humbly bow;
Oh! do not our suit disdain;—
Shall we seek thee, Lord! in vain?

2.
Lord! on thee our souls depend,
In compassion, now descend;
Fill our hearts with thy rich grace;
Tune our lips to sing thy praise.

3.
In thine own appointed way,
Now we seek thee, here we stay;
Lord! we know not how to go,
Till a blessing thou bestow.

4.
Send some message, from thy word,
That may joy and peace afford;
Let thy Spirit now impart
Full salvation to each heart.

5.
Comfort those who weep and mourn,
Let the time of joy return;
Those who are cast down, lift up;
Make them strong in faith and hope.

6.
Grant, that all may seek and find
Thee, a God supremely kind:
Heal the sick, the captive free—
Let us all rejoice in thee.

FISK. 7s. — Prof. C. S. Harrington.

1. Teach me, O my gracious Lord,
By thy spirit and thy word;
All thou dost require of me,
All my duty, Lord, to thee.

2.
Let my proud aspiring mind,
By thy Spirit be refined;
All thy lovely lowness see
All thy sweet simplicity.

3.
May the pattern thou hast shown,
Set by thee and thee alone;
Ever shine before my eyes,
Light me to the upper skies.

4.
Let no earthly grandeur dim,
Glories that shine forth in Him;
Whose bright glory was to be
Sample of humility.

5.
O, thou suff'ring Lamb of God,
Thou didst bear the Father's rod,
Meekly toil, and meekly bleed,
The proud sinner's cause to plead.

SECOND HYMN.

1.
Come, said Jesus' sacred voice,
Come, and make my paths your choice;
I will guide you to your home;
Weary wanderer, hither come!

2.
Thou who, homeless and forlorn,
Long hast borne the cold world's scorn,
Long hast roamed the barren waste,
Weary wanderer, hither haste.

3.
Ye who, tossed on beds of pain,
Seek for ease, but seek in vain;
Ye, by fiercer anguish torn,
In remorse for guilt who mourn:—

4.
Hither come! for here is found
Balm that flows for every wound:
Peace that ever shall endure.
Rest eternal, sacred, sure.

THIRD HYMN.

1.
People of the living God,
I have sought the world around,
Paths of sin and sorrow trod,
Peace and comfort nowhere found.

2.
Now to you my spirit turns—
Turns, a fugitive unblest;
Brethren! where your altar burns,
Oh, receive me into rest!

3.
Lonely I no longer roam,
Like the cloud, the wind, the wave:
Where you dwell shall be my home,
Where you die shall be my grave.

4.
Mine the God whom you adore,
Your Redeemer shall be mine;
Earth can fill my soul no more,
Every idol I resign.

PRAISE. 7s.

ASA HULL.

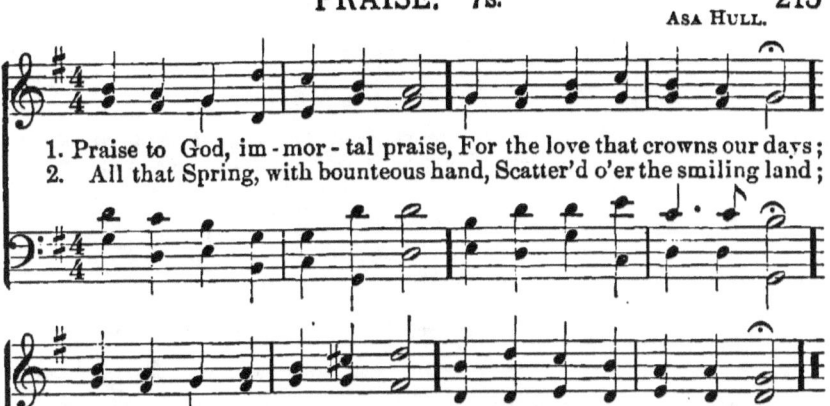

1. Praise to God, im-mor-tal praise, For the love that crowns our days;
Bounteous Source of ev'-ry joy, Let thy praise our tongues employ.
2. All that Spring, with bounteous hand, Scatter'd o'er the smiling land;
All that lib'-ral Autumn pours From his rich, o'erflow-ing stores.

3.
These to that dear Source we owe
Whence our sweetest comforts flow;
These, through all my happy days,
Claim my cheerful songs of praise.

4.
Lord, to thee my soul should raise
Grateful, never-ending praise;
And, when every blessing's flown,
Love thee for thyself alone.

SECOND HYMN.

1.
SLEEP not, soldier of the Cross!
  Foes are lurking all around;
Look not here to find repose:
  This is but thy battle ground.

2.
Up! and take thy shield and sword;
  Up! it is the call of Heaven:
Shrink not faithless from thy Lord;
  Nobly strive as he hath striven.

3.
Break through all the force of ill;
  Tread the might of passion down,—
Struggling onward, onward still,
  To the conqu'ring Saviour's crown!

4.
Through the midst of toil and pain,
Let this thought ne'er leave thy
Every triumph thou dost gain [breast:
Makes more sweet thy coming rest.

THIRD HYMN.

1.
SONGS of praise the angels sang,
Heaven with hallelujah's rang,
When Jehovah's work begun,
When he spoke, and it was done.

2.
Songs of praise awoke the morn,
When the Prince of Peace was born:
Songs of praise arose, when he
Captive led captivity.

3.
Heaven and earth must pass away;
Songs of praise shall crown that day:

God will make new heav'ns and earth;
Songs of praise shall hail their birth.

4.
Saints below, with heart and voice,
Still in songs of praise rejoice;
Learning here, by faith and love,
Songs of praise to sing above.

5.
Borne upon their latest breath
Songs of praise shall conquer death;
Then, amid eternal joy,
Songs of praise their powers employ.

SABBATH. 7s.

Dr. L. Mason.

1. Safely thro' another week God has brought us on our way;
Let us now a blessing seek, Waiting in his courts to day.
Day of all the week the best, Emblem of eternal rest;
Day of all the week the best, Emblem of eternal rest.

2. While we seek supplies of grace, Thro' the dear Redeemer's name,
Show thy reconciling face; Take away our guilt and shame.
From our worldly cares set free, May we rest this day in thee;
From our worldly cares set free, May we rest this day in thee.

3.
Here we come thy name to praise;
  Let us feel thy presence near:
May thy glory meet our eyes,
  While we in thy house appear:
Here afford us, Lord, a taste
  Of our everlasting feast;
Here afford us, Lord, a taste
  Of our everlasting feast.

4.
May the gospel's joyful sound
  Conquer sinners, comfort saints,
Make the fruits of grace abound,
  Bring relief from all complaints;
Thus let all our Sabbaths prove,
  Till we join the church above;
Thus let all our Sabbaths prove,
  Till we join the church above.

TOPLADY. 7s.

Dr. T. Hastings.

1. Rock of a-ges, cleft for me, Let me hide myself in thee;
D. C. Be of sin the dou-ble cure, Save from wrath, and make me pure.
Let the wa-ter and the blood, From thy wounded side which flow'd,

2.
Could my tears forever flow,
Could my zeal no languor know,—
These for sin could not atone;
Thou must save, and thou alone:
In my hand no price I bring;
Simply to the cross I cling.

3.
While I draw this fleeting breath,
When my eyes shall close in death,
When I rise to worlds unknown,
And behold thee on thy throne,—
Rock of ages, cleft for me,
Let me hide myself in thee.

SECOND HYMN.

1.
From the cross uplifted high,
Where the Saviour deigns to die,
What melodious sounds we hear
Bursting on the ravish'd ear:—
Love's redeeming work is done—
Come and welcome, sinner, come!

2.
Sprinkled now with blood the throne,
Why beneath thy burdens groan?
On his pierced body laid,
Justice owns the ransomed paid;
Bow the knee,—embrace the Son—
Come and welcome, sinner, come!

THIRD HYMN.

1.
Weary souls, that wander wide
From the central point of bliss:
Turn to Jesus crucified;
Fly to those dear wounds of his:
Sink into the purple flood;
Rise into the life of God.

2.
Find in Christ the way of peace,
Peace unspeakable, unknown;
By his pain he gives you ease,
Life by his expiring groan:
Rise, exalted by his fall;
Find in Christ your all in all.

3.
O believe the record true,
God to you his Son hath given;
Ye may now be happy too,
Find on earth the life of heaven:
Live the life of heaven above,
All the life of glorious love.

4.
This the universal bliss,
Bliss for every soul design'd;
God's original promise this,
God's great gift to all mankind;
Blest in Christ this moment be,
Blest to all eternity.

3. Shall we, whose souls are lighted
    With wisdom from on high,—
Shall we to men benighted
    The lamp of life deny?
Salvation, oh, salvation!
    The joyful sound proclaim,
Till earth's remotest nation
    Has learned Messiah's name.

4. Waft, waft, ye winds, his story,
    And you, ye waters, roll,
Till, like a sea of glory,
    It spreads from pole to pole:
Till o'er our ransom'd nature
    The Lamb for sinners slain,
Redeemer, King, Creator,
    In bliss returns to reign.

GOODWIN. 7s & 6s. 219

G. J. Webb.

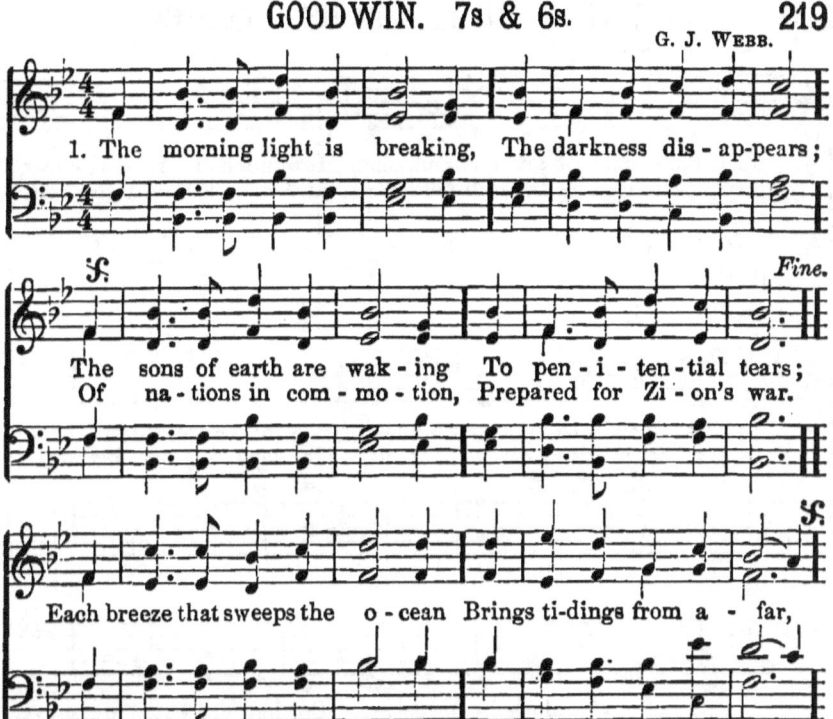

1. The morning light is breaking,
The darkness disappears;
The sons of earth are waking
To penitential tears;
Each breeze that sweeps the ocean
Brings tidings from afar,
Of nations in commotion,
Prepared for Zion's war.

2. Rich dews of grace come o'er us,
In many a gentle shower,
And brighter scenes before us
Are opening every hour;
Each cry to heaven going
Abundant answers brings,
And heavenly gales are blowing,
With peace upon their wings.

3. See heathen nations bending
Before the God we love,
And thousand hearts ascending
And gratitude above:
While sinners, now confessing,
The gospel call obey,
And seek the Saviour's blessing,
A nation in a day.

4. Blest river of salvation,
Pursue thy onward way;
Flow thou to every nation,
Nor in thy richness stay:
Stay not till all the lowly
Triumphant reach their home;
Stay not till all the holy
Proclaim, "The Lord is come."

SECOND HYMN.

1. Through grace I am determined
To conquer, though I die!
And then away to Jesus
On wings of love I'll fly:
Farewell to sin and sorrow,
I bid you all adieu:
And oh, my friends, prove faithful,
And on your way pursue.

2. And if you meet with troubles
And trials on your way,
Then cast your cares on Jesus,
And don't forget to pray:
Gird on the heavenly armor
Of faith, and hope, and love,
And when the conflict's ended
He'll carry you above.

220. THE WAY HE LEADS US. 7s & 6s.

Words by CHISLON.
ASA HULL.

1. How much of joy and com-fort, How much of re-al cheer,
The dear Lord, in his kindness, Gives to his children here;
So gent-ly doth he lead us, So hap-pi-ly we move,
That ev-'ry day our pathway Glows with his ten-der love.

2. Each hour he draweth near-er, And when we need to rest,
He folds his arms a-bout us, He lays us on his breast;
He gives us liv-ing wa-ters, With heav'nly man-na feeds,
And his exhaust-less boun-ty Sup-plies our man-y needs.

3.
Sometimes a passing shadow
 Will flit across the mind,
And dim our hope of heaven,
 Our pleasing prospects blind;
But then his hand he giveth
 To lead us safe along,
And in a moment changeth
 The mourning sigh to song.

4.
And when our loved ones leave us,
 To come to us no more,
He draws aside the curtain,
 And shows the golden shore;
We hear the praise exultant,—
 The harp-strings sweetly ring,
As ransomed friends in glory
 Bow to the loving King.

MORNING, NOON, AND NIGHT. 7s & 6s.

ASA HULL.

1. Go, when the morning shin-eth, Go, when the noon is bright,
Go, when the eve de-clin-eth, Go, in the hush of night;
Go, with pure mind and feel-ing, Fling earthly care a-way,
And, in thy clos-et kneel-ing, Do thou in se-cret pray.

2. Re-mem-ber all who love thee, All who are lov'd by thee;
Pray, too, for those who hate thee, If an-y such there be;
Thou for thy-self, in meek-ness, A bless-ing humbly claim,
And blend with each pe-ti-tion Thy great Redeemer's name.

3.
Or, if 'tis e'er denied thee
 In solitude to pray,
Should holy thoughts come o'er thee
 When friends are round thy way;
E'en then, the silent breathing
 Thy spirit raised above,
Will reach his throne of glory,
 Where dwells eternal love.

4.
Oh, not a joy or blessing
 With this can we compare,—
The grace our Father gave us
 To pour our souls in prayer;
Whene'er thou pin'st in sadness,
 Before his footstool fall;
Remember, in thy gladness,
 His love, who gave thee all.

PENITENCE. 7s, 6s, & 8.

Espressivo. ASA HULL.

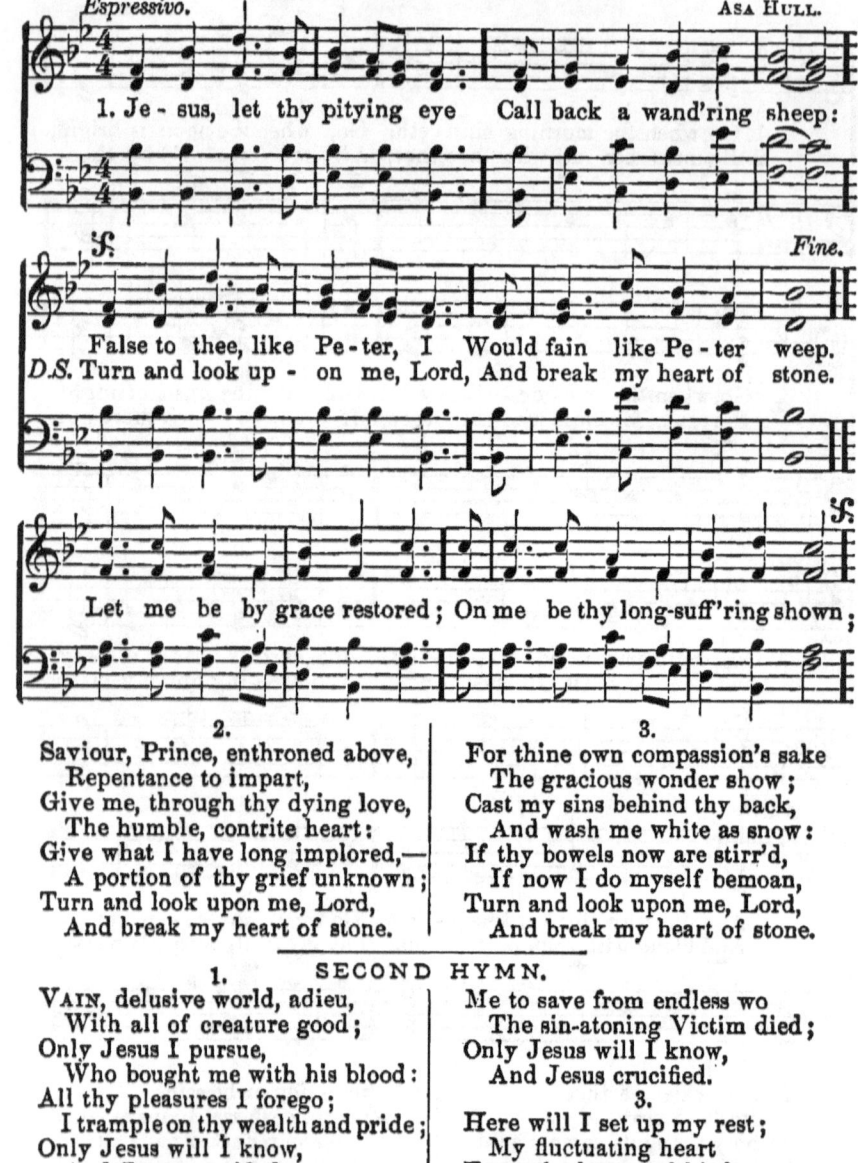

1. Je-sus, let thy pitying eye Call back a wand'ring sheep:
False to thee, like Pe-ter, I Would fain like Pe-ter weep.
D.S. Turn and look up-on me, Lord, And break my heart of stone.
Let me be by grace restored; On me be thy long-suff'ring shown;

2.
Saviour, Prince, enthroned above,
  Repentance to impart,
Give me, through thy dying love,
  The humble, contrite heart:
Give what I have long implored,—
  A portion of thy grief unknown;
Turn and look upon me, Lord,
  And break my heart of stone.

3.
For thine own compassion's sake
  The gracious wonder show;
Cast my sins behind thy back,
  And wash me white as snow:
If thy bowels now are stirr'd,
  If now I do myself bemoan,
Turn and look upon me, Lord,
  And break my heart of stone.

SECOND HYMN.

1.
VAIN, delusive world, adieu,
  With all of creature good;
Only Jesus I pursue,
  Who bought me with his blood:
All thy pleasures I forego;
I trample on thy wealth and pride;
Only Jesus will I know,
  And Jesus crucified.

2.
Other knowledge I disdain;
  'Tis all but vanity;
Christ, the Lamb of God, was slain,
  He tasted death for me:

Me to save from endless wo
  The sin-atoning Victim died;
Only Jesus will I know,
  And Jesus crucified.

3.
Here will I set up my rest;
  My fluctuating heart
From the haven of his breast
  Shall never more depart:
Whither should a sinner go? [wide;
  His wounds for me stand open
Only Jesus will I know,
  And Jesus crucified.

AMSTERDAM. 7s & 6s. 223

1. Rise, my soul, and stretch thy wings: Thy better portion trace;
Rise from transitory things T'ward heav'n thy native place;
Sun and moon and stars decay; Time shall soon this earth remove;
Rise, my soul, and haste away To seats prepar'd above.

2.
Rivers to the ocean run,
 Nor stay in all their course;
Fire, ascending, seeks the sun;
 Both speed them to their source:
So a soul that's born of God
 Pants to view his glorious face;
Upward tends to his abode,
 To rest in his embrace.

3.
Cease, ye pilgrims, cease to mourn;
 Press onward to the prize;
Soon our Saviour will return
 Triumphant in the skies;
There we'll join the heav'nly train,
 Welcomed to partake the bliss;
Fly from sorrow, care, and pain,
 To realms of endless peace.

Concluded from opposite page.

4.
Him to know is life, and peace,
 And pleasure without end;
This is all my happiness,—
 On Jesus to depend;
Daily in his grace to grow,
 And ever in his faith abide;
Only Jesus will I know,
 And Jesus crucified.

5.
Oh, that I could all invite
 This saving truth to prove;
Show the length, the breadth, the height,
 And depth of Jesus' love!
Fain I would to sinners show
 The blood by faith alone applied;
Only Jesus will I know,
 And Jesus crucified.

ZION. 8s, 7s, & 4.

DR. T. HASTINGS.

1. O Thou God of my sal-va-tion, My Redeemer from all sin,
Moved by thy di-vine compassion, Who hast died my heart to win.

I will praise thee; Where shall I thy praise begin? I will praise thee;

Where shall I thy praise be-gin?

2.
Tho' unseen, I love the Saviour;
He hath brought salvation near;
Manifests his pard'ning favor,
And when Jesus doth appear,
:||: Soul and body
Shall his glorious image bear.:||:

3.
While the angel choirs are crying,
Glory to the great I AM,
I with them will still be vying—
Glory, glory to the Lamb!
:||: Oh, how precious
Is the sound of Jesus' name!:||:

4.
Angels now are hov'ring round us,
Unperceived amid the throng;
Wond'ring at the love that crown'd us,
Glad to join the holy song;
:||: Hallelujah!
Love and praise to Christ belong.:||:

SECOND HYMN.

1.
GUIDE me, O thou great Jehovah,
Pilgrim through this barren land;
I am weak, but thou art mighty;
Hold me with thy powerful hand:
:||: Bread of heaven,
Feed me till I want no more.:||:

2.
Open now the crystal fountain
Whence the healing waters flow;
Let the fiery, cloudy pillar
Lead me all my journey through;
:||: Strong Deliv'rer, [Shield.:||:
Be thou still my Strength and

3.
Where I tread the verge of Jordan,
Bid my anxious fears subside;
Bear me through the swelling current;
Land me safe on Canaan's side;
:||: Songs of praises
I will ever give to thee. :||:

GREENVILLE. 8s, 7s & 4s. 225

ROSSEAU.

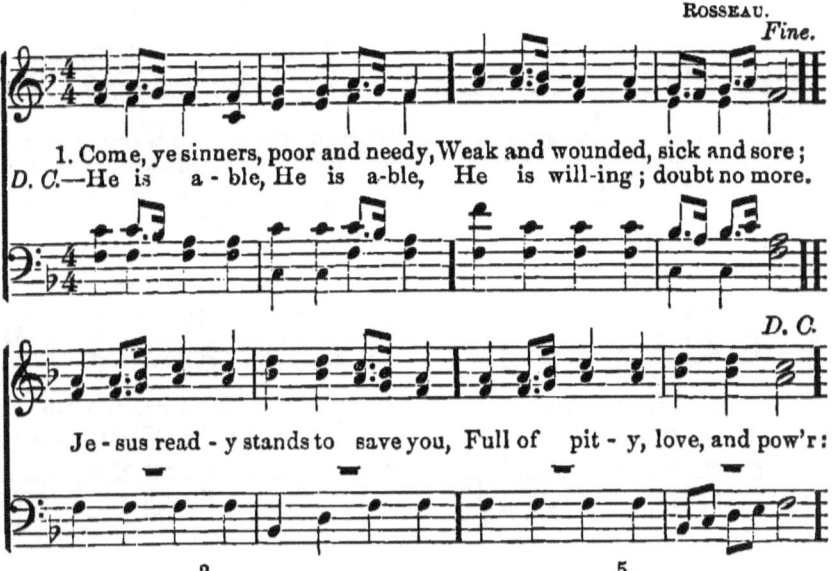

1. Come, ye sinners, poor and needy, Weak and wounded, sick and sore;
   Jesus read-y stands to save you, Full of pity, love, and pow'r:
   D. C.—He is a-ble, He is a-ble, He is will-ing; doubt no more.

2.
Now, ye needy, come, and welcome;
  God's free bounty glorify;
True belief and true repentance,—
  Every grace that brings you nigh,
  :||: Without money, :||:
Come to Jesus Christ and buy.

3.
Let not conscience make you linger;
  Nor of fitness fondly dream:
All the fitness he requireth
  Is to feel your need of him:
  :||: This he gives you,—:||:
'Tis the Spirit's glimm'ring beam.

4.
Come, ye weary, heavy laden,
  Bruised and mangled by the fall,
If you tarry till you're better
  You will never come at all;
  :||: Not the righteousness,—:||:
Sinners Jesus came to call.

5.
Agonizing in the garden,
  Your Redeemer prostrate lies;
On the bloody tree behold him!
  Hear him cry, before he dies,
  :||: It is finished!—:||:
Sinners, will not this suffice?

6.
Lo! th' incarnate God, ascending,
  Pleads the merit of his blood;
Venture on him, venture freely;
  Let no other trust intrude:
  :||: None but Jesus, :||:
Can do helpless sinners good.

7.
Saints and angels, joined in concert,
  Sing the praises of the Lamb;
While the blissful seats of heaven
  Sweetly echo with his name:
  :||: Hallelujah! :||:
Sinners here may do the same.

SECOND HYMN.

1.
Come, thou soul-transforming Spirit,
  Bless the sower and the seed;
Let each heart thy grace inherit;
  Raise the weak—the hungry feed;
  :||: From the gospel :||:
Now supply thy people's need.

2.
Oh, may all enjoy the blessing
  Which the world's design'd to give;
Let us all, thy love possessing,
  Joyfully the truth receive,
  :||: And forever :||:
To thy praise and glory live.

TALMAR. 8s & 7s.

Arranged from I. B. WOODBURY.

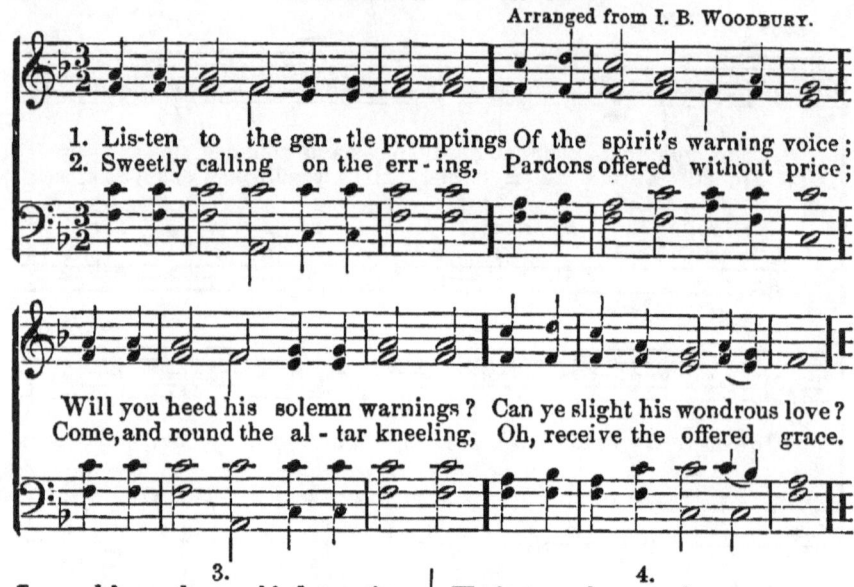

1. Lis-ten to the gen-tle promptings Of the spirit's warning voice;
Will you heed his solemn warnings? Can ye slight his wondrous love?
2. Sweetly calling on the err-ing, Pardons offered without price;
Come, and round the al-tar kneeling, Oh, receive the offered grace.

3.
Joy and hope the troubled conscience
Will allay with soothing peace;
Press ye, then, to realms of glory;
Run with joy the offered race.

4.
Hesitate no longer, sinner,
Lest the spirit, sad and grieved,
Should forsake thee now and ever,
Never more to be deceived.

SECOND HYMN.

1.
DREAD Jehovah! God of nations
From thy temple in the skies,
Hear thy people's supplications;
Now for their deliv'rance rise.

2.
Lo! with deep contrition turning,
In thy holy place we bend;
Hear us, fasting, praying, mourning;
Hear us, spare us, and defend.

3.
Though our sins, our hearts confound-ing,
Long and loud for vengeance call,
Thou hast mercy more abounding;
Jesus' blood can cleanse them all.

4.
Let that mercy vail transgression;
Let that blood our guilt efface:
Save thy people from oppression;
Save from spoil thy holy place.

THIRD HYMN.

1.
LIGHT of those whose dreary dwelling
Borders on the shades of death,
Come, and, by thyself revealing,
Dissipate the clouds beneath.

2.
Thou, new heaven and earth's Creator,
In our deepest darkness rise;
Scatt'ring all the night of nature,—
Pouring day upon our eyes.

3.
Still we wait for thine appearing;
Life and joy thy beams impart,
Chasing all our fears, and cheering
Every poor, benighted heart.

4.
Come, extend, thy wonted favor
To our ruin'd, guilty race;
Come, thou blest, exalted Saviour;
Come, apply thy saving grace.

5.
By thine all-atoning merit,
Every burden'd soul release;
By the teachings of thy Spirit,
Guide us into perfect peace.

CHRIST OUR FRIEND. 8s & 7s. 227

Words by Rev. Thos. L. Poulson. Music by J. G. Robinson.

1. Though the night o'erhang our dwelling, And the tempests round us rave; And the wintry blasts are swelling, Till we fear there's none to save.

2.
Still the gospel streamlets flowing
 To the hearts of all mankind,
And the heavenly breezes blowing,
 Cheer the waiting, trusting mind.

3.
In the cause of God engaged,
 Wrongs of Satan to redress,
When the battle hottest raged,
 We have always won success.

4.
With the Christian's banner o'er us,
 As to duty we attend;
In the wide world spread before us
 Christ shall ever be our friend.

5.
In the morning of his coming,
 When the warfare all is past,
We'll be counted in the morning
 Of his jewels at the last.

SECOND HYMN.

1.
Saviour, breathe an ev'ning blessing,
 Ere repose our spirits seal;
Sin and want we come confessing;
 Thou canst save, and thou canst heal.

2.
Though destruction walk around us,
 Though the arrows past us fly,
Angel guards from thee surround us;
 We are safe, if thou art nigh.

3.
Though the night be dark and dreary,
 Darkness cannot hide from thee;
Thou art he who, never weary,
 Watchest where thy people be.

4.
Should swift death this night o'ertake
 And command us to the tomb, [us,
May the morn in heaven awake us,
 Clad in bright, eternal bloom.

THIRD HYMN.

1.
Jesus, while our hearts are bleeding
 O'er the spoils that death has won,
We would, at this solemn meeting,
 Calmly say, Thy will be done.

2.
Though cast down, we're not forsaken;
 Though afflicted, not alone;
Thou didst give, and thou hast taken;
 Blessed Lord,—Thy will be done.

3.
Tho' to-day we're filled with mourning
 Mercy still is on the throne;
With thy smiles of love returning,
 We can sing,—Thy will be done.

4.
By thy hands the boon was given;
 Thou hast taken but thine own;
Lord of earth, and God of heaven,
 Evermore,—Thy will be done.

WILMOT. 8s & 7s.

From C. M. Von WEBER.

1. In the cross of Christ I glo-ry, Tow'ring o'er the wrecks of time;
2. When the woes of life o'ertake me, Hopes deceive, and fears an-noy,

All the light of sa-cred sto-ry Gathers round its head sublime.
Nev-er shall the cross forsake me: Lo! it glows with peace and joy.

3.
When the sun of bliss is beaming
  Light and love upon my way,
From the cross the radiance streaming,
  Adds new luster to the day.

4.
Bane and blessing, pain and pleasure,
  By the cross are sanctified;
Peace is there that knows no measure,
  Joys that through all time abide.

SECOND HYMN.

1.
Know, my soul, thy full salvation;
  Rise o'er sin, and fear, and care;
Joy to find in every station
  Something still to do or bear:

2.
Think what Spirit dwells within thee;
Think what Father's smiles are thine;
Think that Jesus died to win thee:
  Child of heaven, canst thou repine?

3.
Haste thee on from grace to glory,
Armed by faith, and winged by prayer;
Heaven's eternal day before thee—
God's own hand shall guide thee there.

4.
Soon shall close thine earthly mission,
  Soon shall pass thy pilgrim days;
Hope shall change to glad fruition,
  Faith to sight, and prayer to praise.

THIRD HYMN.

1.
Praise to thee, thou great Creator!
  Praise to thee from every tongue:
Join, my soul, with every creature,
  Join the universal song.

2.
Father, source of all compassion,
  Pure, unbounded grace is thine:
Hail the God of our salvation!
  Praise him for his love divine.

3.
For ten thousand blessings given,
  For the hope of future joy,
Sound his praise thro' earth and heav'n,
  Sound Jehovah's praise on high.

4.
Joyfully on earth adore him,
  Till in heaven our song we raise;
There, enraptured, fall before him,
  Lost in wonder, love, and praise.

SICILIAN HYMN. 8s & 7s.

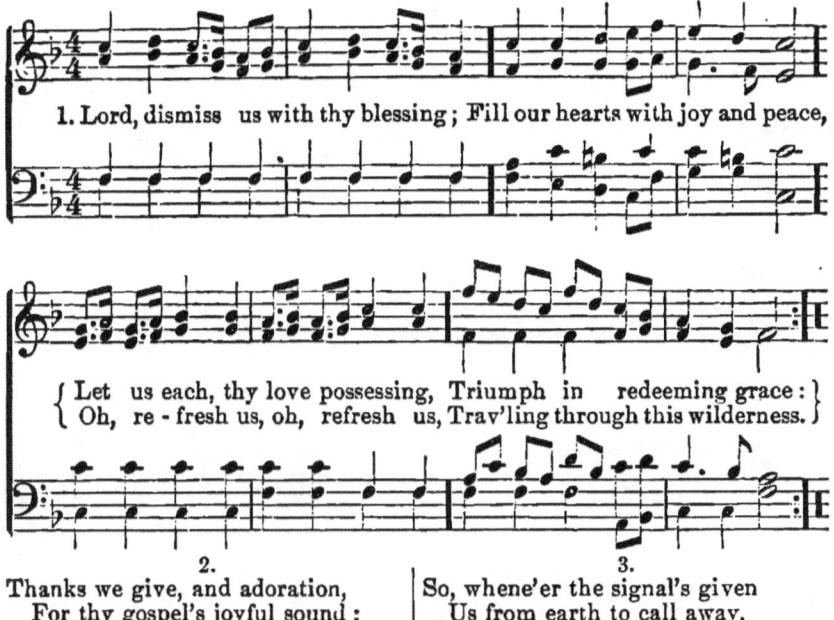

1. Lord, dismiss us with thy blessing; Fill our hearts with joy and peace, Let us each, thy love possessing, Triumph in redeeming grace: Oh, re-fresh us, oh, refresh us, Trav'ling through this wilderness.

2.
Thanks we give, and adoration,
 For thy gospel's joyful sound;
May the fruits of thy salvation
 In our hearts and lives abound:
:||: May thy presence :||:
 With us evermore be found.

3.
So, whene'er the signal's given
 Us from earth to call away,
Borne on angels' wings to heaven,
 Glad the summons to obey,
:||: May we ever :||:
 Reign with Christ in endless day.

SECOND HYMN.

1.
LOVE divine, all love excelling,
 Joy of heaven, to earth come down,
Fix in us thy humble dwelling;
 All thy faithful mercies crown.
2.
Jesus, thou art all compassion,—
 Pure unbounded love thou art;
Visit us with thy salvation;
 Enter every trembling heart.
3.
Breathe, O breathe thy loving Spirit
 Into every troubled breast;
Let us all in thee inherit;
 Let us find that second rest.
4.
Take away our bent to sinning;
 Alpha and Omega be;
End of faith, as its beginning,
 Set our hearts at liberty.

5.
Come, almighty to deliver,
 Let us all thy life receive;
Suddenly return, and never,
 Never more thy temples leave:
6.
Thee we would be always blessing,
 Serve thee as thy hosts above,
Pray, and praise thee without ceasing,
 Glory in thy perfect love.
7.
Finish then thy new creation;
 Pure and spotless let us be;
Let us see thy great salvation,
 Perfectly restored in thee:
8.
Changed from glory into glory,
 Till in heaven we take our place,—
Till we cast our crowns before thee,
 Lost in wonder, love, and praise.

230. SWEET THE MOMENTS. 8s & 7s.

Asa Hull.

Moderato.

1. Sweet the moments, rich in blessing, Which before the cross I spend;
Life and health and peace possessing From the sinner's dy-ing Friend:
D.S. Still in faith and hope a-bid-ing, Life de-riv-ing from his death.
Love and grief my heart di-vid-ing, With my tears his feet I'll bathe;

2.
Oh, how blessed is the station,
  Low before the cross to lie,
While I see divine compassion
  Beaming from his gracious eye:
Here I'll sit forever, viewing
  Mercy streaming in his blood;
Precious drops my soul bedewing,
  Plead and claim my peace with God.

3.
Here it is I find my heaven,
  While upon the Lamb I gaze;
Here I see my sins forgiven,
  Lost in wonder, love, and praise:
May I still enjoy this feeling,
  In all need to Jesus go,
Prove each day his blood more healing,
  And himself more deeply know.

SECOND HYMN.

1.
Vain are all terrestrial pleasures;
  Mix'd with dross the purest gold;
Seek we, then, for heavenly treasures,
  Treasures never waxing old;
Let out best affections center
  On the things around the throne:
There no thief can ever enter;
  Moth and rust are there unknown.

2.
Earthly joys no longer please us;
  Here would we renounce them all;
Seek our only rest in Jesus,—
  Him our Lord and Master call:
Faith, our languid spirits cheering,
  Points to brighter worlds above:
Bids us look for his appearing,—
  Bids us triumph in his love.

BETHLEHEM. 8s & 7s. 231

1. Come, thou Fount of ev'-ry blessing, Tune my heart to sing thy grace;
Streams of mer-cy, nev-er ceasing, Call for songs of loudest praise:
D.S. Praise the mount, I'm fix'd upon it, Mount of thy re-deem-ing love.
Teach me some melodious sonnet, Sung by flaming tongues above:

2.
Here I'll raise mine Ebenezer;
 Hither, by thy help, I'll come;
And I hope, by thy good pleasure,
 Safely to arrive at home.
Jesus sought me when a stranger,
 Wandering from the fold of God;
He, to rescue me from danger,
 Interposed his precious blood.

3.
Oh, to grace how great a debtor
 Daily I'm constrained to be!
Let thy goodness, like a fetter,
 Bind my wandering heart to thee:
Prone to wander, Lord, I feel it,
 Prone to leave the God I love;
Here's my heart—oh, take and seal it,
 Seal it for thy courts above.

Concluded from opposite page.

3.
May our light be always burning,
 And our loins be girded round,
Waiting for our Lord's returning,—
 Longing for the welcome sound:
Thus the Christian life adorning,
 Never need we be afraid,
Should he come at night or morning,
 Early dawn, or evening shade.

Dismission.
LORD, dismiss us with thy blessing,
 Bid us now depart in peace;
Still on heavenly manna feeding,
 Let our faith and love increase:
Fill each breast with consolation;
 Up to thee our hearts we raise:
When we reach our blissful station,
 Then we'll give thee nobler praise.

ABBA. 8s & 7s.

1. Hark! what mean those holy voices, Sweetly sounding thro' the skies?
Lo! th' angelic host rejoices; Heavenly hallelujahs rise.
Listen to the wondrous story, Which they chant in hymns of joy:—
Glory in the highest, glory, Glory be to God most high!

2.
Peace on earth, good will from heaven,
　Reaching far as man is found;
Souls redeemed, and sins forgiven!
　Loud our golden harps shall sound.
Christ is born, the great Anointed;
　Heaven and earth his praises sing;
Oh, receive whom God appointed
　For your Prophet, Priest, and King.

3.
Hasten, mortals, to adore him;
　Learn his name, and taste his joy,
Till in heaven ye sing before him,—
　Glory be to God on high!
Praise the God of our salvation;
　Hosts on high his power proclaim;
Heaven and earth, and all creation,
　Laud and magnify his name.

HAPPY ZION. 8s, & 7s. 233

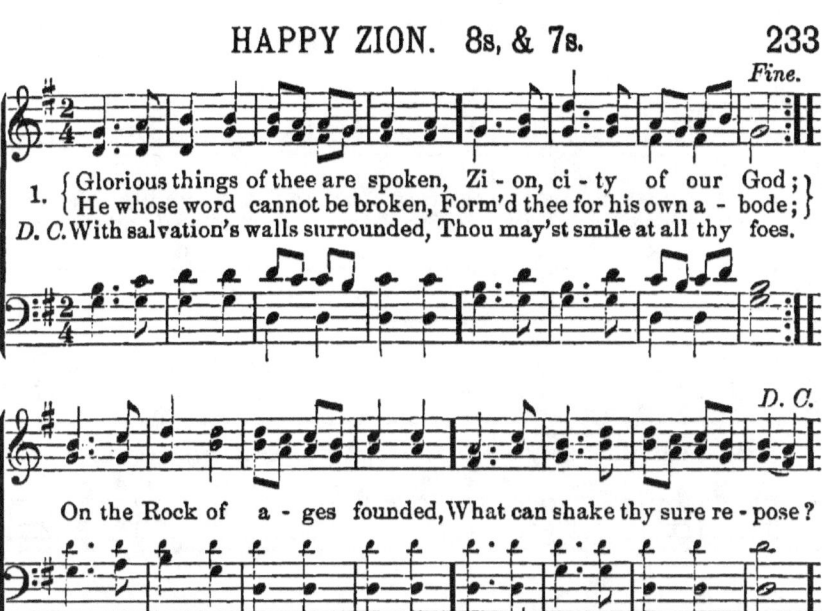

1. Glorious things of thee are spoken, Zi-on, ci-ty of our God;
He whose word cannot be broken, Form'd thee for his own a-bode;
D. C. With salvation's walls surrounded, Thou may'st smile at all thy foes.

On the Rock of a-ges founded, What can shake thy sure re-pose?

2.
See, the streams of living waters,
Springing from eternal love,
Still supply the sons and daughters,
And all fear of want remove:
Who can faint while such a river
Ever flows our thirst t'assuage?
Grace which, like the Lord, the Giver,
Never fails from age to age.

3.
Round each habitation hov'ring,
See the cloud and fire appear!
For a glory and a cov'ring,
Showing that the Lord is near:
He who gives us daily manna,
He who listens when we cry,
Let him hear the loud hosanna,
Rising to his throne on high.

SECOND HYMN.

1.
HAIL, thou once despised Jesus!
Hail, thou Galilean King!
Thou didst suffer to release us;
Thou didst free salvation bring.
Hail, thou agonizing Saviour,
Bearer of our sin and shame!
By thy merits we find favor;
Life is given through thy name.

2.
Paschal Lamb, by God appointed,
All our sins on thee were laid:
By almighty love anointed,
Thou hast full atonement made.
All thy people are forgiven,
Through the virtue of thy blood;
Open'd is the gate of heaven;
Peace is made 'twixt man and God.

3.
Jesus, hail! enthroned in glory,
There forever to abide;
All the heavenly hosts adore thee,
Seated at thy Father's side:
There for sinners thou art pleading;
There thou dost our place prepare:
Ever for us interceding,
Till in glory we appear.

4.
Worship, honor, power, and blessing,
Thou art worthy to receive:
Loudest praises, without ceasing,
Meet it is for us to give.
Help, ye bright angelic spirits;
Bring your sweetest, noblest lays;
Help to sing our Saviour's merits;
Help to chant Immanuel's praise.

CALVARY. H. M.

ASA HULL.

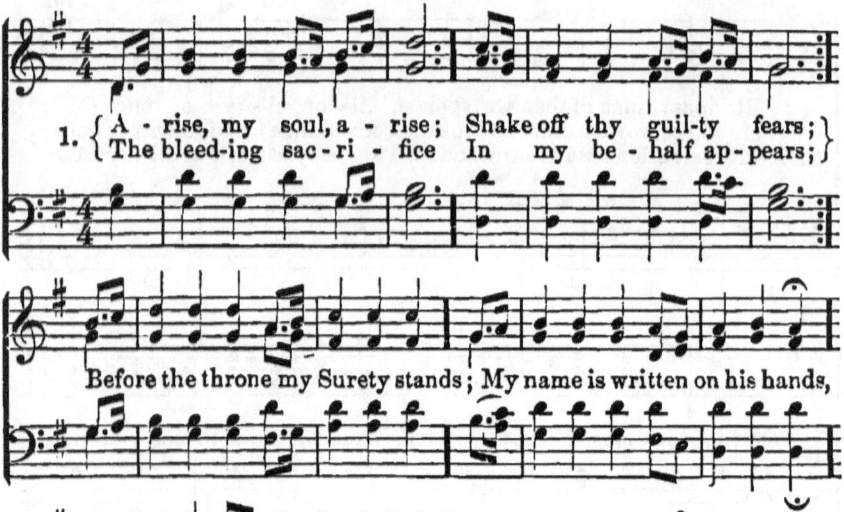

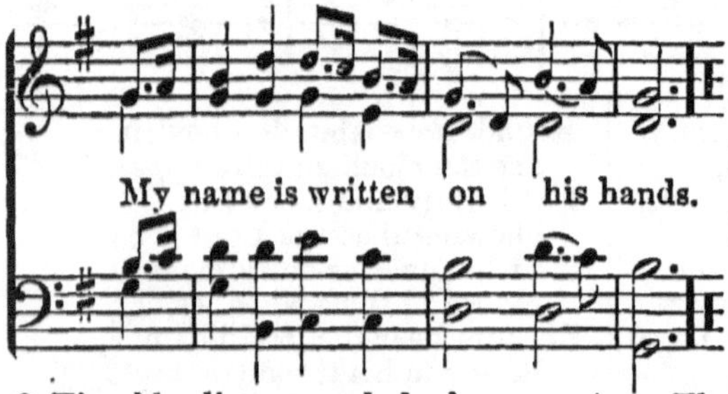

1. { A-rise, my soul, a-rise; Shake off thy guil-ty fears;
   The bleed-ing sac-ri-fice In my be-half ap-pears; }
Before the throne my Surety stands; My name is written on his hands,
My name is written on his hands.

2. He ever lives above,
For me to intercede;
His all redeeming love,
His precious blood to plead;
His blood atoned for all our race,
And sprinkles now the throne of grace.

3. Five bleeding wounds he bears,
Received on Calvary;
They pour effectual prayers,
They strongly plead for me:
Forgive him, oh, forgive, they cry,
Nor let that ransomed sinner die.

4. The Father hears him pray,
His dear anointed One;
He cannot turn away
The presence of his Son;
His Spirit answers to the blood,
And tells me I am born of God.

5. My God is reconciled,
His pard'ning voice I hear,
He owns me for his child,
I can no longer fear:
With confidence I now draw nigh,
And Father, Abba, Father, cry.

SECOND HYMN.

1. THE Lord Jehovah reigns,
His throne is built on high;
The garments he assumes
Are light and majesty:
His glories shine with beams so bright,
No mortal eye can bear the sight.

2. The thunders of his hand
Keep the wide world in awe;
His wrath and justice stand
To guard his holy law;
And where his love resolves to bless,
His truth confirms and seals the grace.

3. Through all his mighty works
Amazing wisdom shines;
Confounds the powers of hell,
And all their dark designs;
Strong is his arm, and shall fulfil
His great decrees and sov'reign will.

LENOX. H. M.

Edson.

1. Blow ye the trumpet, blow The gladly solemn sound; Let all the nations know, To earth's remotest bound, The year of jubilee is come, The year of jubilee is come, Return, ye ransom'd sinners, home.

2.
Jesus, our great High Priest,
  Hath full atonement made;
Ye weary spirits, rest;
  Ye mournful souls, be glad:
The year of jubilee is come;
Return, ye ransom'd sinners, home.

3.
Extol the Lamb of God,
  The all-atoning Lamb;
Redemption in his blood,
  Throughout the world proclaim:
The year of jubilee is come;
Return, ye ransom'd sinners, home.

4.
Ye slaves of sin and hell,
  Your liberty receive,
And safe in Jesus dwell,
  And blest in Jesus live:
The year of jubilee is come;
Return, ye ransom'd sinners, home.

5.
Ye who have sold for naught
  Your heritage above,
Shall have it back unbought,
  The gift of Jesus' love:
The year of jubilee is come;
Return, ye ransom'd sinners, home.

6.
The gospel trumpet hear,—
  The news of heav'nly grace;
And, saved from earth, appear
  Before your Saviour's face:
The year of jubilee is come;
Return, ye ransom'd sinners, home.

Doxology.
To God the Father's throne
  Perpetual honors raise;
Glory to God the Son,
  And to the Spirit praise:
With all our pow'rs, eternal King,
Thy everlasting praise we sing.

LISCHER. H. M.

From the German, by L. MASON.

1. { Welcome, delightful morn, Thou day of sacred rest!
   I hail thy kind return; Lord, make these moments blest: }
   From low delights, and mortal toys, I soar to reach immortal joys,
   I soar to reach immortal joys.

2.
Now may the King descend,
 And fill his throne of grace;
Thy scepter, Lord, extend,
 While saints address thy face;
Let sinners feel thy quick'ning word,
And learn to know and fear the Lord.

3.
Descend, celestial Dove,
 With all thy quick'ning powers,
Disclose a Saviour's love,
 And bless these sacred hours;
Then shall may soul new life obtain,
Nor Sabbaths be indulged in vain.

SECOND HYMN.

1.
To heaven I lift mine eyes;
 From God is all my aid—
The God who built the skies,
 And earth and nature made;
God is the tower to which I fly;
His grace is nigh in every hour.

2.
My feet shall never slide,
 And fall in fatal snares,
Since God, my Guard and Guide,
 Defends me from my fears.
Those wakeful eyes, which never sleep,
Shall Israel keep when dangrs rise.

3.
No burning heats by day,
 Nor blast of evening air,
Shall take my health away,
 If God be with me there;
Thou art my sun, and Thou my shade,
To guard my head by night or noon.

4.
Hast Thou not pledged Thy word
 To save my soul from death?
And I can trust my Lord
 To keep my mortal breath.
I'll go and come, nor fear to die,
Till from on high Thou call me home.

SEA CLIFF. H. M.

Asa Hull.

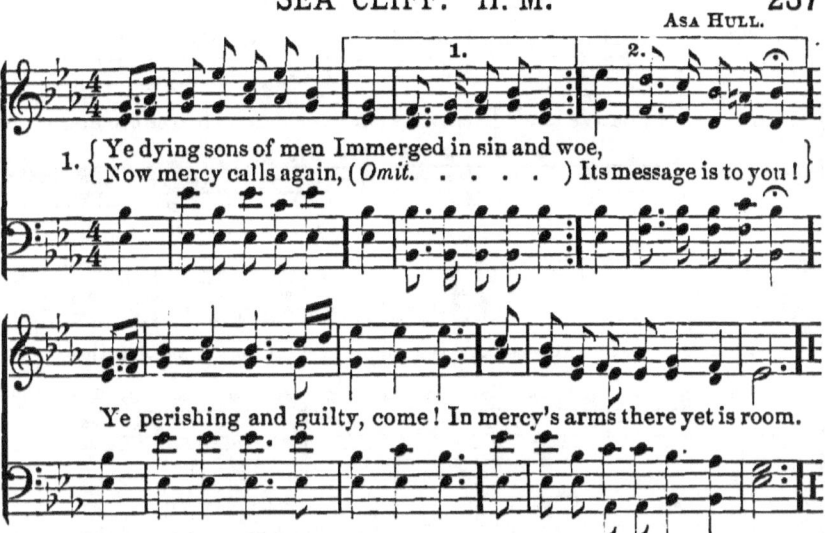

1. Ye dying sons of men Immerged in sin and woe,
Now mercy calls again, (*Omit* . . . . .) Its message is to you!
Ye perishing and guilty, come! In mercy's arms there yet is room.

2.
No longer now delay,
  Nor vain excuses frame;
Christ bids you come to day,
  Though poor, and blind, and lame:
All things are ready, sinner, come!
For ev'ry trembling soul there's room.

3.
Drawn by his dying love,
  Ye wand'ring sheep, draw near;
Christ calls you from above;
  His charming accents hear;
Let whosoever will, now come:
In mercy's arms there still is room.

SECOND HYMN.

1.
Great King of glory, come,
  And with thy favor crown
This temple as thy home,—
  This people as thine own:
Beneath this roof, O deign to show
How God can dwell with men below.

2.
Here may thine ears attend
  Our interceding cries,
And grateful praise ascend
  Like incense to the skies:
Here may thy soul-converting word
With faith be preach'd, in faith be heard.

3.
Here may our unborn sons
  And daughters sound thy praise,
And shine, like polish'd stones,
  Through long-succeeding days:
Here, Lord, display thy saving pow'r,
While temples stand and men adore.

4.
Here may the list'ning throng
  Receive thy truth in love:
Here Christians join the song
  Of the redeem'd above;
Till all, who humbly seek thy face,
Rejoice in thy abounding grace.

THIRD HYMN.

1.
Baptized into thy name,
  Mysterious One in Three,
Our souls and bodies claim
  A sacrifice to thee:
And let us live our faith to prove,
The faith which works by humble love.

2.
O that our light may shine,
  And all our lives express
The character divine,
  The real holiness:
And then receive us up t' adore
The triune God for evermore.

AMERICA. 6s & 4s.

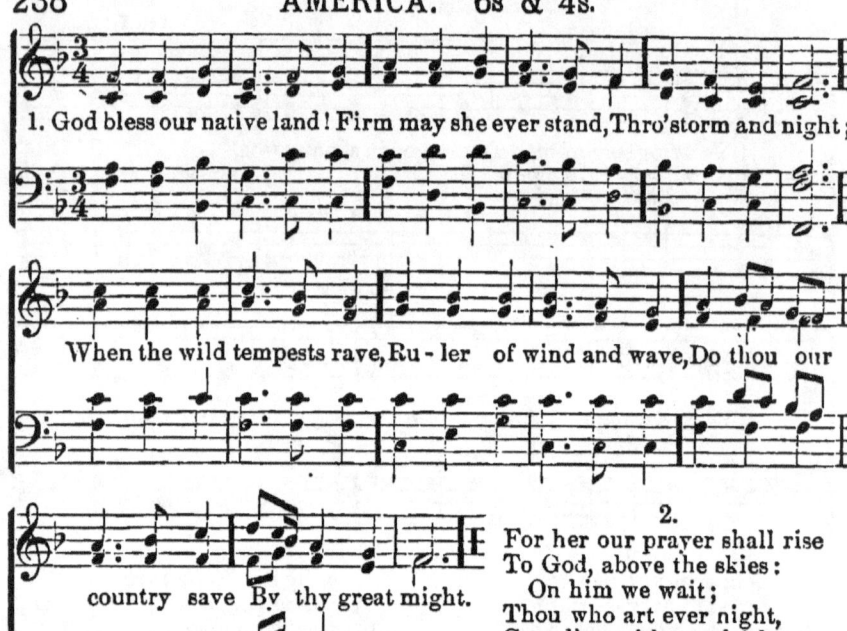

1. God bless our native land! Firm may she ever stand, Thro' storm and night; When the wild tempests rave, Ru-ler of wind and wave, Do thou our country save By thy great might.

2. For her our prayer shall rise
To God, above the skies:
On him we wait;
Thou who art ever night,
Guarding with watchful eye,
To the aloud we cry,
God save the State!

SECOND HYMN.

1. My country, 'tis of thee,
Sweet land of liberty,
Of thee I sing;
Land where my fathers died,
Land of the pilgrim's pride,
From ev'ry mountain side
Let freedom ring.

2. My native country! thee,
Land of the noble free,
Thy name I love;
I love thy rocks and rills,
Thy woods and templed hills
My heart with rapture thrills
Like that above.

3. Let music swell the breeze,
And ring from all the trees
Sweet freedom's song!
Let mortal tongues awake;
Let all that breathe partake;
Let rocks their silence break;
The sound prolong!

4. Our fathers' God! to thee,
Author of liberty,
To thee we sing:
Long may our land be bright
With freedom's holy light;
Protect us by thy might,
Great God, our King!

THIRD HYMN.

1. Sound, sound the truth abroad!
Bear ye the word of God
Through the wide world;
Tell what our Lord hath done;
Tell how the day was won;
And from his lofty throne
Satan is hurled.

2. Far over sea and land,
'Tis our Lord's own command,
Bear ye his name:
Bear it to every shore;
Regions unknown explore;
Enter at every door—
Silence is shame.

ITALIAN HYMN. 6s & 4s. 239
GIARDINI.

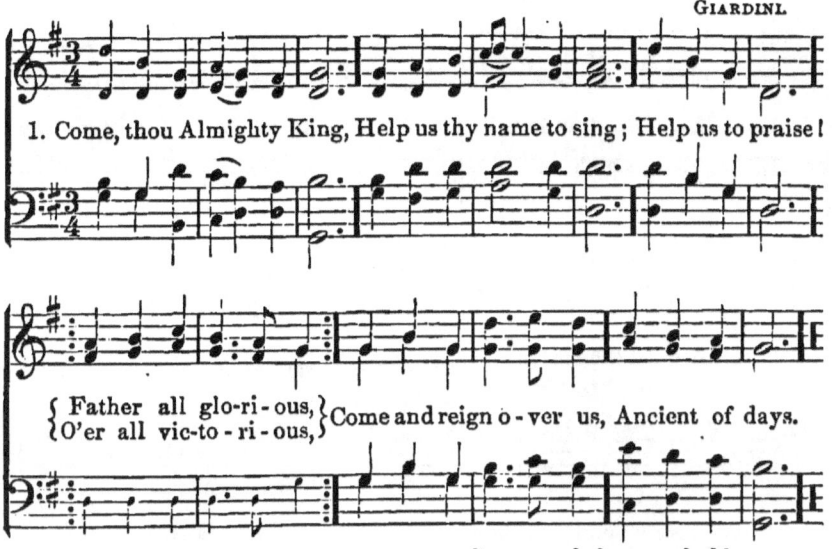

1. Come, thou Almighty King, Help us thy name to sing; Help us to praise! Father all glo-ri-ous, O'er all vic-to-ri-ous, Come and reign o-ver us, Ancient of days.

2.
Jesus, our Lord, arise,
Scatter our enemies,
 And make them fall;
Let thine almighty aid
Our sure defense be made;
Our souls on thee be stay'd;
 Lord, hear our call.

3.
Come, thou incarnate Word,
Gird on thy mighty sword,
 Our pray'r attend;

Come, and thy people bless,
And give thy word success:
 Spirit of holiness,
 On us descend.

4.
Come, holy Comforter,
Thy sacred witness bear
 In this glad hour:
Thou who almighty art,
Now rule in ev'ry heart,
And ne'er from us depart,
 Spirit of power.

SECOND HYMN.

1.
PRAISE ye Jehovah's name,
Praise through his courts proclaim;
 Rise and adore;
High o'er the heavens above
Sounds his great acts of love,
While his rich grace we prove,
 Vast as his power.

2.
Now let the trumpet raise
Sounds of triumphant praise,
 Wide as his fame:
There let the harp be found;
Organs, with solemn sound,
Roll your deep notes around,
 Filled with his name.

3.
While his high praise ye sing,
Strike every sounding string;
 Sweet the accord!
He vital breath bestows;
Let every breath that flows,
His noblest fame disclose;
 Praise ye the Lord.

DOXOLOGY.
To God—the Father, Son,
And Spirit—Three in One—
 All praise be given;
Crown him, in every song;
To him your hearts belong,
Let all his praise prolong,
 On earth—in heaven.

240 OLIVET. 6s & 4s. DR. L. MASON.

1. Come, Holy Ghost, in love Shed on us from above Thine own bright ray! Divinely good thou art; Thy sacred gifts impart To gladden each sad heart; Oh, come to-day!

2.
Come, tend'rest Friend, and best,
Our most delightful guest,
　With soothing power:
Rest, which the weary know,
Shade, 'mid the noontide glow,
Peace, when deep griefs o'erflow,—
　Cheer us, this hour!

3.
Come, Light serene, and still
Our inmost bosoms fill;
　Dwell in each breast:
We know no dawn but thine,
Send forth thy beams divine,
On our dark souls to shine,
　And make us blest!

4.
Exalt our low desires;
Extinguish passion's fires;
　Heal every wound:
Our stubborn spirits bend;
Our icy coldness end;
Our devious steps attend,
　While heavenward bound.

5.
Come, all the faithful bless;
Let all, who Christ confess,
　His praise employ:
Give virtue's rich reward;
Victorious death accord,
And, with our glorious Lord,
　Eternal joy!

SECOND HYMN.

1.
My faith looks up to thee,
Thou Lamb of Calvary,
　Saviour Divine!
Now hear me while I pray;
Take all my guilt away;
Oh, let me, from this day,
　Be wholly thine!

2.
May thy rich grace impart
Strength to my fainting heart,
　My zeal inspire!
As thou hast died for me,
Oh, may my love to thee
Pure, warm, and changeless be—
　A living fire!

3.
While life's dark maze I tread,
And griefs around me spread,
　Be thou my guide;
Bid darkness turn to day,
Wipe sorrow's tears away,
Nor let me ever stray
　From thee aside.

4.
When ends life's transient dream,
When death's cold, sullen stream
　Shall o'er me roll,
Blest Saviour! then, in love,
Fear and distrust remove;
Oh, bear me safe above—
　A ransomed soul!

UNITY. 6s & 5s. 241
Dr. L. Mason.

1. When shall we meet again? Meet ne'er to sever? When will peace wreathe her chain Round us forever? Our hearts will ne'er repose, Safe from each blast that blows, In this dark vale of woes: Never, no, never!
2. When shall love freely flow Pure as life's river? When shall sweet friendship glow, Changeless forever? Where joys celestial thrill, Where bliss each heart shall fill, And fears of parting chill, Never, no, never!

3.
Up to that world of light,
  Take us, dear Saviour!
May we all there unite,
  Happy forever!
Where kindred spirits dwell,
There may our music swell,
And time our joys dispel
  Never, no, never!

4.
Soon shall we meet again,
  Meet ne'er to sever;
Soon will peace wreathe her chain
  Round us forever:
Our hearts will then repose,
Secure from worldly woes:
Our songs of praise shall close
  Never, no, never!

THIRD HYMN for "Olivet."

1.
Come, all ye saints of God,
Wide through the earth abroad
  Spread Jesus' fame:
Tell what his love hath done;
Trust in his name alone;
Shout to his lofty throne,
  "Worthy the Lamb!"

2.
Hence, gloomy doubts and fears!
Dry up your mournful tears;
  Swell the glad theme;
To Christ, our gracious King,
Strike each melodious string;
Join heart and voice to sing,
  "Worthy the Lamb!"

COME, YE DISCONSOLATE.

WEBBE.

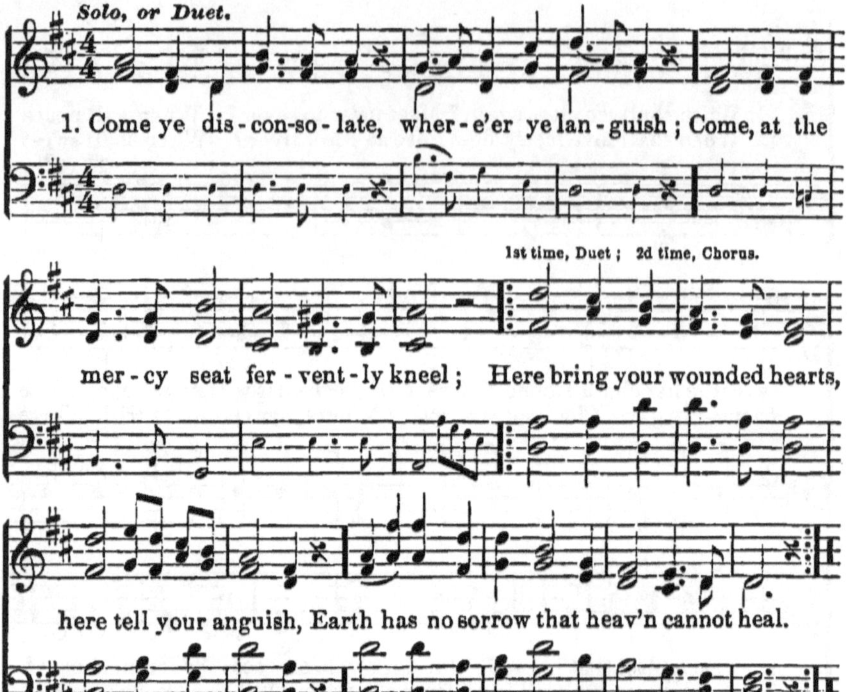

Solo, or Duet.
1. Come ye dis - con-so - late, wher - e'er ye lan - guish ; Come, at the
1st time, Duet ; 2d time, Chorus.
mer - cy seat fer - vent - ly kneel ; Here bring your wounded hearts,
here tell your anguish, Earth has no sorrow that heav'n cannot heal.

2. Joy of the desolate, light of the straying,
Hope of the penitent, fadeless and pure ;
:||: Here speaks the Comforter, tenderly saying :
Earth has no sorrow that Heaven cannot cure. :||:

3. Here see the Bread of Life ; see waters flowing
Forth from the throne of God, pure from above ;
:||: Come to the feast of love ; come, ever knowing,
Earth has no sorrow but Heaven can remove. :||:

FADING, STILL FADING.

Arranged.

Duet.
1. Fa-ding, still fad - ing, the last beam is shining ; Fa - ther in
2. Fa - ther in heav - en, oh, hear when we call, Hear for Christ's

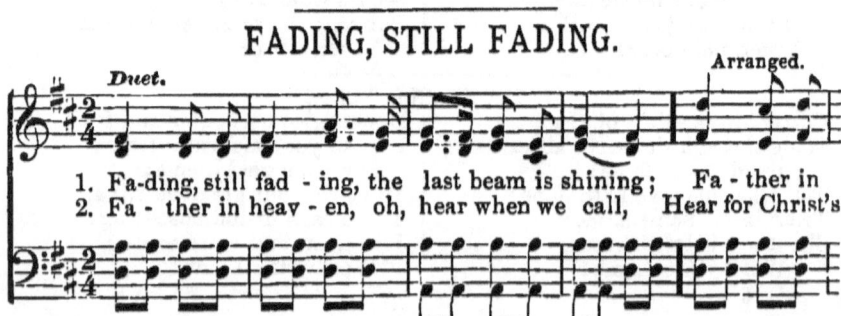

FADING, STILL FADING.

PORTUGUESE HYMN. 10s & 11s.

1. Tho' troubles assail, and dangers affright, Tho' friends should all fail, and foes all unite, Yet one thing secures us, whatever betide, The promise assures us, The promise assures us, The promise assures us, The Lord will provide.

2. The birds without barn or storehouse are fed;
From them let us learn to trust for our bread:
His saints what is fitting shall ne'er be denied,
So long as 'tis written, The Lord will provide.

3. When Satan appears to stop up our path,
And fills us with fears, we triumph by faith;
He cannot take from us, tho' oft he has tried,
The heart-cheering promise, The Lord will provide.

4. He tells us we're weak,—our hope is in vain;
The good that we seek we ne'er shall obtain:
But when such suggestions our graces have tried,
This answers all questions,—The Lord will provide.

5. No strength of our own, or goodness, we claim:
Our trust is all thrown on Jesus's name;
In this our strong tower for safety we hide;
The Lord is our Power; The Lord will provide.

LYONS. 10s & 11s. 245

1. Ye servants of God, your Master proclaim, And publish abroad his wonderful name: The name all-victorious of Jesus extol; His kingdom is glorious; he rules over all.

2. God ruleth on high, almighty to save,
And still he is nigh; his presence we have;
The great congregation his triumph shall sing,
Ascribing salvation to Jesus, our King.

3. Salvation to God, who sits on the throne;
Let all cry aloud, and honor the Son;
The praises of Jesus the angels proclaim,
Fall down on their faces and worship the Lamb.

4. Then let us adore, and give him his right,—
All glory, and power, and wisdom, and might,
All honor and blessing, with angels above,
And thanks never ceasing for infinite love.

Concluded from opposite page.

6. When life sinks apace, and death is in view,
The word of his grace shall comfort us through:
Not fearing or doubting, with Christ on our side,
We hope to die shouting, The Lord will provide.

DELAY NOT. 11s.

Asa Hull.

1. De-lay not, de-lay not, O sinner, draw near! The waters of life are now flowing for thee; No price is de-mand-ed, the Saviour is here; Redemption is purchas'd, sal-va-tion is free.
2. De-lay not, de-lay not, O sinner, to come, For mer-cy still lin-gers, and calls thee to-day; Her voice is not heard in the vale of the tomb; Her message, unheed-ed, will soon pass a-way.

3. Delay not, delay not! the spirit of grace,
   Long griev'd and resisted, may take its sad flight,
   And leave thee in darkness to finish thy race,
   To sink in the vale of eternity's night.

4. Delay not, delay not! the hour is at hand,—
   The earth shall dissolve, and the heavens shall fade;
   The dead, small and great, in the judgment shall stand,
   What pow'r, then, O sinner, shall lend thee its aid?

SECOND HYMN.

1. Oh, turn ye! oh, turn ye! for why will ye die,
   When God, in his mercy, is coming so nigh;
   Since Jesus invites you; the Spirit says, Come,
   And angels are waiting to welcome you home.

2. How vain the delusion, that while you delay,
   Your hearts may grow better by staying away;
   Come wretched, come starving, come just as you be,
   While streams of salvation are flowing so free.

FREDERICK. 11s. 247
G. Kingsley.

1. I would not live alway; I ask not to stay, Where storm after
storm ris-es dark o'er the way: The few lu-cid mornings that
dawn on us here, Are enough for life's woes, full enough for its cheer.

2. I would not live alway; no! welcome the tomb, Since Jesus has
lain there, I dread not its gloom; There, sweet be my rest, till he
bid me a-rise, To hail him in triumph de-scending the skies.

3. Who, who would live always away from his God,—
Away from yon heaven, that blissful abode,
Where the rivers of pleasure flow o'er the bright plains,
And the noontide of glory eternally reigns.

4. There the saints of all ages in harmony meet;
Their Saviour and brethren transported to greet;
While the anthems of rapture unceasingly roll,
And the smile of the Lord is the feast of the soul.

Concluded from opposite page.

3. And now Christ is ready your soul to receive;
Oh, how can you question, if you will believe;
If sin is your burden, why will you not come?
'Tis he bids you welcome,—he bids you come home.

4. In riches, in pleasure, what can you obtain
To soothe your affliction, or banish your pain?
To bear up your spirit when summon'd to die,
Or waft you to mansions of glory on high?

SCOTLAND. 12s.
Dr. Clarke.

1. The voice of free grace, cries, escape to the mountain! For Adam's lost race, Christ hath open'd a fountain; For sin and uncleanness, and ev'ry transgression, His blood flows most freely, in streams of salvation, His blood flows most freely, in streams of salvation.

CHORUS.—Hal-le-lu-jah to the Lamb, who hath purchased our pardon! We'll praise him a-gain when we pass o-ver Jordan, We'll praise him again, when we pass o-ver Jordan.

2. Now glory to God in the highest is given;
Now glory to God is re-echoed in heaven;
Around the whole earth let us tell the glad story,
And sing of his love, his salvation, and glory.—Hallelujah, etc.

3. O Jesus, ride on,—thy kingdom is glorious;
O'er sin, death, and hell, thou wilt make us victorious;
Thy name shall be praised in the great congregation,
And saints shall ascribe unto thee their salvation.—Hallelujah, etc.

INDEX OF FIRST LINES.

Abide with me; fast falls the eventide.	29
Abraham, when severely tried,	161
According to thy gracious word	180
A charge to keep I have	206
A home in heaven! what a joyful	52
Alas! and did my Saviour bleed	132
All for Jesus! all for Jesus!	5
All glory to the dying Lamb	185
All hail the power of Jesus' name	166
Am I a soldier of the cross	132
Amid the hours that rapid fly	133
And am I born to die	206
And are we yet alive	198
And can it be that I should gain	23
And can I yet delay	203
And let this feeble body fail	90
Another day is past	202
Anywhere with Jesus, says the	30
Arise, my soul, arise;	234
Arise, my soul, to Pisgah's height,	83
Assembled, at thy great command	153
Author of faith, eternal word	142
Awake, and sing the song.	197
Awake my soul! stretch every nerve	171
Baptized into thy name	237
Bear thy cross cheerfully	69
Beautiful mansion, home of blest	47
Before Jehovah's awful throne	141
Beautiful Zion, built above	80
Behold a fountain deep and wide	12
Behold! behold the Lamb of God	111
Behold the sure foundation stone	183
Behold the throne of grace	197
Blessed Bible! how I love it	108
Blest are the sons of peace	204
Blest be the tie that binds	207
Blow ye the trumpet, blow	235
Brethren in Christ, and well beloved	155
Children of the heavenly King	212
Come, all ye saints of God	241
Come, brethren, don't grow weary,	116
Come, Holy Ghost, in love	240
Come, Holy Ghost, our hearts inspire	188
Come, humble sinner, in whose breast	182
Come, let us anew, our journey pursue	65
Come, let us lift our joyful eyes	181
Come on my partners in distress	192
Come, poor pilgrim, sad and weary	93
Come, said Jesus' sacred voice	214
Come, sing the praise of Jesus	73
Come, sing to me of heaven	121
Come, sinners, to the gospel feast	134, 150
Come, sound his praise abroad	195
Come, thou Almighty King	239
Come, thou fount of every blessing	231
Come, thou soul-transforming Spirit	225
Come to Jesus, just now	109
Come to the fountain of mercy	21
Come unto me when shadows darkly	96
Come up hither! come away!	42
Come, weary sinner, come,	200
Come, ye disconsolate	242
Come, ye sinners, poor and needy	225
Come, ye that love the Lord	121, 136
Come, ye that love the Saviour's name	177
Dear Jesus, I long to be perfectly whole	14
Deep are the wounds which sin has	144
Delay not, delay not, O sinner	246
Delightful work! young souls to win	185
Depth of mercy! can there be	57
Dread Jehovah! God of nations!	226
Equip me for the war	196
Eternal beam of light divine	159
Eternal depth of love divine	156
Extended on the cursed tree	144
Fade, fade each earthly joy	101
Fading, still fading, the last beam	242
Far from my tho'ts vain world be gone	152
Far from these scenes of night	202
Far from the world, O Lord, I flee	171
Father of mercies, in thy word	178
Father, whate'er of earthly bliss	178
Flee as a bird to your mountain	118
For a season called to part	210
Forever here my rest shall be	139
Forever with the Lord	194
From all that dwell below the skies	141
From Greenland's icy mountains	218
From every stormy wind that blows	155
From the cross uplifted high	217
Give me the wings of faith to rise	122, 170

INDEX OF FIRST LINES.

Glad as the morning, swift as the light.	89
Glorious things of thee are spoken,	233
Glory to thee, my God, this night	143
God bless our native land	233
God is the refuge of his saints	146
God moves in a mysterious way	188
God's holy law, transgressed,	51
Go, when the morning shineth	221
Go, ye messengers of God	211
Grace! tis a charming sound	205
Great God, attend while Zion sings	150
Great God, indulge my humble claim	157
Great God! the nations of the earth	176
Great God, to thee my evening song	157
Great God, to thee my evening. C. M.	172
Great King of glory, come	237
Guide me, O thou great Jehovah	224
Hail, gentle peace, good-will to man	149
Hail, thou ever rolling ocean	41
Hail, thou once despised Jesus	233
Hark! the glad sound! the Saviour.	170
Hark! what mean those holy voices	232
Hasten, sinner, to be wise	77
He dies, the Friend of sinners dies	145
He wills that I should holy be	160
High on a throne of light, O Lord	175
Ho! ev'ry one that thirsts draw nigh	135
How beauteous are their feet	199
How blest the righteous when he dies	146
How blest the sacred tie that binds	161
How gentle God's commands	207
How helpless nature lies	206
How happy every child of grace	166
How much of joy and comfort	220
How pleasant, how divinely fair	148
How sweetly flowed the gospel's sound,	158
How sweet the hour of closing day	158
How sweet the name of Jesus sounds	167
How tedious and tasteless the hours	125
How vain is all beneath the skies	145
I am coming to the cross	59
I am so glad that our Father in heav'n.	17
If human kindness meets return	187
If we cannot plant our cottage	85
I gave my life for thee	3
I heard the voice of Jesus say,	95
I hear the Saviour say	50
I know her walls are Jasper	102
I'll praise my Maker while I've breath	164
I love thee, I love thee, I love thee my.	55
I love the Lord, he heard my cries.	180
I love thy kingdom, Lord	203
I love to steal awhile away	172
I love to tell the story	36
I'm but a stranger here	127
I'm a pilgrim, and a stranger	110
In God I have found a retreat	39
In some way or other	15
In the Christian's home in glory	104
In the cross of Christ I glory	228
In the silent midnight watches	22
In thy presence we appear	212
I seem to hear a voice within	43
I thirst, thou wounded Lamb of God	154
It may be far, it may be near	8
I've been thinking of my home	128
I want a principle within	182
I was a wand'ring sheep	198
I will follow thee, my Saviour	115
I will sing for Jesus	62
I will sing you a song	63
I would be thine; O take my heart	186
I would not live alway:	247
Jerusalem, my glorious home	169
Jesus, and shall it ever be	159
Jesus, I fain would walk with thee	146
Jesus! I hear thee knocking	114
Jesus, immortal King, arise	189
Jesus, let thy pitying eye	222
Jesus, lover of my soul	208
Jesus my all to heaven is gone	151
Jesus saves me every day	105
Jesus, Saviour, pilot me,	16
Jesus shall reign where'er the sun	152
Jesus, the Life, the Truth the Way	186
Jesus, the word bestow	199
Jesus, the name high over all	117, 138
Jesus! the name that charms our fears.	138
Jesus, thine all-victorious love	173
Jesus, to thy dear wounds we flee	175
Jesus, where'er thy people meet	148
Jesus, while our hearts are bleeding	227
Just as I am, with one plea	49
Kingdoms and thrones to God belong	147
Know, my soul, thy full salvation	228
Land ahead! its fruits are waving	100
Let him to whom we now belong	179
Let not the wise their wisdom boast	160

INDEX OF FIRST LINES.

Let worldy minds the world pursue	168
Let Zion's watchman all awake	184
Lift your eyes of faith, and see	211
Light of life, seraphic fire	209
Light of those whose dreary dwelling	226
Like the sea that cannot rest	26
Listen to the gentle promptings	226
Live on the field of battle	51
Lord, dismiss us with thy blessing	229
Lord, how secure and blest are they	154
Lord, I am thine, entirely thine	143
Lord, I hear of showers of blessings	92
Lord, in the morning thou shalt hear	179
Lord of hosts, how lovely fair	213
Lord of hosts! to thee we raise	213
Lord of the harvest hear	200
Lord of the Sabbath, hear us pray	157
Lord, we come before thee now	213
Lord, while for all mankind we pray	188
Lo! on a narrow neck of land	192
Lo! round the throne a glorious band	153
Love divine, all love excelling	229
Love has a ready ear	45
Mary to the Saviour's tomb	209
More love to thee, O Christ,	127
'Mid pleasures and palaces tho' we may	124
'Mid scenes of confusion and	124
Must Jesus bear the cross alone	189
My country, 'tis of thee	238
My days are gliding swiftly by	123
My faith looks up to thee	240
My foot is on the threshold	24
My God, I am thine, what a comfort	107
My God, O can it be, that I	160
My God, the spring of all my joys	190
My hope is built on nothing less	61
My latest sun is sinking fast	88
My life flows on in endless song	13
My Saviour, my almighty Friend	184
My soul, be on thy guard	196
My soul is now united	54
My soul, repeat his praise	197
My soul with rapture waits for thee	56
My son, know thou the Lord	204
Nearer, my God, to thee	137
No night shall be in heaven	35
Nothing but leaves! the spirit grieves	7
Now from the altar of our hearts	179
Now, O God, thine own I am	105
O bliss of the purified! bliss of the free	75
O God, of good th' unfathom'd sea	164
O God, unseen, yet ever near	174
O happy day, that fix'd my choice	135
O, love divine, what hast thou done	163
O, my offended God	201
O, think of a home over there	38
O, thought full of sweetness to those	20
O, thou God of my salvation	224
O thou, that wouldst not have	203
O thou, to whom all creatures bow	183
O, who'll stand up for Jesus	33
O'er the hills the sun is setting,	64
Of Him who did salvation bring	151
Oh, blessed feet of Jesus	66
Oh, come the stream that never runs	81
Oh, could I speak the matchless worth	193
Oh, for a glance of heavenly day	145
Oh, for a heart to praise my God	174
Oh, for a thousand tongues to sing	167
Oh, for that flame of living fire	143
Oh, my house is builded upon the Rock	70
Oh, now I am a soldier	37
Oh, now I see the crimson wave	11
Oh, turn ye, oh, turn ye, for why will ye	246
Oh, what amazing words of grace	92
Oh, what hath Jesus bought for me	107
Oh, when shall I see Jesus	103
Oh, where shall rest be found	200
Oh, why should gloomy thoughts arise	180
Once more, my soul, the rising day	173
Once more we come before our God,	176
On every sunny mountain	87
One sweetly solemn thought	48
On Jordan's stormy banks I stand	191
Onward, forward, pilgrim trav'lers	34
Peace, troubled soul, whose plaintive	165
People of the living God	214
Praise God, from whom all blessing flow	141
Praise the Lord; ye heav'ns adore him	65
Praise to God, immortal praise	215
Praise to thee, thou great Creator	228
Praise ye Jehovah's name	239
Praise ye the Lord, ye heav'nly choirs	187
Praise waits in Zion, Lord, for thee	152
Prayer is appointed to convey	142
Prince of peace, control my will	212
Pris'ners of hope, be strong, be bold	163
Quiet as a peaceful river	27

INDEX OF FIRST LINES.

Rise, my soul, and stretch thy wings.... 223
Rock of ages, cleft for me.................... 217

Sad and weary with my longing 67
Safely through another week................. 216
Salvation! oh, the joyful sound............. 184
Saviour, breathe an evening blessing... 227
Saviour, like a shepherd lead us........... 129
Saviour of the sin-sick soul.................. 59
Shall we gather at the river 84
Show pity, Lord! O Lord, forgive 149
Sinners obey the heavenly call 154
Sinners, turn ; why will ye die............. 211
Sleep not, soldier of the cross.............. 215
Soldiers of Christ, arise 205
Soldiers on life's battle field................. 77
So let our lips and lives express 161
Songs of praise the angels sang............ 215
Sound, sound the truth abroad............. 238
Sow in the morn thy seed..................... 196
Stand up for Jesus, Christian............... 60
Sweet is the work, my God, my King... 159
Sweet hour of prayer 140
Sweet the moments rich in blessing..... 230

Teach me, O, my gracious Lord............ 214
The cross! the cross! the blood-stain'd.. 32
The day is past and gone...................... 202
The great Physician now is near.......... 79
The Lord, Jehovah reigns..................... 234
The Lord my pasture shall prepare...... 162
The morning light is breaking 219
The night is dark the storm is loud...... 61
The pity of the Lord............................. 207
There are joys we fondly cherish.......... 19
There are lonely hearts to cherish........ 9
There is a beautiful world 136
There is a fountain filled with blood..33,139
There is a gate that stands ajar............ 18
There is an hour of peaceful rest, ... 172
There is a land that is fairer than day. 58
There is a land of pure delight........69, 168
There is a radiant sunny clime,............ 90
There is a spot to me more dear........... 113
There is beauty all around 74
There is no name so sweet on earth...... 123
There's a crown in heav'n for the........ 82
These are the crowns that we shall...... 106
The voice of free grace, cries escape..... 248
The world is overcome 96
They have reached the sunny shore..... 94
This is not my place of resting.............. 101

Thou art my portion, O, my God.......... 176
Thou art the way: to thee alone........... 173
Thou dear Redeemer, dying Lamb 186
Though clouds arise, and storms prevail. 71
Though the night o'erhang our............ 227
Though troubles assail, and dangers 244
Thou rock of my salvation, haste......... 189
Through grace I am determined 219
Through heaven's clear arch the echoes. 53
Thus far the Lord hath led me on........ 142
Time is earnest, passing by.................. 31
To day the Saviour calls....................... 134
To God the Father's throne.................. 235
To God the Father, Son........................ 239
To heaven I lift mine eyes 236
To Jesus, our exalted Lord 155
To Jesus, the crown of my hope 125
To our Redeemer's glorious name....... 169
To the cross of Christ, my Saviour....... 6
Try us, O God, and search the ground... 183
'Twas Jesus, my Saviour, who died...... 120

Unto the Lord, unto the Lord 148
Unvail thy bosom, faithful tomb.......... 158

Vain are all terrestrial pleasures.......... 230
Vain, delusive world, adieu.................. 222

Wake, O my soul, and hail the morn.... 153
Watch for the time is short................... 78
Watchman, tell me, does the morning.. 112
Watchman, tell us of the night............. 209
We are out on the ocean sailing 131
We are waiting by the river................. 97
Weary souls, that wander wide............ 217
Weary wanderer o'er the main............ 86
We know, by faith we know................ 195
Welcome, delightful morn 236
Welcome, sweet day of rest.................. 195
We may spread our couch with........... 25
We're going home to glory 91
We shall meet in that beautiful land ... 98
What a friend we have in Jesus........... 28
What am I, O thou glorious God.......... 149
What glory gilds the sacred page......... 177
What sinners value I resign................. 147
What to me are earth's pleasures........ 72
When all thy mercies, O my God,........ 177
Whence came the armies of the sky 132
When I can read my title clear............ 68
When Israel trod the desert way 156
When I survey the wondrous cross...... 144

When I think of that city of light	126	With joy we hail the sacred day	178
When marshaled on the nightly	130	With joy we lift our eyes	201
When mountains of doubt hem me in	4	With stately towers and bulwark strong	171
When power divine, in mortal form	140	Wondrous cross! thy glory beaming	40
When shall I see the day	109	Work, for the night is coming	119
When shall we meet again	241	Would Jesus have the sinner die	165
When the tempest rages high	46	Ye Christian heralds go proclaim	156
When we hear the music ringing	44	Ye dying sons of men	237
While clinging to Jesus with	10	Ye golden lamps of heaven! farewell	185
While life prolongs its precious light	147	Ye praying souls rejoice	204
While shepherds watched their flocks	181	Ye servants of God, your Master	245
While through this world we roam	205	Yes, I will bless thee, O my God	174
While with ceaseless course the sun	210	Yes, O yes, I'm trusting in my	99
Who, who are these beside the chilly	76	Ye who know your sins forgiven	112
Why should we boast of time to come	175	Ye wretched, starving poor	201

FIRST LINES OF CHORUSES.

All I have I leave for Jesus	67	Oh, lead me to the Rock	4
Amazing love, how can it be	18	Oh, may that crown in heaven	82
Beautiful vale of rest	56	Oh, help me sing for Jesus	62
By and by, yes, by and by	8	Oh, sing of his mighty love	75
Far beyond the rolling billows	41	Oh, sing the praise of Jesus	73
Far and wide the Sabbath music rolls	89	Oh, the blood, the precious blood	32
For, oh, we stand on Jordan's strand	123	Oh, we'll die on the field	37
For my Rock is firm	70	Onward, onward to glory	77
For thee, He is praying for thee	20	Pressing on toward the prize	34
For the Lion of Judah shall break	120	Rocks and storms I'll fear no more	100
God is love, I know, I feel	57	Shall we know each other	44
Glory, glory be to Jesus	6	Stand up for Jesus, nobly stand	60
Help me, dear Saviour, thee to own	132	The cleansing stream, I see, I see	11
I am so glad that Jesus loves me	17	The cross, for Christ, I'll cherish	33
I am trusting in the Lord	59	There's glory in my soul	54
In a bright happy home we shall	98	The fountain lies open	12
I'm glad salvation's free	121	There are lights along the shore	110
I'm nearer my home, nearer	48	There is free grace and never-dying	134
I'm watching, waiting, hoping	128	There is no other name in earth or sky	138
I love to tell the story	36	There is rest for the weary	104
In the sweet by and by	58	There is sweet rest in heaven	116
I know her walls are jasper	102	They'll sing their welcome home to me	122
It is the voice of love divine	43	'Tis well, 'tis well, 'tis with the	87
I will follow thee, my Saviour	115	'Tis a song from the home of the	72
Jesus died for you	92	Trav'ling on, so glad and free	52
Jesus paid it all	50	We are waiting by the river	97
Lead me to thee	47	We'll be there, we'll be there	136
Live on the field of battle	51	We will stand the storm	68
My Jesus and I, my Jesus	10	We will walk thro' the valley	106
My all is on the altar	114	Whiter than snow; yes, whiter than	14
Oh, come to the crimson flood	81	Yes, we'll gather at the river	84
Oh, come, angel band, come	88	Zion, Zion, beautiful Zion	80
Oh, how I love Jesus	117		

INDEX OF TUNES.

Tune	Meter	Page
Abba	8s & 7s	232
Abide with me	10s	29
A home beyond the tide	8s & 7s	131
A home in heaven	L. M.	52
Altar and sacrifice	7s & 6s	114
All for Jesus	8s & 7s	5
All to Christ I owe		50
Antioch	C. M.	170
Anywhere with Jesus		30
Amsterdam	7s & 6s	223
America	6s & 4s	238
Ariel	C. P. M.	193
Arlington	C. M.	173
Azmon	C. M.	174
Balerma	C. M.	188
Bear thy cross	6s & 4s	69
Beautiful city	L. M.	80
Beautiful river	8s & 7s	84
Beautiful vale		56
Be in earnest	7s	31
Benevento	7s	210
Bethany		137
Bethlehem	8s & 7s	231
Bethlehem's star	L. M.	130
Boylston	S. M.	206
Bridgewater	L. M.	150
Brighton	L. M. 6 lines	163
Calvary	H. M.	234
Cambridge	C. M.	184
Celestial army	C. M.	132
Celestial city	7s & 6s	102
Christmas	C. M.	181
Christain hero		51
Christ our friend	8s & 7s	227
Christ our Intercessor		66
Cleansing fountain	C. M.	139
Cleansing stream		81
Cleansing wave	C. M.	11
Clinging to the cross		67
Clinging to Jesus		10
Clinging to the rock		46
Come up hither	7s	42
Come to Jesus		109
Come, ye disconsolate		242
Coronation	C. M.	166
Creation	L. M. 6 lines	162
Cross and crown	C. M.	189
Defence	7s	208
Delay not	11s	246
Dennis	S. M.	207
Depth of mercy	7s	57
Downs	C.M.	176
Duane street	L. M.	151
Duke street	L. M.	148
Dundee	C. M.	175
Elim	C. M.	187
Emmons	C. M.	186
Evening	L. M.	158
Even me		92
Exhortation	C. M.	191
Fading, still fading		242
Faith in God		99
Federal street	LM.	149
Fisk	7s	214
Flee to your mountain	8s & 7s	118
Forever with the Lord	S. M.	194
Fountain of mercy		120
Fountain lies open	C. M.	12
Frederick	11s	247
Free grace	L. M.	134
Fugitive moments		65
Gate that stands ajar		18
Geneva	C. M.	177
Gerar	S. M.	205
Glory to the Lamb		96
Golden shore		98
Glorious by and by		8
Glorious treasure	8s & 7s	108
Glorious prospect		133
Goodwin	7s & 6s	219
Greenville	8s, 7s, & 4s	225
Hallowed cross	C. M.	32
Hallowed spot	8s & 7s	113
Hamburg	L. M.	147
Happy day	L. M.	135
Happy Zion	8s & 7s	233
Heaven is my home	6s & 4s	127
Heavenly visitor		22
Heavenly feast	11s & 12s	107

INDEX OF TUNES.

Heavenly vision	C. M.	106
Heber	C. M.	171
Hebron	L. M.	142
Hendon	7s	212
Henley	11s	96
Heralds of Zion		89
Home of the soul		63
Home, sweet home		124
Howard	C. M.	180
How can I keep from singing	8s & 7s	13
I long to be there		126
I love thee	11s	55
I love to tell the story		36
I'm nearer my home	6s	48
Infinite grace	8s	23
Italian hymn	6s & 4s	239
I will follow thee		115
I will sing for Jesus		62
Jesus died for you	C. M.	92
Jesus is mine	6s & 4s	101
Jesus loves even me		17
Jesus, Saviour, pilot me	7s	16
Jesus saves me	7s	105
Jerusalem	C. M.	169
Keep Christ in view		71
Laban	S. M.	196
Land of Beulah	C. M.	88
Lead me to the rock		4
Leavenworth	7s	211
Lebanon	L. M.	159
Lenox	H. M.	235
Let there be light		53
Lischer	H. M.	236
Life's battle field	7s	77
Lights along the shore		110
Like the sea	7s	26
Lord, lead me to thee		47
Love's attributes		45
Love at home		74
Lyons	10s & 11s	245
Martyn	7s	209
Mercy's gate	8s & 7s	19
Meribah	C. P. M.	192
Merton	C. M.	185
Missionary chant	L. M.	156
Missionary hymn	7s & 6s	218
Mornington	S. M.	195
Morning, noon, and night	7s & 6s	221
My spirit name in heaven	C. M.	90
My title clear	C. M.	68
Naomi	C. M.	178
Nazlar	L. M.	160
Nearer home	8s & 7s	64
Newcourt	L. P. M.	164
Newton ?		125
No night in heaven		35
Northfield	C. M.	167
Ocean grove	8s & 7s	41
Oh, don't stay away		91
Oh, how I love Jesus		117
Old hundred	L. M.	141
Olivet	6s & 4s	240
Olmutz	S. M.	200
Olney	S. M.	203
On the cross		111
Ortonville	C. M.	182
Our mission	8s & 7s	75
Over there		38
Palestine	L. P. M.	165
Park street	L. M.	153
Pearly gate	L. M.	61
Penitence	7s, 6s & 8s	222
Portuguese hymn	10s & 11s	244
Praise	7s	215
Praise of Jesus	C. M.	73
Pleyel's hymn	7s	213
Pressing toward the prize		34
Resting at the cross		6
Resting on the promises	8s & 7s	27
Resting place	C. M.	95
Rest for the weary	8s & 7s	104
Retreat	L. M.	155
Rockingham	L. M.	154
Rothwell		152
Sabbath	7s	216
Safe within the vail	8s & 7s	100
Salvation's free		121
Saviour, like a shepherd	8s & 7s	129
Scotland		248
Sea cliff	H. M.	237
Seeking joys immortal		54
Sessions	L. M.	143

INDEX OF TUNES.

Title	Meter	No.
Seir	S. M.	201
Shall we know each other		44
Shirland	S. M.	204
Sicilian hymn	8s & 7s	229
Sing of his mighty love		75
Sorrow is o'er		72
Stand up for Jesus		60
St. Martin's	C. M.	183
St. Thomas	S. M.	197
Stonefield	L. M.	161
Sweet by and by		58
Sweet the moments	8s & 7s	230
Sweeping thro' the gates		76
Sweet hour of prayer	L. M.	140
Sweet rest in heaven		116
Take it all to the Lord	8s & 7s	28
Talmar	8s & 7s	226
The alter and sacrifice	7s & 6s	114
The beautiful city	L. M.	80
The beautiful vale		56
The celestial army	C. M.	132
The celestial city	7s & 6s	102
The Christian hero		51
The cleansing fountain	C. M.	139
The cleansing stream		81
The cleansing wave	C. M.	11
The fountain of mercy		120
The fountain lies open	C. M.	12
The gate that stands ajar		18
The glorious by and by		8
The glorious prospect		133
The glorious treasure	8s & 7s	108
The golden shore		98
The hallowed cross	C. M.	32
The hallowed spot	8s & 7s	113
The heavenly feast		107
The heavenly visitor		22
The home of the soul		63
The invitation		21
The Land of Beulah	C. M.	88
The Lord will provide		15
The only plea		49
The pearly gate	L. M.	61
The penitent	7s & 6s	24
The polar star		86
The praise of Jesus		73
The resting place	C. M.	95
The rock on which I build		70
The royal way		25
The sabbatic year		109
The Saviour's call		134
Thy Saviour is praying for thee		20
The shining shore	8s & 7s	123
The sinners friend	C. M.	138
The sunny shore		94
The sweetest name	8s & 7s	79
The wanderer	S. M.	198
The way he leads us	7s & 6s	220
The welcome home	C. M.	122
The wondrous cross	8s & 7s	40
The world of light		136
The voice within	L. M	43
Thoughts of home		128
'Tis well with the righteous		87
There, there is rest		93
Time	S. M.	202
Toplady	7s	217
Treasures of heaven		82
Trusting in the Lord	7s	59
Turner	C. M	190
Under his wings	8s.	39
Unity		241
Uxbridge	L. M.	144
Varina	C. M.	168
Voice within	L. M.	43
Waiting by the river	8s & 7s	97
Ward	L. M.	146
Watch and pray		78
Watchman	8s & 7s	112
Ware	L. M.	145
Warwick	C. M.	179
Welcome home	C. M.	122
We'll die on the field		37
We'll stand the storm		83
What hast thou done		3
Whiter than snow		14
Who'll stand up for Jesus	7s & 6s	33
Williamsville	S. M.	199
Wilmot	7s	228
Withered leaves		7
Wondrous cross	8s & 7s	40
Woodland	C. M.	172
Work for the night is coming		119
Work while the day lasts		9
World of light	S. M.	136
Zephyr	L. M.	157
Zion	8s, 7s, & 4s	224

www.ingramcontent.com/pod-product-compliance
Lightning Source LLC
Chambersburg PA
CBHW021358230426
43666CB00006B/567